WITHDRAWN

First Freedom

FIRST FREEDOM

The Responses of Alabama's Blacks to
Emancipation and Reconstruction

Peter Kolchin

Contributions in American History, Number 20

The Publishing Division of
GREENWOOD PRESS, INC., Westport, Connecticut

GREENWOOD PRESS, PUBLISHERS
WESTPORT, CONNECTICUT

Library of Congress Cataloging in Publication Data

Kolchin, Peter.
    First Freedom.

        (Contributions in American history, no. 20)
        Includes bibliographies.
            1. Negroes — Alabama.   2. Reconstruction —
    Alabama. I. Title.
    E185.93.A3K64   301.45'19'60730761   72-816
    ISBN 0-8371-6385-4

Library of Congress Catalog Number: 72-816
ISBN: 0-8371-6385-4

First published in 1972
The Publishing Division of Greenwood Press, Inc.
51 Riverside Avenue, Westport, Connecticut 06880

Manufactured in the United States of America

Designed by Chris Simon

Contents

List of Tables

vii

List of Maps

Acknowledgments

I should like to thank the staffs at the following libraries for their help and consideration: National Archives, Library of Congress, Alabama State Department of Archives and History, Southern Historical Collection at the University of North Carolina, Duke University Library, University of Alabama Library, Talladega College Archives, Fisk University Library, Johns Hopkins University Library, and the State Historical Society of Wisconsin. Special credit is due to Sarah Jackson of the National Archives for her knowledge of the Freedmen's Bureau Papers and her general assistance.

I am grateful to the following for helpful comments, suggestions, and criticisms: Thomas B. Alexander, Anne Boylan, Eugene Genovese, Hugh Davis Graham, Elise Hall, Stanley Kutler, and Grigsby Wotton, Jr. Robert Gilmour has read the entire manuscript in two separate drafts; I have profited greatly from my conversations with him and from his knowledge of Reconstruction in Alabama.

My greatest debt is to David Donald, under whose direction

I first began this project as a doctoral dissertation. His assistance exceeded any I had a right to hope for or expect. At every stage, he gave me the kind of constant instruction, guidance, and support for which he is justly famous, but which only his students can truly appreciate.

Introduction

For many years, when most historians wrote about blacks during Reconstruction, they depicted a topsy-turvy world in which ignorant freedmen, only a stage or two removed from barbarism, wreaked havoc upon the civilized South. Some of these historians believed that Negroes were members of a naturally inferior race while others suggested that they were not yet ready for equality, but all of them saw Reconstruction as a tragic era in which the "bottom rail was on the top." The questions they asked about Negroes during Reconstruction were "did they behave themselves properly," and "if not, why not?" The usual answer to the first question was that there were both good darkeys and uppity niggers throughout the South. The answer to the second question was that there would have been little trouble had not self-seeking Northern whites — the proverbial outside agitators — descended on the South and, for their own nefarious purposes, aroused the naturally submissive Negroes to unnatural thoughts and actions.[1]

This implicitly racist viewpoint was challenged, at first by a handful of Negroes and Marxists, and then by a much larger number of revisionist historians, until, by the late 1960s, the accepted orthodoxy told a story that was in many ways the opposite of the traditional one. There were, to be sure, differences among the revisionists. While some maintained that Reconstruction was a time of slow but steady progress for blacks in their long trek to equality, most believed, like the traditionalist historians they were attacking, that Reconstruction was a tragic era. For them, however, the tragedy lay in its failure rather than in its temporary success. The promise of equality never became a reality for the ex-slaves because Northerners who spoke about civil rights were for the most part unwilling to convert their principles into practice. Southern blacks became the unfortunate pawns of competing forces, buffeted about by Southern planters who wanted their labor, poor whites who feared their competition, and Northerners who promised much but delivered little. When the storm had finally cleared, Southern Negroes remained hopelessly oppressed, free in name only.[2]

The interpretation presented by the revisionists was in general an improvement over that of the traditionalists; certainly it was more in line with the thoughts of an age concerned with civil rights and equality. Almost without exception, the revisionists showed greater sympathy for the plight of the ex-slaves than had previous historians. What is more, the best of the revisionist historians, such as Willie Lee Rose and Joel Williamson, began branching out into new areas, asking — and tentatively offering some answers to — new kinds of questions. There was a new interest in black feelings and attitudes, a new attempt to explore the impact of changed economic and social relationships.

But it is curious how similar in many instances the preoccupations of most revisionists were to those of the traditionalists. If one ignores their divergent normative judgments, one finds that the kinds of problems they were interested in often were the same. Both saw blacks as passive objects. Most revisionists were primarily concerned with how much whites did for blacks, or what they did to them. They emphasized race relations — for example, how quickly patterns of segregation emerged — which of

necessity meant mostly how whites treated blacks. The very idea
of regarding Reconstruction as a failure implied that the key
questions were "how much was done for blacks" and "to what
extent were freedmen given their rights?" Perhaps it is not surprising that many of the best revisionist works dealing with freedmen during Reconstruction focused on how whites perceived of
and treated blacks.[3]

There is much of value in the writings of both the traditionalists and the revisionists. The former, despite their often quite
blatantly racist assumptions, prepared detailed and informative
studies that remain indispensible sources for the history of Reconstruction. The concern of the latter for the freedman's plight
is admirable. Furthermore, the questions that both groups asked
are intrinsically interesting and valid. Blacks were indeed used,
and were, in the end, all too often the victims of the failure of
white Republicans to set aside the struggle for the spoils of office
and unite behind what was supposedly their common goal. And
at the end of Reconstruction, most blacks were still at the bottom
of Southern society, toiling in the fields as they had twenty years
earlier.

The common approach of previous historians — together with
the prevalence of white historical sources and the scarcity of
black ones — has tended, however, to obscure numerous developments of Reconstruction. Many questions still remain largely un-
explored — questions dealing with the structure and behavior of
the Negro community itself rather than with the actions of whites
toward it, and with black social patterns rather than with race
relations. These are the questions that I address myself to in the
following pages. Although my focus is on one state — Alabama —
I believe this work can be considered a case study for the Deep
South as a whole rather than a local study of interest only to
those steeped in Alabama history. The essential problems that
blacks faced — what would be their new position within society,
how would they react to their freedom — were the same throughout the South. Despite differing political climates, most of the
social and economic conditions that would help to shape the outcome of these questions were similar. There is little reason to
doubt that the responses of Alabama's Negroes were in most

respects typical of those in other Southern states as well.

II

A fresh approach to the history of blacks in Reconstruction necessitates putting the problems of the period into proper perspective. The crucial issue was the transition from a slave to a free society. The Civil War and ensuing emancipation shattered the slaveholding economy of the South. Destruction of the established order inevitably produced a period of turmoil, uncertainty, and struggle. The years immediately following the war were revolutionary ones during which new relationships were formed among whites, among blacks, and between the races.

In undergoing this process, Alabama's experience was in many ways typical of that of the newer, Deep South cotton states. Although entering the Union as late as 1819 and continuing to display many of the markings of a frontier region throughout the antebellum period, by 1860 Alabama had a highly stratified society increasingly dominated by a small planter class supported by slave labor.[4] A minority of whites owned slaves, and most of these owners were small farmers with fewer than ten slaves each.[5] But if only a few whites were large slaveholders, it does not follow that their influence was slight or that most slaves were held in small units. Indeed, these planters owned the vast majority of slaves; of the state's 435,080 slaves in 1860, only 80,885 belonged to persons owning fewer than ten blacks each. The planter class controlled Alabama's economy, dominated its politics, and set the tone for the whole society.[6]

The Civil War effectively destroyed Alabama's entire social system without immediately making clear what would follow. The emancipation of the slaves struck at the very basis of planter wealth and power, which were already weakened by wartime economic dislocations. In the uncertain vacuum caused by the destruction of one social system without an obvious replacement, new forces were set in motion and new conflicts erupted. Poor whites who had long chafed at planter hegemony sought to settle old grievances and improve their own status. Freed blacks voiced increasingly militant demands. Northerners — quickly labeled carpetbaggers by bitter ex-Confederates — arrived with their own usually half-formed and frequently conflicting notions of what needed to be done. Some native whites, designated scala-wags by their hostile compatriots, rushed to endorse various Northern plans of Reconstruction; others vowed to struggle to the death for the preservation of old ways; still others embraced an apathy born of defeat and turned inward to brood and culti-vate their gardens.

Reflecting these conflicting currents, Alabama's government rested in a curious limbo for three years, in an uneasy balance between state and federal authorities. Under President Andrew Johnson's provisional governor, Lewis E. Parsons, whites held a Constitutional Convention in 1865 that ratified the Thirteenth Amendment to the Constitution, wrote a new state constitution, and called elections for a new, all-white government, which at-tempted to function as if all were normal. Elections continued to be held; the state legislature met, deliberated, and passed laws; and Governor Robert M. Patton, elected in December 1865, executed most of the functions of his office. The power of the new state government, however, was never complete. Con-gress refused to recognize its legitimacy and did not admit Ala-bama to congressional representation. Union generals exercised their own discretion in countermanding state laws and issuing regulations of their own. The confusion resulting from this divided authority remained until Congress passed the Recon-struction Acts of 1867 setting forth the prescribed path of Re-construction. Under the prodding of these acts, Alabama's Con-stitutional Convention held in 1867 produced a constitution pro-viding for black suffrage. In 1868, the new state government was inaugurated, and Alabama's representatives were readmitted to Congress.

III

In the following pages, I am concerned with how Alabama's blacks adjusted during this chaotic period to the transition from slavery to freedom. The confusion of social relations was reflect-ed in the prevailing uncertainty over the role of the new freed-

men. Although they were no longer slaves, it was not clear during
the tumultuous months after the war what their new position
would be. Many whites proclaimed loudly that the free Negro
was a contradiction in terms, and that the consequence of
emancipation would be the extinction of the black race. Others
argued that the overthrow of slavery would have little or no
practical effect: "We controlled his labor in the *past* (at our expense) and *will* control it in the future (at his)," explained one
Alabama planter of the Negro in 1865. "His condition *before* the
war and *since* are almost identical."[7] Blacks, too, were unsure of
what their new status would be, but they were determined that it
should be as far removed from slavery as possible.

Although this study deals with blacks in Alabama following
the war, it is not a general history of the Negro in Alabama
during Reconstruction. It does not tell — except incidentally — of
atrocities against blacks or of black criminality and thieving; of
the great destitution that gripped much of the state or of the role
of the Freedmen's Bureau in feeding the hungry and caring for
the sick; of the rise of the Ku Klux Klan or of black "contributions" to Reconstruction. In this respect, too, it differs, both in
scope and approach, from the several excellent revisionist
studies that have appeared during the last few years.

Instead, I am primarily concerned with questions involving
black actions and attitudes. What was the impact of emancipation upon the black family? How was black social structure affected? How did the newly freed slaves perceive their relations
with whites? What did the freedmen expect from freedom? How
did they try to achieve their goals? It is, of course, impossible to
discuss Negroes during Reconstruction in total isolation; they
were continually interacting with, influencing, and being influ-
enced by whites. Furthermore, what whites said about blacks —
properly interpreted — serves as one of the best sources of information about what blacks themselves were thinking and doing.
But whatever attention I give to whites is less an effort to understand their attitudes than to use them as a means of explaining
black behavior.

This study also differs from most others in that it covers a
relatively short time span. Most historians have seen Reconstruc-

tion as a long, drawn-out process lasting at least until 1877. This view may be partially justifiable from a primarily political perspective. The struggle over Reconstruction policies continued through much of the 1870s — although in most Southern states the Reconstruction governments were overthrown well before 1877 — and the formal rejection of the Reconstruction constitutions did not occur in most states until the turn of the century. But the term "Reconstruction" has for too long carried a purely political connotation. The Reconstruction with the greatest impact upon the South was not Radical Republican rule, but the rebuilding of patterns of life — often along very new lines — after emancipation. There is much evidence that as far as blacks were concerned — and, I suspect, as far as whites were concerned as well — the new social order took shape and virtually all of the significant new developments of Reconstruction occurred in the immediate postwar years. Emancipation and the establishment of a free labor system produced important and relatively sudden readjustments in men's relationships to each other, but the new patterns rapidly became solidified.

As I suggest in the following pages, emancipation produced a short transition period — one of great flux, hope, and experimentation — during which many old modes of thought and behavior among blacks gave way to new ones. Negroes refused to be treated as slaves and insisted on behaving as they understood free men to behave. Most important, they resisted remaining in a position of complete dependence upon their former masters. Indeed, one of the striking facts of Reconstruction was the failure of freedmen to conform to the stereotype of the good-natured, docile, lazy Sambo.[8] Almost every facet of Negro life, from agriculture to family relations, education, and religion, was affected by the desire of blacks to be as independent as possible. During the four or five years following the war, new black institutions and social patterns emerged that would, with relatively minor alterations, remain intact for the remainder of the nineteenth century.

NOTES

¹For some of the best examples of this school of history, see William A. Dunning, *Reconstruction, Political and Economic, 1865-1877* (New York: Harper and Brothers, 1907); Claude G. Bowers, *The Tragic Era: The Revolution after Lincoln* (Cambridge: Houghton Mifflin Company, 1929); Samuel Denny Smith, *The Negro in Congress, 1870-1901* (Chapel Hill: University of North Carolina Press, 1940); Walter L. Fleming, *Civil War and Reconstruction in Alabama* (New York: Columbia University Press, 1905); and John W. DuBose, *Alabama's Tragic Decade: Ten Years of Alabama, 1865-1874,* ed. James K. Greer (Birmingham, Alabama: Webb Book Company, 1940).

²For the early Negro and Marxist revisionist studies, see W. E. Burghardt Du Bois, *Black Reconstruction in America* (New York: Harcourt, Brace and Co., 1935); Horace Mann Bond, *Negro Education in Alabama: A Study in Cotton and Steel* (Washington, D.C.: The Associated Publishers, Inc., 1939); James S. Allen, *Reconstruction: The Battle for Democracy, 1865-1876* (New York: International Publishers, 1937); and three works by Alrutheus A. Taylor: *The Negro in South Carolina during Reconstruction* (Washington, D.C.: The Association for the Study of Negro Life and History, 1924); *The Negro in The Reconstruction of Virginia* (Washington, D.C.: The Association for the Study of Negro Life and History, 1926); and *The Negro in Tennessee, 1865-1880* (Washington, D.C.: The Associated Publishers, Inc., 1941). More recent studies include Vernon L. Wharton, *The Negro in Mississippi: 1865-1890* (Chapel Hill: University of North Carolina Press, 1947); Willie Lee Rose, *Rehearsal for Reconstruction: The Port Royal Experiment* (New York: The Bobbs-Merrill Company, Inc., 1964); Joel Williamson, *After Slavery: The Negro in South Carolina during Reconstruction, 1861-1877* (Chapel Hill: University of North Carolina Press, 1965); Joe M. Richardson, *The Negro in the Reconstruction of Florida, 1865-1877* (Tallahassee: Florida State University Press, 1965); Lerone Bennett, Jr., *Black Power U.S.A.: The Human Side of Reconstruction, 1867-1877* (Chicago: Johnson Publishing Co., 1967).

³See Henry Swint, *The Northern Teacher in the South, 1862-1870* (Nashville, Tennessee: Vanderbilt University Press, 1941); George R. Bentley, *A History of the Freedmen's Bureau* (Philadelphia: University of Pennsylvania Press, 1955); William S. McFeely, *Yankee Stepfather: General O. O. Howard and the Freedmen* (New Haven: Yale University Press, 1968); C. Vann Woodward, *The Strange Career of Jim Crow* (New York: Oxford University Press, 1955); James M. McPherson, *The Struggle for Equality: Abolitionists and the Negro in the Civil War and Reconstruction* (Princeton: Princeton University Press, 1964); Theodore B. Wilson, *The Black Codes of the South* (University, Alabama: University of Alabama Press, 1965); Claude H. Nolen, *The Negro's Image in the South: The Anatomy of White Supremacy* (Lexington: University of Kentucky Press, 1967); Forrest G. Wood, *Black Scare: The Racist Response to Emancipation and Reconstruction* (Berkeley and Los Angeles: University of California Press, 1970); Allen

W. Trelease, *White Terror: The Ku Klux Klan Conspiracy and Southern Recon-struction* (New York: Harper & Row, 1971); and George M. Fredrickson, *The Black Image in the White Mind: The Debate on Afro-American Character and Destiny, 1817-1914* (New York: Harper & Row, 1971).

[4]For a different view of antebellum Alabama, see Frank and Harriet Owsley, "The Economic Basis of Society in the Late Ante-Bellum South," *Journal of Southern History* 6 (1940): 24-45; see also the refutation by Fabian Linden, "Economic Democracy in the Slave South: An Appraisal of Some Recent Views," *Journal of Negro History* 31 (1946): 140-189. The best recent study exploring planter domination of Southern society is Eugene D. Genovese, *The Political Economy of Slavery: Studies in the Economy and Society of the Slave South* (New York: Random House, 1965).

[5]There were only 33,370 slave owners in a white population of 526,271. Thus, counting 5 persons per family, only 1 out of 3 white families owned slaves. Of the slave owners, 21,803 owned from 1 to 9 slaves each, and 27,709 owned from 1 to 19. Only 6,301 whites in Alabama owned 20 or more slaves. Population statistics in this introduction are from U.S. Census Office, *Eighth Census: Population* (Washington, D.C.: Government Printing Office, 1864).

[6]On antebellum Alabama, see James B. Sellers, *Slavery in Alabama* (University, Alabama: University of Alabama Press, 1950); Charles S. Davis, *The Cotton Kingdom in Alabama* (Montgomery: Alabama State Department of Archives and History, 1939); and Lewy Dorman, *Party Politics in Alabama from 1850 through 1860,* Alabama State Department of History and Archives, Historical and Patriotic Series No. 13 (Wetumpka, Alabama: Wetumpka Printing Co., 1935).

[7]Letter to the Huntsville *Advocate,* 9 November 1865.

[8]For the controversial Sambo thesis, see Stanley Elkins, *Slavery: A Problem in American Institutional and Intellectual Life* (Chicago: The University of Chicago Press, 1959), pt. III.

First Freedom

1

Black Migration

I

Emancipation came with startling suddenness to most of Alabama's black slaves. Except for the Tennessee Valley region in the extreme north, where federal troops had appeared as early as April 1862 and which was the scene of fierce fighting throughout much of the war, the state was relatively untroubled by the wartime havoc and destruction that plagued so much of the South.[1] Although many blacks no doubt had heard murmurings about the Emancipation Proclamation from the slave grapevine, in the blackbelt and surrounding counties, where most of Alabama's Negroes were concentrated, it was not until the spring of 1865 that Union soldiers under General J. H. Wilson arrived bearing with them the tidings of freedom.[2] Within a few days, the war was over. In few other states had it caused so little immediate disruption; in few others was the freeing of the slaves so sudden.

The overturning of the established order was all the more dras-

tic for its very suddenness. In most other areas of the South,
some Negroes had already had several years to experiment with
various forms of freedom and semifreedom. They had flocked to
Union lines and served there as laborers and later as soldiers.
They had worked under contract for both planters and the
United States government. They had sent their sons and daughters to freedmen's schools established by Northern benevolent
societies.[3] For the vast majority of Alabama's blacks, however,
emancipation did not come before April and May of 1865.

II

The first impulse of many newly freed blacks was to test their
freedom, to prove to themselves and their ex-masters that they
really were free. The easiest, most obvious way to do this was to
do what they had never before been allowed: leave home. It did
not really matter where they went; the act of departure itself
proved symbolically they were no longer slaves. "I's want to be
free man, cum when I please, and nobody say nuffin to me, nor
order me roun'," explained a Negro to the Northern traveler and
newspaperman Whitelaw Reid, who found him squatting in an
abandoned tent outside Selma.[4] Negroes seemed to grasp in-
stinctively that if they were to have a new position in Southern
society, they must establish their mobility immediately.[5]

   In northern Alabama, the migratory process had begun earlier.
Thousands of blacks had joined the Union army to fight for their
cause.[6] Others had labored on federal fortifications, and many
more used the federal presence as an opportunity to escape from
their owners. "[O]ur servants have all left us with the exception
of Uncle Tom," lamented a Huntsville resident with unintention-
al irony in 1864. "He will doubtless go next — old as he is; there is
a powerful charm in the word 'Freedom.'"[7] The Tennessee
Valley was not militarily secure, however, until the last months
of the war, and Negroes there could not be sure of their status
until the fall of the Confederacy. Even in northern Alabama,
then, the urge to test their new condition was frequently irresistible during the spring and summer of 1865.

   This initial postwar mass movement of the freedmen was undertaken in the face of the determined and persistent opposition of all authorities — local, state, and federal, official and unofficial. Planters warned their hands not to give up the friendly, comfortable life on the old plantation for the illusory benefits of an unknown freedom, and threatened dire consequences should their advice go unheeded. "Some of you have left with the enemy," Tuscaloosa planter-politician Robert Jemison told his newly freed slaves. "Those who left me to go with the enemy have chosen their lot and must abide by it. They will not be permitted to return."[8] Some whites tried reverse psychology. An agent of an absent planter told the freedmen on one blackbelt plantation that it was in the planter's "int[erest]s for *all* to leave but to their ints that they should stay & behave as they had done."[9] When persuasion failed, planters sometimes resorted to force. In the western blackbelt area around Livingston, Negroes still were not allowed off their plantations without passes.[10] An army officer stationed across the border in Mississippi reported that in Alabama "[w]hipping and the most severe modes of punishment are being resorted to to compell [*sic*] the Freedmen to remain at the old plantations and the negro kept in ignorance of his real condition [his freedom]."[11]

Federal officials also joined in the effort to convince the freedmen to remain where they were (in most cases, on the plantation). Especially effective were the efforts of the Bureau of Refugees, Freedmen, and Abandoned Lands, usually known as the Freedmen's Bureau. Established in 1865 as a welfare agency to aid blacks in the transition from slavery to freedom, the Bureau exercised a myriad of functions. It fed the hungry, set up hospitals, aided in establishing an educational system for blacks, and supervised labor relations between planters and agricultural laborers. The Freedmen's Bureau, headed in Washington by Commissioner O. O. Howard, was staffed largely by Union officers. In Alabama, the chief of the Bureau was Assistant Commissioner Wager Swayne, a man of generally moderate temperament who was sympathetic with the plight of the freedmen but also sometimes cooperated with planters and state authorities. Under him were a small number of sub-assistant commissioners, superintendents, and assistant superintendents, located in six regional offices across the state.[12]

Shortly after Union forces captured Selma, a general gathered the blacks of the area together and advised them to remain at work.[13] A Freedmen's Bureau official gave a similar speech to freedmen in the blackbelt town of Greensboro.[14] The first circular issued from Bureau headquarters in Montgomery, on 7 September 1865, urged Negroes not to change employers, and even the conservative Mobile *Advertiser and Register* praised the "liberal and enlightened Chief of the Freedmen's Bureau in this State," Wager Swayne, for his efforts to keep Negroes laboring on the plantations.[15] Everywhere blacks were urged to "behave" themselves and prove that they were worthy of their freedom by continuing to toil in the cotton fields.

That such a concerted effort was necessary is evidence that the freedmen had different ideas. Many — on some plantations, most — did stay at home, but more still left their plantations, at least temporarily.[16] One resident of the blackbelt community of Greensboro described the departure of former slaves from his brother-in-law's plantation and added: "On some plantations *all* the negroes have left. I don't know anyone who has not lost more or less."[17] Another planter in the same area agreed that "[t]he negroes are leaving the plantations here in squads."[18] Other reports from newspapers, planters, army officers, and Freedmen's Bureau officials confirmed the picture.[19]

Many of the freedmen who left their plantations during the spring and summer of 1865 crowded into Mobile, Montgomery, Selma, Huntsville, and numerous smaller towns, where life was different and exciting and federal garrisons provided comforting reassurance. It is impossible to tell precisely how many blacks did go to the cities during the first few months of freedom since there are no statistics from 1865. A New York *Tribune* correspondent arriving in Montgomery with Union troops on 25 April reported that he had heard estimates of as many as 5,000 new black migrants in the capital city alone. Freedmen "thronged the highways, almost impeding our march," he wrote. "In many cases we advised them to stay with their old masters, but they said, 'No, da was going to be free,' and that their old masters had treated them too cruelly." Urban whites repeatedly complained about the swarms of invading blacks. One letter to Montgomery's leading newspaper stated that the city was "crowded, crammed, packed with multitudes of lazy, worthless negroes." The Selma *Daily Times* was equally annoyed by hundreds of "impudent and noisy" Negroes parading through the streets, and Baptist minister Basil Manly noted that Tuscaloosa was "daily filled with idle vagrant negroes."[20]

It is likely that the urban migration would have been considerably greater had it not been for the strenuous efforts of city authorities to reverse the tide. Mayor R. H. Slough ordered Mobile's police to arrest all "vagrants" and announced that if troublesome Negroes did not leave the city they would be forced to labor on the streets.[21] The mayor's language was so strong that the generally cooperative Swayne, assistant commissioner of the Freedmen's Bureau, felt compelled to protest this "denial of the right peaceably to assemble, and the right to choose a place of habitation and industry."[22] Similar measures were taken, however, in other cities. In Montgomery, a group of "vagrant" blacks was put to work on the city streets. "This is a movement in the right direction," editorialized the Montgomery *Daily Advertiser*, "as the streets are in a wretched condition and need the levelling influence of 'de shubel and de hoe.'"[23] In December, a Selma city ordinance, ostensibly designed to protect against the influx of smallpox, barred any freedman from entering the city without the written approval of his employer.[24]

By that time, however, the initial migratory movement of the freedmen was coming to an end. In January, Swayne wrote that he had "no further fear of the wandering propensities of the negro." He explained that "[t]he removal of forced restraint was naturally followed by a jubilee. But that is over now."[25] Economic necessity also played a role in inducing blacks to return to the plantations, for as whites delighted in telling them, if they would eat they must work, and most of the work was to be found in the cotton fields. "Contrary to general expectations," declared the Eufaula *News* in early January, "the freedmen in this community are manfully coming up to contract for work during the year. Every one of them seems now to be anxious to make some arrangement for their future sustenance."[26]

But if the jubilee was over, its effects were of longer duration. In demonstrating his mobility, the Negro had shown planters that his labor could not be taken for granted, that they would have to offer him adequate compensation, and indeed, that they would have to bid for his labor. No planter in 1866 was able to employ hands "for the consideration of . . . victuals and clothing" as farmer Benjamin Blasingame had during the previous summer.[27] Instead, Swayne now reported, "those men who used their freedmen badly last year find proportionate difficulty this year and some of them have had to give it [planting] up."[28]

III

If early 1866 found most freedmen again toiling in the cotton fields, they continued to move about in order to better their condition. Their ability to move constituted one of the principal safeguards of their freedom, as well as one of its principal elements. Plantation turnover remained extraordinarily high throughout the remainder of the 1860s. An almost continuous local, plantation-to-plantation migration occurred, which probably had more significance for the lives of most blacks than the statistically more measurable interregional movements.

In many cases, planters themselves expelled Negroes from their plantations. Frequently, after the main labor on the crop was done, employers drove away their laborers without wages, usually charging them with a technical violation of contract. Others discharged blacks for voting Republican or taking part in political meetings. Some planters, dissatisfied with the quality of work received or the wages demanded, sought vainly for more docile and obedient hands and even experimented with white labor.[29]

Even more widespread were the efforts of blacks, facilitated by the shortage of labor that prevailed throughout the state and in most of the Deep South, to improve their position by leaving unsatisfactory employers. The labor scarcity became so acute that some whites concluded that without the protecting hand of slavery the black race was rapidly dying out and would soon become extinct. "What Has Become of the Freedmen?" inquired one newspaper in 1867. "That there are nothing like the number of negroes in this section, that there were two years ago, is quite certain. Death, immigration, or some other cause is rapidly thinning their ranks." The Mobile *Advertiser and Register* estimated that there had been a "depreciation of [Negro] laborers, by death alone, of nearly or quite one-half."[30]

Despite such talk, there was no substantial "dying off" of Negroes; the shortage of labor resulted from a variety of other causes.[31] As a newly settled, semifrontier society, Alabama had experienced chronic labor shortages even before the war. Wartime disruption and the ensuing changes in social relations served sharply to accentuate this shortage. Black women, who had once constituted a sizable portion of the labor force, frequently forsook the cotton field for the home. Many children who had previously toiled beside their parents now spent much of their time in school. The migration to the towns and cities further reduced the number of hands available for hire in the country. Finally, although no doubt one planter's complaint that "[t]he laborers do not do half their former work" was an exaggeration, some freedmen simply did not work as hard or as long as they had in slavery.[32]

The labor situation, then, remained fluid during the first few years after emancipation. While examples of faithful servants standing loyally by their old masters can be cited, most freedmen were not prepared to remain at work on the old plantation under conditions that they perceived as similar to those prevailing before the war. About the first of each year, when new contracts were made, many blacks left their employers. A few went to the cities, and a few others were able to secure land of their own, either as homesteaders or, more frequently, through outright purchase. But most of those who moved simply contracted with different planters in their home county or region. "[T]he freedmen are mostly leaving their former masters and old homes for new places," complained one small planter in his diary in January 1866.[33] Throughout that year and subsequent ones, planters issued similar complaints. One wrote that he had fifty or sixty laborers who, he had supposed, were all happy, but now "to my surprise they are leaving."[34] Another informed his son that all his hands had quit, but added, "I am not sorry for it for they had got above their business. I am fast filling their places."[35]

IV

Although much of the immediate postwar flocking to the cities was a temporary affair which ended by early 1866, Negroes continued to move to urban areas throughout the 1860s. In 1867, the Selma *Times* complained that despite the need for agricultural laborers "[t]he disposition to leave the plantations, and move to the towns and cities, is increasing every day."[36] Between 1860 and 1870, the black population of Alabama's four largest cities — Mobile, Montgomery, Selma, and Huntsville — jumped 57.8 percent.[37] Smaller towns grew rapidly as well, some with startling suddenness. Between 1860 and 1870, the number of blacks in the mountain town of Jacksonville increased from 8 to 355, and in the blackbelt town of Demopolis, where a regional Freedmen's Bureau office was located, the Negro population leapt from 1 to 965. By 1870, 40,199, or over 8 percent of the state's blacks, lived in towns and cities of over 500 inhabitants.

This migration of freedmen to the cities was more than just an element of a general nineteenth-century urban trend. Before the war, from 1850 to 1860, the black population of the state's four largest cities had increased only 20.6 percent, while the white population had increased 31.9 percent (see Table 1). During the 1860s, however, while the number of blacks in the four cities rose 57.8 percent, the number of whites remained stationary, largely because of a sharp decrease in the number of whites living in Mobile.[38] In many of the smaller towns that experienced such a dramatic growth in black population, the number of white residents increased only moderately.[39]

Cities and towns offered various attractions to Negroes that caused them to leave the plantations despite the shortage of agricultural labor. They had traditionally looked upon the city as a refuge in a hostile world. Before the war, most of the state's 2,690 free Negroes had made their homes there, more than a third of them in Mobile alone. Fugitive slaves, too, had sometimes managed to lose themselves in the urban throng and elude

Table 1 *Black and White Population of Four Alabama Cities, 1850-1870*

BLACKS	1850	1860	Change, 1850-1860	1870	Change 1860-1870
Mobile	7,518	8,404	+ 11.8%	13,919	+ 62.7%
Montgomery	2,217	4,502	+107.6%	5,183	+ 15.1%
Huntsville	1,377	1,654	+ 20.9%	2,375	+ 43.6%
Selma	2,100	1,368	- 34.9%	3,660	+167.6%
Total	13,212	15,928	+ 20.6%	25,137	+ 57.8%
WHITES					
Mobile	12,997	20,854	+69.8%	18,115	- 13.1%
Montgomery	6,511	4,341	- 33.3%	5,405	+24.5%
Huntsville	1,500	1,980	+32.0%	2,532	+27.8%
Selma	973	1,809	+85.9%	2,824	+56.1%
Total	21,981	28,984	+31.9%	28,876	- 0.4%

SOURCE: U.S. Census Office, *Eighth Census: Population* (Washington, D.C.: Government Printing Office, 1864), p. 9, and its *Ninth Census: Population* (Washington, D.C.: Government Printing Office, 1872), pp. 77-83.

their pursuers.[40] Blacks could live more independently there than under the watchful eye of the plantation overseer. Despite changes in plantation management after the war, the cities continued to offer Negroes greater independence, freedom, and excitement.

The city was also a much safer place for the independent-minded freedman than many of the more remote rural areas where it was relatively easy for hostile whites to take the law into their own hands with little chance of exposure or prosecution. Blacks who made themselves too prominent through political or religious leadership sometimes found it necessary to take refuge in Montgomery or some other city.[41] In 1866 the Mobile *Nationalist,* Alabama's leading Republican paper, asserted that most of the port city's new Negro residents were refugees who had fled from persecution in the surrounding area.[42] Although this claim was certainly an exaggeration, the rapid increase of the black urban population was no doubt in part the product of the security afforded by cities, especially those with Freedmen's Bureau offices or federal troops.

V

Despite the rapid increase in the number of blacks living in urban areas, only a very small minority of the state's Negroes moved to the towns and cities during the 1860s. More than nine-tenths of the black population remained rural in 1870. But "rural" does not necessarily imply "immobile." In addition to the constant local movement from plantation to plantation, there was considerable interregional migration within the boundaries of the state.

By the late antebellum period, geographical variations had produced several distinct regions within Alabama with strikingly different economies.[43] In the extreme north of the state lay the Tennessee Valley, a generally fertile area where both large plantations and smaller farms abounded, and the population was evenly divided between whites and blacks. South of the Tennessee Valley was a generally mountainous region rich in as yet untapped natural resources. These mountain counties were unsuited for large-scale planting operations, and small, self-sufficient farms predominated. The region was overwhelmingly white; in none of the mountain counties did blacks constitute as much as 20 percent of the population and in many they comprised less than 10 percent. Both the mountain region and the Tennessee Valley, which together occupied the northern third of Alabama, were isolated from the rest of the state by lack of an effective transportation system. As a result of this isolation and of the small farming economy prevalent throughout much of the north, regional feelings there were strong. North Alabamians increasingly resented the dominance of the state by south Alabama planters, and during the war Unionist sentiment was strong in much of the north.

A piedmont region served as a buffer zone between northern Alabama and the blackbelt. The upper piedmont resembled the mountain counties in geography, economy, and population; farther south, the land became less hilly, the farms larger, and slaveholding more prevalent. The piedmont gradually merged with the blackbelt, a thin tier of cotton-producing counties, where the plantation system reached its peak of development. In 1860, almost half of Alabama's slaves lived in these ten counties, which occupied less than one-fifth of the state's area. In almost

Map 1

The Regions of Alabama, with Blacks as a Percentage of Total Population by County, 1860

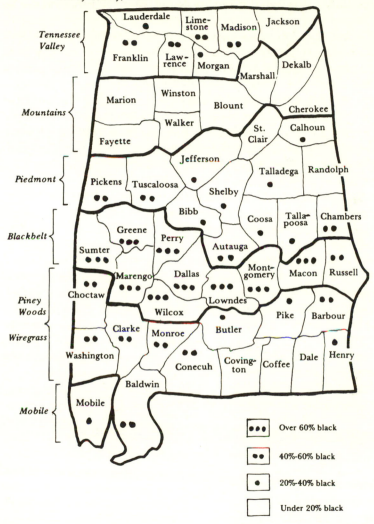

SOURCE: U.S. Census Office, *Eighth Census: Population* (Washington: Government Printing Office, 1864).

all blackbelt counties more than two-thirds of the population were slaves, and in many more than three-quarters were.[44]

South of the blackbelt lay the piney woods-wiregrass region. In the western portion of this region, pine land alternated with fertile farming soil. While large plantations were less numerous than in the blackbelt, the number of blacks and whites was fairly even. In the southeastern, wiregrass counties, the land was much less fertile, settlement often sparse, and slaves relatively few. Finally, Mobile County differed so greatly from the surrounding piney woods counties that it must be considered as a separate region. Originally settled by the French and Spaniards, the county was dominated by Mobile city, the state's largest, most cosmopolitan city and only major seaport.

Migration among these several regions during the 1860s is difficult to measure, because, in addition to possible inaccuracies in the state census of 1866 and the federal census of 1870, most of Alabama's county boundaries changed between 1866 and 1868. Fortunately, nineteen counties remained intact, and eight more can be combined into three units whose boundaries remained unchanged. By using these twenty-two counties and combinations of counties as samples, it is possible to derive a fairly accurate picture of interregional migration.

The most obvious trend was the increasing concentration of Negroes in the southern part of the state, especially in the blackbelt and Mobile County. Much of this movement occurred during

Table 2   *Black Population by Regions, 1860, 1866*

	1860	1866	Change	
Tennessee Valley	52,162	43,187	- 8,975	- 17.2%
Mountains	10,069	9,091	- 978	- 9.7%
Piedmont	82,987	77,015	- 5,972	- 7.8%
Blackbelt	205,009	216,323	+11,314	+ 5.5%
Piney woods-wiregrass	74,972	74,582	- 384	- 0.5%
Mobile County	12,571	16,664	+ 4,093	+32.6%
Total	437,770	436,862	- 908	- 0.2%

SOURCES: U.S. Census Office, *Ninth Census: Population*, pp. 11-12; Alabama state census of 1866, Montgomery *Daily Advertiser*, 21 March 1868.

Table 3 *Black Population of Counties with Unchanged Boundaries, 1866, 1870*

	1866	1870	Change
Tennessee Valley counties			
Colbert/Franklin	5,744	5,952	+ 3.4%
Lauderdale	5,094	5,170	+ 1.5%
Limestone	7,518	7,253	- 3.4%
Lawrence	6,210	6,562	+ 5.7%
Morgan	3,282	3,358	+ 2.3%
Madison	12,685	15,740	+22.5%
Jackson	2,654	3,060	+15.5%
Total	43,187	47,095	+ 9.1%
Mountain counties			
Winston	31	21	- 30.3%
Walker	486	308	- 36.5%
Marion/Fayette/Sandford	3,070	2,864	- 7.0%
Total	3,587	3,193	- 11.0%
Piedmont counties			
Jefferson	2,601	2,506	- 3.5%
Pickens	9,938	9,638	- 3.0%
Total	12,539	12,144	- 3.2%
Blackbelt counties			
Sumter	17,969	18,907	+ 5.2%
Wilcox	17,019	21,610	+26.9%
Dallas	29,610	32,152	+ 8.6%
Total	64,598	72,669	+12.5%
Piney woods-wiregrass counties			
Henry	4,491	4,657	+ 3.2%
Choctaw	6,575	6,872	+ 4.3%
Clarke	9,277	7,565	- 18.4%
Washington	2,215	1,787	- 15.5%
Baldwin/Conecuh/Escambia	7,119	7,697	+ 7.5%
Monroe	6,694	7,572	+12.9%
Total	36,371	36,150	- 0.6%
Mobile County	16,664	21,107	+26.1%

SOURCES: U.S. Census Office, *Ninth Census: Population*, pp. 11-12; Alabama state census of 1866, Montgomery *Daily Advertiser*, 21 March 1868.

the war, when the federal occupation of northern Alabama no doubt led some slave owners to move their blacks to safer portions of the state.[45] Some Negroes from the occupied area enlisted in the Union army; of these, some were killed and others chose not to return after the war.[46] As a result, the black population of both the Tennessee Valley and mountain counties declined sharply between 1860 and 1866.[47]

A study of those counties whose boundaries remained unchanged reveals that the concentration of Negroes into the blackbelt and Mobile continued during the immediate postwar years.[48] This southward shift of the black population — away from the mountains and toward the blackbelt and Mobile — was in direct contrast to a general movement of Alabama's whites from the southern to the northern part of the state.[49] As a result, those areas of the state which had been predominantly black in 1860 were even more heavily black in 1870, while the white areas — especially the mountains — were still more white.[50]

Economic incentives were in part responsible for this black migration. It was in the cotton fields of the blackbelt and surrounding counties that blacks were most needed for plantation

Table 4   *Blacks as a Percentage of the Population in Counties with Unchanged Boundaries, 1860, 1870*

	1860	1870
Counties in which blacks constituted over 65% in 1870		
Dallas	76.9%	79.0%
Sumter	75.3%	78.0%
Wilcox	71.9%	76.2%
Counties in which blacks constituted under 25% in 1870		
Jackson	18.9%	15.2%
Winston	3.4%	0.5%
Walker	6.5%	4.7%
Marion/Fayette/Sandford	12.4%	12.9%
Jefferson	22.7%	20.3%

SOURCE: U.S. Census Office, *Ninth Census: Population*, pp. 11-12.

Map 2

Black Migration by County, 1860-1866

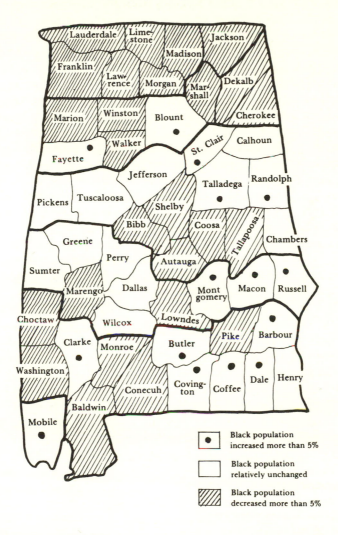

SOURCES: U.S. Census Office, *Ninth Census: Population* (Washington: Government Printing Office, 1872); Alabama State Census of 1866, in Montgomery *Daily Advertiser*, 21 March 1868.

labor. Throughout the latter half of the 1860s, planters complained of a shortage of labor. There was, on the other hand, little demand for Negro laborers in the piney woods-wiregrass region of the south, and less still in the mountain country, where small, self-sufficient farms predominated.

If economic opportunities were greatest in the blackbelt, political and social pressures also induced Negroes to leave the white-dominated counties. The hostility of poor whites, many of whom felt a keen sense of economic rivalry with the freedmen, made it intensely uncomfortable for blacks to live in areas where they were greatly outnumbered. Although the Ku Klux Klan and other terroristic organizations which arose in the 1860s were not confined entirely to the white counties, there was a qualitative difference between their operations there and in regions where blacks predominated. In the blackbelt, the Klan acted primarily as an agent of social control, aiming at insuring a cheap and obedient labor force, but in the mountain country the goal was often to exclude Negroes altogether.[51] In the isolated mountain county of Winston, whites met and passed a resolution barring Negroes from entering the county,[52] and the black population there declined from 122 in 1860 to 21 in 1870. "[I]n some portions of my circuit they will not let a negro live," declared Circuit Judge William S. Mudd to a congressional investigating committee; "that is, it is a white population, and they do not want to come in contact with the negro. They want to cultivate the lands themselves, and they want to have an exclusively white society."[53]

Even in some nonmountain counties, poor white hostility led to black emigration. Tallapoosa, a piedmont county just north of the blackbelt, witnessed a general exodus of freedmen under pressure from the Ku Klux Klan. Many fled southward to Opelika and other blackbelt towns.[54] According to one Tallapoosa planter, the Klan raids ran "the negroes out of certain beats." As a result, planters found it difficult to obtain labor "and many men there that were considered rich before the war have not a negro about them, and they cannot get them."[55]

Map 3

Black Migration by County, 1866-1870

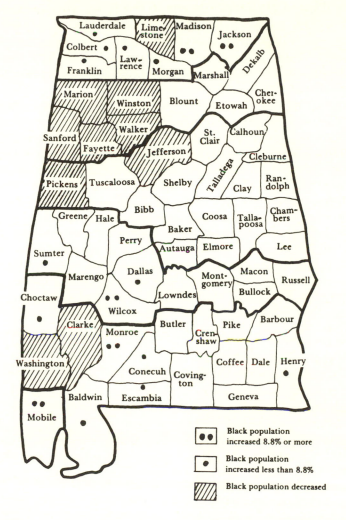

SOURCES: U.S. Census Office, *Ninth Census: Population* (Washington: Government Printing Office, 1872); Alabama State Census of 1866, in Montgomery *Daily Advertiser*, 21 March 1868. Only those counties with unchanged borders are included.

VI

There was relatively little migration of blacks into or out of Alabama during the early postwar years.[56] In some Southern states, such as Florida and Texas, the number of blacks was growing much more rapidly than in Alabama, and in Virginia there was actually a slight decrease in the Negro population. But the 8.6 percent increase in Alabama's black population during the 1860s was remarkably close to the average increase of 8.4 percent for eleven Southern states, and suggests that there was little migration between Alabama and other states.[57]

Immediately after the war, it seemed probable that blacks could be induced to migrate to labor-hungry Alabama from the upper South, which had long had a surplus of black workers. Ex-Confederate General James Longstreet recommended precisely such a policy to the assistant commissioner of the Freedmen's Bureau in Louisiana when he urged that freedmen from Virginia, North Carolina, and Kentucky be transported from those states, where they were not needed, to the gulf states, where they were.[58] The Bureau assistant commissioner in Virginia suggested that 50,000 idle Negroes be sent from his state to Florida.[59] In 1866, when Congress passed a Southern Homestead Act de-

Table 5 *Black Population of Eleven Southern States, 1860, 1870*

STATE	1860	1870	CHANGE	
Florida	62,677	91,689	29,012	46.3%
Texas	182,921	253,475	70,554	38.5%
Georgia	465,698	545,142	79,444	17.1%
Tennessee	283,019	322,331	39,312	13.8%
Arkansas	111,259	122,169	10,910	9.8%
Alabama	437,770	475,510	37,740	8.6%
North Carolina	361,522	391,650	30,128	8.3%
Louisiana	350,373	364,210	13,837	3.9%
Mississippi	437,404	444,201	6,797	1.6%
South Carolina	412,320	415,814	3,494	0.8%
Virginia	527,763	512,841	-15,122	-2.8%
Total	3,632,726	3,939,032	306,206	8.4%

SOURCE: U.S. Census Office, *Ninth Census: Population*, p. 5.

signed to help blacks and poor whites obtain land in Alabama, Arkansas, Florida, Louisiana, and Mississippi, it appeared likely that a considerable number of blacks desiring land of their own would migrate from the upper South to those states.

Despite the shortage of labor and the lure of free land, there was no mass migration of blacks to Alabama following the war. It soon became clear that few freedmen would be able to secure land in Alabama under the Homestead Act.[60] Equally important, the very factors that produced a labor shortage in Alabama during Reconstruction acted to reduce the apparent surplus of workers in the upper South. Finally, the demand for hands was even greater in some of the more recently settled Southern states than it was in Alabama. While some Negroes from Virginia and South Carolina did move south, the bulk of these went to Florida and Texas, where land was still plentiful and labor in great demand. Only in Virginia was there anything approaching a black exodus, and few of the emigrants moved to Alabama. Elsewhere, a Freedmen's Bureau official reported in late 1866 that, despite expectations, Negroes were not leaving North Carolina, South Carolina, or Georgia in order to take advantage of homesteading opportunities. They lacked the funds to move, and in any case their labor was in demand in their own states.[61]

Equally few blacks left Alabama for other states during the early Reconstruction period. It is difficult to agree with historian Vernon Wharton that the postwar years saw a substantial migration of Negroes in search of higher wages from Alabama to Mississippi.[62] True, Mississippi planters did attempt, sometimes with success, to recruit laborers in Alabama.[63] Equally often, however, they met with failure. One irate Mississippi planter wrote Wager Swayne that "I visited Huntsville some ten days since, for the purpose of employing hands to work on my plantation in this county — I only succeeded in getting two, although I offered to pay them fifteen dollars per month."[64] From the statistical evidence, it appears extremely unlikely that there was any very large-scale migration from Alabama to Mississippi. While Alabama's Negro population increased 8.6 percent between 1860 and 1870, Mississippi's grew only 1.6 percent.

White violence and intimidation were probably greater factors

than was economic incentive in causing the departure of the few
Negroes who did leave Alabama, where the demand for labor
consistently outran the supply. In the later years of Reconstruction, as whites marshaled their forces to overthrow Radical rule,
terrorism against blacks grew increasingly severe, especially in
certain counties in the western part of the state. An emigration
movement of sorts from western Alabama did get under way
toward the end of the 1860s. Robert Fullerlove, a Negro farmer
from Choctaw County, testified that he planned to leave the
state, possibly for Kansas. "I believe all the people in this neighborhood are fixing to go," he said. "[T]here is no peace in the
neighborhood."[65] In neighboring Sumter County, a similar
sentiment was developing. One black woman reported that people were talking about going to "[a] place called Kansas, way up
here somewhere. I've got it mighty strong in my head."[66] As of
1870, however, the movement was more talk than action; between 1866 and 1870, the black population increased in both
Choctaw and Sumter counties. In 1870, only 168 native black Alabamians resided in Kansas.[67]

VII

Alabama Negroes, then, exercised and experimented widely with
their new-found geographic mobility during the early postwar
years. Immediately after their liberation, tens of thousands left
their plantations, roamed over the countryside, settled on neighboring plantations, and crowded into towns and cities. They continued throughout the 1860s to move from plantation to plantation. The number of urban blacks increased sharply, although the
great bulk of the population remained rural. A few left the state,
but a great many more moved from one region of the state to
another. The result was an increasing racial polarization. As
blacks and poor whites were forced together into competitive
situations for the first time, both frequently drew back in alarm.
The black response to white harassment was to move into areas
where Negroes predominated, as well as the cities, and away
from regions in which they were heavily outnumbered. This migration pattern mirrored the development of separate institu-

tions and separatist sentiment in other areas of black life, such as religion, politics, and education.

That freedmen did move so much is indicative of the general weakness of the bonds between planters and blacks. However strong feelings of community may have been under slavery, such ties were usually not able to withstand the shock of emancipation. True, some freedmen did stand loyally by their old masters, at least for a while. In January 1866, for example, Mary F. Clay, wife of the once wealthy planter-politician Clement Claiborne Clay, wrote her sister that her old and trusted servants were still with her. Later she added that "[t]he servants are kind and attentive. . . . They are infinitely better than strangers."[68] Such affectionate ties, however, were rare even among house servants; among most field hands, who had had little or no personal contact with their owners, they were nonexistent. More common among planters than joyful elegies on the loyalty of their freedmen was the blunt comment of Tuscumbia planter-lawyer J. B. Moore. "Our freedmen will leave us," he wrote. "They will not agree to work and be controlled by me, hence, I told them I would not hire them."[69] Most blacks did not want to be controlled by anyone, and they were willing to migrate to insure that they were not.

For the blacks, the migration itself was of even greater significance than any changes in population distribution that resulted from it. They migrated to improve their economic position, and they migrated to protect themselves from physical abuse. But more than that, they migrated to affirm their freedom, because free movement was one of the most obvious earmarks of their new status. No matter what else might happen to him, the Negro who could move was in an important sense master of his own destiny.

Notes

1. See Walter L. Fleming, *Civil War and Reconstruction in Alabama* (New York: Columbia University Press, 1905), pp. 61-143 *passim*.

2. *Ibid.*, pp. 71-74.

3. See Bell I. Wiley, *Southern Negroes, 1861-1865* (New Haven: Yale University Press, 1938), pp. 175-344; David Dudley Cornish, *The Sable Arm: Negro Troops in the Union Army, 1861-1865* (New York: Longmans, Green and Co., 1956); Henry Lee Swint, *The Northern Teacher in the South* (Nashville: Vanderbilt University Press, 1941); John W. Blassingame, "The Union Army as an Educational Institution for Negroes, 1862-1865," *Journal of Negro Education* 34 (1965): 152-159; Willie Lee Rose, *Rehearsal for Reconstruction: The Port Royal Experiment* (New York: The Bobbs-Merrill Company, 1964).

4. Whitelaw Reid, *After the War: A Tour of the Southern States, 1865-1866* (Cincinnati: Moore, Wilstach and Baldwin, 1866), p. 389.

5. Carl Schurz was practically alone among whites in recognizing this social process. He recommended that the freedmen be encouraged to move to new plantations, as the "new relation [of free labor] would establish itself more naturally and easily if no other individual relation had ever existed between the employer and the laborer." Schurz to Andrew Johnson, Montgomery, 21 August 1865, Johnson Papers, Library of Congress.

6. Official records show 4,969 Negro recruits from Alabama. This figure represented a smaller proportion of the state's slave population than that provided by any other Confederate state except Texas and Georgia. *The War of the Rebellion: A Compilation of the Official Records of the Union and Confederate Armies* (Washington: Government Printing Office, 1897; hereafter cited as OR), ser. III, vol. IV, pp. 1269-1270. According to Fleming, however *(Civil War and Reconstruction*, p. 88), many Alabama Negroes "were credited to the northern states" and at least 10,000 blacks from Alabama enlisted. If so, there is no reason to doubt that Negroes from other Confederate states served in Northern regiments as well.

7. Mrs. W. D. Chadick, diary, 27 March 1864, typed copy, Alabama State Department of Archives and History.

8. Robert Jemison, proclamation to his slaves, April 1865, typed copy, Southern Historical Collection, University of North Carolina.

9. John A. Wemyss to Henry Watson, Mobile, 14 July 1865, Watson Papers, Duke University Library.

10. A. L. Mock, Lieutenant General, to C. Cadle, Assistant Adjutant General, Gainsville, 12 October 1865, Freedmen's Bureau Papers (hereafter cited as FBP), Alabama Letters Received, National Archives.

11. C. W. Clarke, Lieutenant and Provost Marshal, District of East Mississippi, to Wager Swayne, Meridian, Mississippi, 14 July 1865, FBP, Alabama Letters Received.

12. See George R. Bentley, *A History of the Freedmen's Bureau* (Philadelphia: University of Pennsylvania Press, 1955); William S. McFeely, *Yankee Stepfather: General O. O. Howard and the Freedmen* (New Haven: Yale University Press, 1968); and Elizabeth Bethel, "The Freedmen's Bureau in Alabama," *Journal of Southern History* 14 (1948): 49-92.

13. C. C. Andrews to the freedmen of Selma and vicinity, 9 May 1865, OR, ser. I, vol. XLIX, pt. 2, pp. 728-729.

14. *Alabama Beacon* (Greensboro), 23 June 1865.

15. Montgomery *Daily Advertiser,* 9 September 1865; Mobile *Advertiser and Register,* 9 September 1865.

16. See, for example, the letter of Baptist minister Basil Manly to his sister Jane, Tuscaloosa, 8 June 1865, Manly Family Papers, University of Alabama Library. Manly wrote that in part because the "commander of the forces that came here, after the surrender, was a Kentuckian," without "any wish to interfere with our servants," there had been relatively little disruption of "domestic arrangements." He rejoiced that his Negroes had not run off and commented that "things go on, as before."

17. John H. Parrish to Henry Watson, Greensboro, 19 June 1865, Watson Papers.

18. F. C. Taylor to Robert Jemison, Greensboro, 18 May 1865, Jemison Papers, University of Alabama Library.

19. See, for example, L. F. Hubbard, Colonel Commanding, to Captain W. H. F. Randall, Demopolis, 20 May 1865, OR, ser. I, vol. XLIX, pt. II, p. 855; James Mallory, diary, 10 June 1865, Southern Historical Collection; *Clarke County Journal* (Grove Hill), 29 June 1865.

20. New York *Daily Tribune,* 3 June 1865; Montgomery *Daily Advertiser,* 5 August 1865; Selma *Daily Times,* 5 August 1865; Manly's addition to a letter from S. L. Manly to his mother, sister, and brother, Tuscaloosa, 22 July 1865, Manly Papers.

21. Newspaper clipping, 24 July 1865, Lewis E. Parsons Papers, Alabama State Department of Archives and History.

22. Swayne to Provisional Governor Parsons, 31 July, 1865, Parsons Papers.

23. Montgomery *Daily Advertiser,* 26 July 1865.

24. Selma *Morning Times,* 9 December 1865.

25. Swayne to Commissioner O. O. Howard, 31 January 1866, FBP, Alabama Weekly Reports.

26. Quoted in the Mobile *Advertiser and Register,* 9 January 1866.

27. Contract between Benjamin Blasingame and 13 former slaves, Chambers County, 24 July 1865, FBP, Alabama Letters Received.

28. Swayne to Howard, 2 January 1866, FBP, Alabama Weekly Reports.

29. See chap. 2 for relations between freedmen and planters. See Robert Gilmour, "The Other Emancipation: Studies in the Society and Economy of Alabama Whites during Reconstruction" (Ph.D. diss., Johns Hopkins University, 1972), pp. 32-43, for the futile efforts of planters to secure white laborers.

30. *Alabama Beacon,* 12 January 1867; Mobile *Advertiser and Register,* 7 April 1866.

31. According to the census, the black population of Alabama increased from 437,770 to 475,502. U.S. Census Office, *Ninth Census: Population* (Washington: Government Printing Office, 1872), pp. 11-12. In fact, the black population may have increased even more substantially than is indicated by the census returns, since it appears that the 1870 census undercounted the number of Southern blacks. See U.S. Department of the Interior, Census Office, *Tenth Census: Population* (Washington: Government Printing Office, 1883), p. xxxviii, and its *Eleventh Census: Population* (Washington: Government Printing Office, 1895), pp. xi-xii, xciv.

32. Henry Watson to W. A. and G. Maxwell and Company, Northampton, Mass., 11 July 1866, Watson Papers.

33. James Mallory, diary, 1 January 1866, Southern Historical Collection.

34. John G. Harris to Governor Robert M. Patton, Chambers County, 21 April 1866. Patton Papers, Alabama State Department of Archives and History. Harris complained that "[l]aborers without any cause or provocation are leaving their employers and are encouraged to do so for the reason that they find no difficulty in getting employment."

35. Benjamin Fitzpatrick to his son, Oak Grove, 19 January 1869, Benjamin Fitzpatrick Papers, Southern Historical Collection.

36. Quoted in the Mobile *Advertiser and Register,* 17 December 1867.

37. See Table 1. Unless otherwise stated, population statistics for 1860 and 1870 are derived from the U.S. Census Office, *Ninth Census: Population.* All 1866 population figures are derived from the state census of that year. There are at least two slightly varying published versions of this census. Because it is more complete, I have used the version printed in the Montgomery *Daily Advertiser,* 21 March 1868. For two counties, however, Greene and Jackson, this version is clearly inaccurate, and I have consequently found it necessary to substitute figures from the version published in the U.S. Senate, Ex. Doc. No. 6, 39th Cong., 2d sess., pp. 21-22.

38. See Table 1. Even excluding Mobile, the white population of the other three cities increased only 27 percent during the 1860s, compared with an increase of 49 percent for the black population.

39. In Jacksonville, for example, the white population actually decreased between 1860 and 1870 from 695 to 603. In Demopolis, it increased from 472 to 574.

40. See Richard C. Wade, *Slavery in the Cities: The South, 1820-1860* (New York: Oxford University Press, 1964), pp. 215-225.

41. James Alston, for example, a political leader in Macon County, fled to Montgomery in 1870 after being shot in his home by a group of whites. See U.S., Congress, *Testimoy Taken by the Joint Select Committee to Inquire into the Condition of Affairs in the Late Insurrectionary States* (Washington: Government Printing Office, 1872), IX, 1017-1018. This testimony is hereafter cited as *Ku Klux Conspiracy.*

42. Mobile *Nationalist,* 18 January 1866.

43. Historians and geographers have used several different systems of geo-graphical classification, dividing the state into as many as ten regions. See the discussion in Horace Mann Bond, *Negro Education in Alabama: A Study in Cotton and Steel* (Washington, D.C.: The Associated Publishers, Inc., 1939), pp. 1-3. For the purposes of this study, a simpler version, consisting of six regions, is most useful. See Figure 1. The regional boundaries were never as sharp as any system of classification must suggest. Although regions sometimes cut across county lines, I have, for convenience, placed every county entirely in one region or another.

44. Of the state's 435,080 slaves, 205,009 lived in blackbelt counties. Only 22,657 of these were held in units of fewer than 10 slaves.

45. Wiley, *Southern Negroes,* p. 47.

46. Robert Somers, *The Southern States Since the War: 1870-1* (London: Mac-Millan and Co., 1871), p. 115.

47. See Table 2 and Figure 2. During these years, the black population of the state as a whole remained almost unchanged, decreasing from 437,770 to 436,862, or 0.2 percent. The white population decreased from 526,271 to 522,799.

48. See Table 3 and Figure 3. Although the black population of the Tennessee Valley increased 9.1 percent between 1866 and 1870, this growth paralleled the increase of the black population in the state as a whole, which was 8.8 percent. About three-quarters of the growth of the Negro population in the Tennessee Valley occurred in Madison County, which included the city of Huntsville. The black population of three sample mountain counties and combinations of counties declined 8.5 percent. The number of Negroes in two piedmont counties declined 3.2 percent. On the other hand, the black population of three blackbelt counties increased 12.5 percent, and in Mobile County it increased 26.1 percent. As a re-sult of migration to Mobile from the surrounding piney woods counties, the Ne-gro population of the sample piney woods-wiregrass counties decreased 0.6 per-cent.

49. See Gilmour, "The Other Emancipation," p. 83.

50. See Table 4. There was a coefficient of correlation of +0.592 between the percentage of blacks in the twenty-two sample counties in 1870 and the percent-age increase in black population from 1860 to 1870. In other words, blacks were migrating to counties which were already heavily black and away from those which were predominantly white. Only in the mixed farming and planting region of the Tennessee Valley were blacks and whites frequently moving into the same areas. The correlation was figured according to the Spearman (rank-order) for-mula,

$$P = 1 - \frac{6\sum(d^2)}{n^3 - n}$$

where n=the number of counties and d=the difference in their ranks.

51. Fleming, *Civil War and Reconstruction*, p. 692. On the Klan in Alabama, see Allen W. Trelease, *White Terror: The Ku Klux Klan Conspiracy and Southern Reconstruction* (New York: Harper & Row, 1971), passim.

52. Fleming, *Civil War and Reconstruction*, pp. 691-692. On Winston County, see Wesley S. Thompson, *"The Free State of Winston," A History of Winston County, Alabama* (Winfield, Alabama: Pareil Press, 1968).

53. *Ku Klux Conspiracy*, X, 1757.

54. *Ibid.*, testimony of Daniel Taylor, IX, 1126-1128.

55. *Ibid.*, testimony of John J. Holley, IX, 1137.

56. It is even more difficult to measure interstate migration of blacks between 1860 and 1870 than it is to determine their regional movements within a single state. Since the federal census of 1860 did not record the state of birth of slaves, it is impossible to compare the number of blacks born out-of-state residing in Alabama in 1860 with the number in 1870, or to compare the number of Alabama-born Negroes living in other states in 1860 with the number in 1870. Conclusions concerning interstate migration of blacks during this decade are, therefore, rough estimates only, based on population figures of Alabama and other Southern states, and on scattered nonstatistical evidence.

57. This is not to suggest that there was not considerable local migration across state lines. In moving from one plantation to another, freedmen paid little more attention to state than to county boundaries. Net immigration or emigration, however, was very slight. See Table 5. The decline in the number of blacks in the Tennessee Valley between 1860 and 1866, coupled with the 13.8 percent increase of Tennessee's Negro population between 1860 and 1870, suggests, as noted by Swayne, that during the war years there was a substantial northward movement from the Valley into Tennessee. See Swayne to Howard, Montgomery, 31 October 1866, FBP, Assistant Adjutant General's Office. Annual Report.

58. Longstreet to General A. Baird, Assistant Commissioner of Louisiana, New Orleans, 31 January 1866, FBP, Assistant Adjutant General's Office, Letters Received. Longstreet recommended that blacks be hired as sharecroppers for one-sixth of the crop.

59. Colonel O. Brown, Assistant Commissioner of Virginia, to Howard, Richmond, December 1865, FBP, Assistant Adjutant General's Office, Letters Received.

60. See chap. 6, for an analysis of the failure of the Homestead Act in Alabama.

61. Report of Bvt. Brigadier General F. D. Sewell, Inspector General, Washington, D.C., 15 December 1866, FBP, Assistant Adjutant General's Office, Letters Received.

62. See Vernon L. Wharton, *The Negro in Mississippi: 1865-1890* (Chapel Hill: University of North Carolina Press, 1947), p. 107.

63. For example, early in 1867 ninety-four Alabama freedmen bound themselves to work on any of R. M. Robertson's plantations in Mississippi or Louisiana

for the year 1867. They also promised to obey all orders and not to leave the plantation without permission. Contract, Uniontown, Alabama, 1 January 1867, FBP, Alabama Letters Received.

64. Lawrence H. Moore to Swayne, Noxubee County, Mississippi, 12 April 1866, FBP, Alabama Letters Received.

65. *Ku Klux Conspiracy*, X, 1056.

66. *Ibid.*, Testimony of Jane Killens, X, 1739.

67. U.S. Census Office, *Ninth Census: Population*, p. 328.

68. Mary F. Clay to sister, Huntsville, 21 January, 12 February 1866, Clement Claiborne Clay Papers, Duke University Library. In the first letter, however, she also wrote that "Aunt M. often says she is tired of cooking & Alfred told Lawson that he intended to move. I make no remarks, give few orders, never interfere with their duties & need no attention for my room from them."

69. Moore, diary, 23 December 1865, typed copy, Alabama State Department of Archives and History.

2

Free Plantation Labor

I

Despite the migration of Negroes to Alabama's towns and cities, the most important question to blacks in 1865 concerned the role of the rural freedmen. The end of the Civil War found general confusion as to their status. "You have been told by the Yankees and others that you are free," one planter declared to his Negroes in April 1865. "This may be so! I do not doubt that you will be freed in a few years. But the terms and time of your ultimate freedom is not yet fully and definitely settled. Neither you nor I know what is to be the final result."[1] Even if free, the Negroes' position in society remained to be determined. Presumably they would continue to till the land, for agriculture, especially cotton, was the mainstay of the state's economy and would continue as such for years. But it was not clear under what new system the land would be cultivated.

In the spring of 1865, before the arrival of Freedmen's Bureau officials, Union officers played the greatest role in establishing

30

the new order.² Throughout the state, they informed whites that the Negroes really were free and gathered blacks together to tell them of their new rights. "All persons formerly held as slaves will be treated in every respect as entitled to the rights of freedmen, and such as desire their services will be required to pay for them," announced Lieutenant Colonel C. T. Christensen in a typical statement from Mobile.³

The army also served as the precursor of the Freedmen's Bureau in establishing the new agricultural labor system, according to which freedmen were to work under yearly contracts with their employers, supervised by federal officials. Varieties of this contract system had already been tested in certain Union-occupied portions of the South before the end of the war, and in April Thomas W. Conway, general superintendent of freedmen for the Department of the Gulf, arrived in Montgomery to inaugurate it in Alabama.⁴ But it was late summer before the Freedmen's Bureau was fully established throughout the state, and until then the task of supervising relations between planters and freedmen rested primarily with the army. Officers advised blacks to remain on their plantations "whenever the persons by whom they are employed recognize their rights and agree to compensate them for their services."⁵ Similar circulars, although not always so friendly in tone, were issued from other parts of the state. Brevet Major General R. S. Granger ordered that all contracts between freedmen and planters must be in writing. He added bluntly that "[t]hose found unemployed, will be arrested and set to work."⁶ But officers were usually vague in recommending what the compensation of the freedmen, or their working relations with planters, should be. Conditions varied widely from one location to another during the first few months after the war as individual army officers, Freedmen's Bureau officials, and planters exercised their own discretion.

Observers generally noted a demoralization of labor during the spring and summer of 1865, which they frequently associated with the early migration of freedmen. Upon his arrival in Montgomery, Conway noted a "perfect reign of idleness on the part of the negroes."⁷ Other Bureau officials joined planters in declaring that blacks either would not work or would at best make feeble

symbolic gestures toward work.[8] Southern whites, and some
Northern ones as well, complained that Negroes refused to work
and were "impudent and defyant."[9] In one piedmont county, the
commander of the local militia warned that "[t]he negroes are
becoming very impudent and unless something is done very soon
I fear the consequences."[10] White Alabamians frequently confused black "impudence" with outright revolt, but organized
violence did occasionally occur.[11]

Events on the Henry Watson plantation, a large estate in the
blackbelt county of Greene, illustrate the behavior of freedmen
during the first few months after the war. "About the first of
June," wrote John Parrish to his brother-in-law Henry Watson,
who was vacationing in Germany, "your negroes rebelled
against the authority" of the overseer George Hagin. They refused to work and demanded his removal. As Parrish was ill at
the time, he induced a friend of Watson's, J. A. Wemyss, to go to
the plantation and attempt to put things in order. "He made a
sort of compromise bargain with the negroes," Parrish reported,
"agreeing that if they would remain he would give them part of
the crop, they should be clothed and fed as usual, and that Mr.
Hagan [sic] should have no authority over them. . . . All hands
are having a good easy time, not doing half work." Six days later
Parrish reported that "they have again rebelled." When Wemyss
informed them firmly that they must submit to the overseer's
authority, at first they "amiably consented," but soon they once
again objected — "their complaints were universal, very ugly" —
and seventeen of them left for nearby Uniontown, where a
federal garrison was stationed. Meanwhile, a Freedmen's Bureau agent had arrived in Greensboro. Parrish brought him to the
plantation, where he "modified the contract in the negroes[']
fav[or] & made them sign it with their marks." The modified contract granted the laborers one-eighth of the crop.[12]

When Watson finally returned from Germany to take charge of
matters himself, he was totally disgusted with what he found.
The Negroes "claim of their masters full and complete compli-
ance on their part," he complained, "but forget that they agreed
to do anything on theirs and are all idle, doing nothing, insisting
that they shall be fed and are eating off their masters." Finding

such a state of affairs more than he could tolerate, he decided to rent the plantation to overseer Hagin and "have nothing to do with the hiring of hands or the care of the plantation." Hagin, in turn, later broke up the plantation and sublet individual lots to Negro families.[13]

II

Southern whites, long accustomed to thinking of their slaves as faithful and docile servants, were quick to blame outsiders for any trouble. As early as April 1862, a north Alabama planter had noted that the Union soldiers "to a great extent demoralized the negroes. . . . The negroes were delighted with them and since they left enough can be seen to convince one that the Federal army[,] the negroes and white Southern people cannot inhabit the same country."[14] After the war, planters continued to complain about the harmful influence of the army.[15] The presence of black troops was especially unpalatable to former slave owners. "[N]egroes will *not work* surrounded and encouraged with black troops encouraging them to insubordination," complained one outraged resident of a blackbelt community.[16]

Although Alabama whites were deeply humiliated by the presence of Yankees and black troops in their midst, there was little foundation to the complaints about outside agitation. Indeed, federal officials often cooperated directly with planters and local authorities in attempting to keep blacks in line. Army officers urged Negroes to stay on their plantations. Freedmen's Bureau agents frequently assisted in keeping order, too. "My predecessors here worked with a view to please the white citizens, at the expense of, and injustice to, the Freedmen," complained a shocked Bureau assistant superintendent shortly after his arrival in Tuskegee. "They have invariably given permission to inflict punishment for insolence or idleness, and have detailed soldiers to tie up and otherwise punish the laborers who have, in the opinion of the employers, been *refractory*."[17] Commissioner Howard later explained that the Bureau "came to the assistance of the Planters" and succeeded in making the blacks "reliable laborers under the free system." He added that "[t]he good conduct of the millions of freedmen is due to a large extent to our officers of the Army and the Bureau."[18]

A more substantial cause of the demoralization of labor was the mistrust existing between freedman and planter. Where this mistrust was minimal — that is, where planters and freedmen had relatively close ties and where planters readily acknowledged the changed condition of their relations — Negroes continued to work well.[19] More often than not it was the small planter, who worked in the field beside his employees and knew them personally, who managed to remain on good terms with them.[20] But few planters were willing to accept all the implications of the overthrow of slavery. "Thus far," pronounced the state's leading newspaper in October, "we are sorry to say that experience teaches that the negro, in a free condition will not work on the old plantations."[22] Another newspaper agreed that freedom had made the blacks "dissatisfied, listless, improvident, and unprofitable drones."[22] Throughout the state, whites refused to believe that Negroes would work without the compulsion of slavery.[23]

Some planters continued to hope that emancipation could either be rescinded or delayed, and "consequently told the negroes they were not free."[24] Others recognized the de jure passing of slavery and concentrated on making the condition of the freedmen as near as possible to that of slaves. Upon his arrival in Montgomery, Conway noted that "the Planters appeared disinclined to offer employment, except with guarantees that would practically reduce the Freedmen again to a state of bondage."[25]

Early contracts between planters and freedmen reflected the disbelief of whites in the possibility of free black labor and their desire to maintain slavery in fact, if not in name. Some planters reached "verbal agreements" with freedmen to continue as they had, without recompense. It was also relatively easy, before the Freedmen's Bureau was firmly established, for planters to lure former slaves into signing contracts that essentially perpetuated their condition. "Today I contracted with Jane and Dick to serve the remainder of the year, such being the federal law," Sarah Espy of the mountain county of Cherokee wrote in her diary in July. "I give them their victuals and clothing, the proceeds of their patches[,] and they are to proceed as heretofore."[26] Similar contracts were made in other regions, and numerous Freedmen's Bureau officials reported upon arrival at their posts that Negroes were working without pay.[27] The practice was summarized in a report to Swayne: "We find that the agreements they [the freedmen] have been working under (some of them since last April) are merely a paper drawn up by their late owners," wrote Captain J. W. Cogswell, "in which the negro promises to work for an indefinite time for nothing but his board and clothes, and the white man agrees to do nothing."[28]

When some compensation was provided, as was the case more often than not, it almost always involved a share of the crop. There seems to have been little or no experimentation with wage labor during the first few months after the war. The initial reason for the immediate widespread adoption of sharecropping was simple: the defeated South did not have sufficient currency to pay laborers in cash. Cropping provided a convenient mode of paying freedmen without any money transactions.[29]

Partly for the same reason and partly from tradition, most early contracts specified that food and medical care would be provided by the planter. In addition to being a continuation of the old plantation paternalism, this provision also conformed to the wishes of the Freedmen's Bureau. Shortly after his arrival in Montgomery, Swayne drew up a list of proposed labor regulations. One was that "[p]art of the compensation is required to be in food and medical attendance, lest the improvident leave their families to suffer or the weak are obliged to purchase at unjust rates what they must immediately have."[30] The concern of the Freedmen's Bureau for the welfare of the freedmen, superimposed upon the legacy of slave paternalism and combined with the shortage of currency, insured that early contracts would give Negroes, in addition to their share of the crop, "quarters, fuel, necessary clothes, [and] medical attendance in case of sickness."[31]

Although the size of the shares freedmen received in 1865 varied considerably, it was almost always very small. W. C. Penick agreed to pay his laborers one-quarter of the crop, but such liberality was rare during the summer of 1865. More typical was the contract between Henry Watson and his more than fifty

adult blacks, which promised them one-eighth of the crop. In
other cases shares varied from one-quarter to one-tenth of the
crop.[32]

In addition to appropriating the greater portion of the freedmen's labor, planters were concerned with maintaining control
over their lives. "I look upon slavery as gone, gone, gone, beyond
the possibility of help," lamented one planter. He added reas-
suringly, however, that "we have the power to pass stringent
police laws to govern the negroes — This is a blessing — For they
must be controlled in some way or white people cannot live
amongst them."[33] Such an outlook did not necessarily represent
a conscious effort to thwart the meaning of freedom, for whites
had been conditioned by years of slavery to look upon subservience as the only condition compatible with Negro, or any plantation, labor. Nevertheless, the effect was the same. Early contracts often included provisions regulating the behavior of laborers. A typical one provided that "all orders from the manager are
to be promptly and implicitly obeyed under any and all circumstances" and added "[i]t is also agreed that none of the said negroes will under any circumstances leave the plantation without
a written permission from the manager." If any of them quit work
before the expiration of the contract, he was to forfeit all his
wages.[34] Some contracts gave planters authority to whip refractory Negroes.[35]

It is only as a response to such attempts to perpetuate slave conditions that the seeming demoralization of black labor can be
understood. Although whites pointed at idle or turbulent Negroes and repeated that they did not comprehend the meaning
of freedom, the lack of comprehension was on the part of Alabama's whites. Blacks lost little time in demonstrating their grasp
of the essentials of freedom and the tactical flexibility their new
condition provided. Just as many felt compelled to leave their
old plantations immediately after the war to prevent old relations
from being perpetuated, so did they find it necessary to establish
at the outset that they would not labor under conditions that made
them free in name but slave in fact.

III

In December 1865 events reached something of a crisis as planters continued to strive for a return to the methods of prewar days and blacks continued to resist. Planter-laborer relationships were tense during the summer and fall, but with contracts entered into after the war due to expire on 31 December, the approach of the new year heralded an especially difficult time. Negroes now had the experience of over half a year as freedmen in dealing with planters. They also had the backing of the Freedmen's Bureau, which, if generally ambivalent about the precise position of the freedman in Southern society, refused to sanction his essential reenslavement. The culmination of the demoralization of labor and the mass migrations of 1865 was the refusal of many blacks to contract for the following year.

One reason Negroes were slow to contract was that many of them expected the plantations of their ex-masters to be divided among them at the start of the year.[36] While this idea proved to be a total misconception, it was neither so ludicrous nor so far-fetched a notion as white Alabamians portrayed it. Southern whites themselves had contributed greatly to the expectation by warning during the war that defeat would result in the confiscation of their lands.[37] Commissioner Howard had originally intended to turn over confiscated and abandoned lands to the freedmen, and it was only when President Johnson directly countermanded this policy in the autumn of 1865 that the Bureau reversed itself and began restoring the lands in its possession to the original owners.[38] As the end of the year approached, Freedmen's Bureau officials carefully explained to Negroes that they were not to be given land and advised them to contract for moderate wages.[39]

White Alabamians responded to the black desire for land by exaggerating the extent to which the freedmen expected confiscation, playing up every minor incident, and predicting ominously that New Year's would bring a black uprising. They complained of Negroes arming themselves, and in at least one area whites organized armed patrols to defend themselves against an imagined impending Negro insurrection.[40] Other observers, however, denied any threat of an uprising, and according to Carl Schurz rumors were "spread about impending negro insurrections evidently for no other purpose than to serve as a pretext for annoying police regulations concerning the colored people."[41]

The refusal of the freedmen to contract in December in no way presaged a rebellion, but merely expressed their reluctance to repeat their unhappy experience of the past half-year. Without careful Freedmen's Bureau supervision, the contract system threatened to become little more than an opportunity for whites to take advantage of illiterate and ignorant blacks. As Swayne wrote, with what turned out to be something of an underestimation of the abilities of the newly freed slaves, "[c]ontracts imply bargaining and litigation, and at neither of these is the freedman a match for his Employer." For this reason, the assistant commissioner reported, planters "so vigorously demanded contracts there was danger they would not undertake to plant at all without them."[42]

That the fears of insurrection consisted chiefly of groundless rumors became evident when New Year's day passed without the slightest hint of trouble. To the astonishment and relief of whites, freedmen rushed to contract during the first few days of 1866 and then settled down to work. "The praiseworthy conduct of the negroes has surprised many," declared the Selma *Morning Times* in an editorial that typified the general white response.[43] The demoralizing effects of emancipation about which whites had complained so bitterly vanished in a matter of days. "One thing is obvious," recorded a surprised planter; "the negroes, who are hired are farming and working much better than any one predicted they would work." Other white Alabamians agreed.[44] From Tuskegee, the local Freedmen's Bureau agent boasted that "the Freedmen have commenced work with such a zeal as to merit the praise and approbation of the Planters. Planters say to me [']my negroes have never done so well as they are doing now[']"[45]

But if planters rejoiced that their laborers were hard at work, the freedmen had won a signal victory that was noticed by the more perceptive whites. "I think the negro hire was very high," complained future Democratic Governor George S. Houston;

"[I] never had any idea of paying that much for negroes."[46] He was right. Gone were the days when a typical contract gave the laborers one-eighth of the crop, or merely bed and board. By refusing to contract until the last moment, the freedmen had thrown their prospective employers into a panic and forced a significant alteration in the terms of the ultimate settlement. Although neither so well concerted nor organized, the process had essentially the same effect as a massive general strike.[47]

Aside from the presence of the Freedmen's Bureau, which made blatant cheating by planters more difficult, the prevailing shortage of labor proved an inestimable boon to the freedmen. In 1866, as throughout most of the early postwar period, the pressure was on the planter to find laborers rather than on the Negro to find employment. Freedmen could feel relatively free in refusing to contract on what they regarded as unsatisfactory terms or in leaving employers with whom they were unhappy. Labor stealing, or enticing freedmen to change employers for higher wages, was a persistent complaint among planters.[48] Occasionally, blacks were even able to strike for higher wages, as in the mountain county of Cherokee, "where they bound themselves together, under a penalty of fifty lashes, to be laid on the naked back, not to contract to work for any white man during the present harvest, for less than two dollars per day."[49]

As had been the case in 1865, the terms of working arrangements varied widely among plantations. Both the lower and upper limits of the pay scale, however, were substantially higher than they had been. Half, or perhaps slightly more than half, of the contracts provided for a division of the crop. In such cases, the laborer almost always received a larger share than he had in 1865. Although there are examples of freedmen receiving as little as one-sixth of the crop, the prevailing portion — when, as was usual in 1866, the laborer provided nothing but his own labor — was one-quarter.[50] For the first time, many planters contracted to pay their employees money wages rather than a portion of the crop. A typical small planter recorded that he paid his eight field hands an average of ten dollars per month for men and fifty dollars a year for women, in addition to food.[51] In other cases where Negroes worked for wages, the rate of compensation

usually ranged from seven to fifteen dollars per month for men,
and somewhat less for women.[52]

IV

The economic disadvantage of sharecropping to the Negro became evident in 1866 as the bright prospects of winter and spring
faded in the summer. By August the cotton crop, which once
seemed so promising, had been reduced by unseasonal rains to
half its usual size, and autumn saw the second straight crop failure.[53] As the extent of the disaster became clear, whites across
the state began to decide that free blacks were not working well
after all. The *Clarke County Journal,* for example, noted that although freedmen had labored satisfactorily during the winter
and spring, now they seemed stubborn and lazy. "What is the
matter with the freedmen?" it queried.[54]

The contract system provided innumerable opportunities for
friction between planters and freedmen — especially sharecroppers — in time of crisis. True, there were occasional touching instances when planters looked after former slaves. One white
wrote to Swayne that an ex-slave of his who had left him after
the war "because he would not 'feel free' if he did not" was
"about to be imposed upon by an unprincipled man, who is about
to employ him for the next year for far less than he is worth. . . .
Please write to me," begged the distressed planter in a letter
asking the assistant commissioner for advice. "I am willing to put
myself to some trouble to protect my former faithful slave."[55]
Most planters, however, were primarily interested in receiving
the maximum possible labor from the freedmen at minimal cost,
even if it involved cheating, violence, and brutality.

The most common complaint of the freedmen was that either
after the main labor on the crop was done or when it came time to
divide the crop, planters would drive them off the plantations,
frequently charging them with some technical violation of contract.[56] Unlike wage earners, who were relatively secure, sharecroppers could be discharged and deprived of any compensation
whatsoever. Temporary laborers could then be hired either by the
day or week to finish up any remaining work.[57] From Greene

County, in the blackbelt, a Freedmen's Bureau agent reported "I find many, many men who employed them [freedmen] are arresting them . . . in a large majority of cases without cause" and sending them to sit in jail until the crop was sold.[58] Although in some instances Bureau officials, or even the courts, mediated between planters and freedmen and were able to secure for the latter some payment, many injustices went unnoticed or unredressed.[59]

The cyclical pattern established in 1865-1866 was repeated with some variations the following year. In December 1866, blacks once again were reluctant to contract.[60] Although many of them now had the additional experience of being cheated out of their share of the crop, the absence of any illusions over the possibility of land confiscation enabled most blacks and planters to come to agreements more quickly and with less bitter feeling on both sides than they had the previous year.[61] By spring, whites were rejoicing over Alabama's good fortune and praising her Negroes for their hard work and reliability.[62] "The freedmen, according to universal testimony, are working better than they did last year," reported the *Daily Selma Messenger* with satisfaction.[63]

There was an almost universal return to sharecropping in 1867, although a very few planters and freedmen continued, despite the shortage of currency, to experiment with wages.[64] Some Freedmen's Bureau officials, who felt that Negroes fared better economically on wages, and some white Alabamians, who supported the system under which blacks were most carefully supervised, continued to advocate wage labor.[65] With very few exceptions, however, planters and freedmen ignored their pleas. Arrangements granting the laborers one-quarter of the crop were most widespread, although in a few instances freedmen contracted to provide their own food and receive half the crop.[66]

Sharecropping triumphed because both planters and freedmen favored the system. To the average planter it continued to be a more feasible labor system than wages, if for no other reason than the shortage of currency.[67] In addition, many whites felt that shares gave blacks an interest in the crop, thus providing them with an incentive to work. Most blacks apparently preferred cropping, despite the economic disadvantages, because it allowed them greater control of their own lives. Because of his interest in the crop, the sharecropper required less supervision.[68] In contrast to the wage laborer, who was a hired hand clearly in a subordinate position to his employer, the cropper was the partner of the landowner in a joint business venture that provided the freedman with opportunities for greater individual discretion, dignity, and self-respect. For this reason, Negroes considered the cropper a notch above the wage laborer in the social scale. "I am not working for wages," declared one freedman to his employer, as he explained why he had a right to leave the plantation at will to attend political meetings, "but am part owner of the crop and as I have all the rights that you or any other man has I shall not suffer them abridged."[69]

V

As in 1866, the cotton crop of 1867 was a poor one. By fall, planters had once again begun to complain about the inefficiencies of freedmen as laborers. "The cause of the cotton crop being so inferior is the inefficiency of labor and the bad season [is] more on account of labor than anything else," lamented George Hagin, the ex-overseer who had rented Henry Watson's plantation. "There has been a few of the old negroes that lived on the place before that have worked very well but the younger ones are worth nothing."[70] A correspondent of the Union Springs *Times* proclaimed free labor a failure.[71]

Once again, planters drove freedmen from their homes without pay.[72] "Negroes are now being dismissed from the plantations[,] there being nothing more for them to do," explained one blackbelt resident. He added calmly that "[t]hey will all be turned loose without homes[,] money or provisions[;] at least no meat."[73] From the northwest corner of the state, 114 Negroes appealed for assistance to Major General John Pope, who in April had assumed command of the Third Military District, comprising Alabama, Georgia, and Florida. They explained that "unless some person, in whom we can place the utmost confidence be appointed to superintend the settling up of our affairs, we do not feel that justice will be done us."[74] In 1867, for the first time, many blacks were also fired for voting Republican or attending political meetings.

Occasionally, through unusual persistence or intelligence, blacks were able to enlist the aid of the Freedmen's Bureau and resist arbitrary discharge. Bernard Houston, a sharecropper on an Athens plantation, told his landlord, "I shall not suffer myself to be turned off[,] and under legal advice and the advice of assistant Commissioner of [the] Freedmans Bureau I shall stay there until the crop is matured[,] gathered and divided according to contract." The planter protested lamely that he objected to the Negro's being "disobedient" and denied that politics had anything to do with the situation, but a month later he complained to Swayne that the freedman was "yet on the place acting in utter and entire disobedience of orders & the necessary discipline of the plantation."[75]

In numerous other cases, freedmen were less fortunate. Freedmen's Bureau agents tried to come to the assistance of persecuted blacks, but there were simply too few agents for the job. Furthermore, since the procedure for handling grievances was not clear, Bureau representatives were not sure how best to dispose of them. Some turned cases over to the civil courts. In general, however, this method proved unsatisfactory. "[B]esides the slow process of the Law, there stands in the way the difficulty of obtaining counsel," explained one Bureau agent. "The Freedmen as a general thing have no mean[s] to pay a fee: consequently they submit to the swindle simply because they cannot purchase justice."[76] The sub-assistant commissioner at Huntsville sent discharged freedmen back to their plantations and told them to stay there.[77] In other locations, officials tried to mediate between laborers and planters. "I notify the parties concerned to appear at this office together, and try either to effect an understanding, or a settlement," explained one Bureau official. He reported that he had "so far been fortunate, to prevent any injustice to be done."[78] But for every such settlement, many other grievances undoubtedly went unheard.

The cumulative effects of three years of substandard crops became increasingly evident during the late autumn and early win-

ter of 1867-1868, a period of considerable tension because of the
meeting of the Radical Constitutional Convention in December
and the election to ratify the new constitution in February. The
problem was no longer that freedmen were reluctant to contract,
but rather that planters were unwilling or unable to plant. Their
universal reaction to poor crops and low profits was to plan to
cut back on planting operations.[79] Unemployment among Negroes threatened to reach serious proportions for the first time
since the war.[80]

Many planters blamed free labor for the trouble, and tension
between planters and freedmen reached a new high. From
Russell County, in the blackbelt, six planters who had employed
750 blacks wrote Swayne that "[t]he disasters of this year force
us to curtail our planting operations another year, and we appre-
hend, from demonstrations already made, much trouble and
probable violence on the part of the freedmen, when they are
requested to leave our plantations." The worried planters reported that many of the blacks were already seizing some of the
plantations.[81] In many areas, planters held conventions to discuss ways to salvage the situation. Almost invariably they recommended lower compensation for laborers and greater control
over them.[82] At one such meeting in Selma, a "large number of
the colored men present voted against the adoption of the report,
but the votes were not considered."[83]

Although the situation appeared to offer little hope, the sea-
sonal cycle continued to operate, and events unexpectedly took a
turn for the better. Once again, despite earlier prophecies of
doom, the spring of 1868 found planters planting and freedmen
working with a determination that surprised all but the most
optimistic. Labor shortage replaced unemployment as planters
reversed earlier decisions to curtail operations. Unlike previous
years, reports that Negroes were working well continued through
the summer.[84]

Once again, some blacks were discharged after the main labor
on the crop was done, and others were dismissed for political reasons.[85] But the effects seemed less serious than they had in the
past. Because of the labor shortage, freedmen fired during the
spring and early summer of 1868 had little trouble finding em-

ployment elsewhere, "and in general upon much better terms."[86] An act of the new Republican state legislature giving agricultural laborers a lien on the crop had a "most beneficial effect among the farming population, influencing the farmer to deal fairly with the freedman."[87] The effective closing of operations by the Freedmen's Bureau, which earlier would have had serious repercussions, came precisely at the time when a new Radical state government committed to the protection of the rights and interests of all citizens was assuming command. For the rural Alabama freedman, the autumn of 1868 was a time of great hopes and expectations.

VI

Hidden behind the daily monotony of agricultural labor, significant changes occurred in the lives of black plantation workers during their first few years of freedom. These changes were evident both in their relations with their employers and in their relations with each other. All of them can, with little inaccuracy and only slight ambiguity, be called moves toward independence. These moves, as much class as racial in nature, represented not only the desire of blacks to be free of white control, but also of ex-slave plantation laborers to be free of planter control.

"Freedom has worked great changes in the negro, bringing out all his inherent savage qualities," proclaimed the Mobile *Daily Register* in 1869.[88] Certainly a growing physical restlessness and self-consciousness among black plantation workers — reinforced by the political emancipation brought about under congressional Reconstruction — were very evident. They were no longer willing to be imposed upon by their former owners. From the end of the war laborers, such as those on the Henry Watson plantation, had revolted against working under their old overseers. But the increasing number of white complaints of Negro "impudence," "insolence," and "insubordination," and the increasing readiness of black laborers to resort to violence and organization when faced with an unpalatable situation, testified to their growing self-assertiveness and confidence. In December 1867, for example, planters in Russell County, who were forced

to cut back on planting operations because of poor crops the previous year, complained that their laborers were "seizing and
holding property upon some of the places. They are generally
armed."[89] A year later, a revolt in the same area had to be put
down by military force.[90]

This desire of agricultural laborers for independence, which
led them to choose sharecropping over wages even though they
usually fared better economically under a wage system, was one
of the greatest causes of other changes in modes of life and labor
on the plantation. Before the war, field hands on large plantations had usually lived in rows of cabins grouped together. They
had worked together in a slave gang, under the authority of an
overseer and perhaps a driver. Their lives had been, by and large,
collective. After the war, black plantation laborers quickly indicated their preference for a more individual form of life. They objected to working under the control of an overseer. They also objected to the regimented nature of the work gang and the Negro
quarters. These had been accepted "in the days of slavery, when
laborers were driven by overseers by day, and penned like sheep
at night, and not allowed to have any will of their own," reported
one Freedmen's Bureau agent. "But now, being *free* to think and
act for themselves, they feel their individual responsibility for
their conduct, and the importance of maintaining a good character." He noted that fights frequently broke out among Negroes
forced to live among others against their will.[91]

Many planters found it necessary or useful to break up the
former slave quarters and allow laborers to have individual huts,
scattered across the plantations. The process was far from complete by the end of the 1860s, but the trend was unmistakable.
As early as the spring of 1867, an article in the Montgomery
Daily Advertiser described certain changes that had occurred in
the appearance of one plantation community. "You do not see as
large gangs together as of old times, but more frequently squads
of five or ten in a place, working industriously without a driver,"
wrote the correspondent. "Several large land owners have broken up their old 'quarters' and have rebuilt the houses at selected
points, scattered over the plantation."[92]

The rise in white tenancy following the war had the further effect of creating smaller individual farming units, with fewer black laborers and less regimentation on each one.[93] While most plantations continued to be owned by large planters, they were frequently managed by several white tenants, who in turn contracted with black sharecroppers. Other planters rented directly to blacks. One planter wrote that he had "rented out all my plantation on shares except forty acres around the house that I intend to take charge of myself."[94] A early as 1867, a Bureau official reported approvingly that some planters in his district had decided to break up their plantations into small farms and rent them to Negroes for a period of several years. Later in the year, he wrote that "the plan . . . of dividing the large plantations into small farms, is gaining favor with farmers."[95]

Although most black sharecroppers continued to provide only their labor and receive food and clothing in addition to their usual quarter of the crop, the late 1860s saw the introduction of a new cropping arrangement that would, in a matter of years, be widely adopted. Early in 1868, a Freedmen's Bureau official noted that there "does not seem to be as much uniformity in the tenor of contracts as last year." He wrote that although "some give the freedmen one-fourth of the crop and provide rations as was customary last year . . . others give one third of [the] crop, and require the laborers to furnish their own rations; and some give one half, the laborers bearing an equal share of the expense."[96] The result was to remove the cropper still further from the wage laborer, and accentuate his role as a partner of the planter in a joint business venture.

Such changes in working and living conditions were sometimes fostered by planters themselves. Some, like Henry Watson, found it impossible to adjust to a new situation in which they did not have total control over their labor force. Under such circumstances, it was tempting for them to adopt whatever system would permit the least contact between employer and laborer, even if it resulted in more of the very independence that so troubled them. A correspondent from the blackbelt county of Hale reported to the Mobile *Daily Register* in 1869 that "everything appears experimental. . . . Many planters have turned their stock, teams, and every facility for farming, over to the negroes, and only require an amount of toll for the care of their land, refusing to superintend, direct, or even, in some cases, to suggest as to their management."[97]

By the late 1860s, then, old patterns of agricultural relationships had been irreparably shattered, and the outlines of new ones had emerged. The logical culmination of emancipation for the plantation workers — the acquisition of their own land — remained for most an illusory dream.[98] But within the confines of the plantation system great changes had occurred in the lives of the black laborers. They themselves had helped bring about most of these changes by demonstrating that they were not willing to continue in a position of complete subservience to their former owners. As one white planter lamented succinctly of the freedmen, "they wish to be free from restraint."[99] That wish was a potent one in the years immediately following the Civil War.

NOTES

1. Robert Jemison, proclamation to his slaves, April 1865, typed copy, Southern Historical Collection, University of North Carolina.

2. On the army's role in Reconstruction, see James E. Sefton, *The United States Army and Reconstruction: 1865-1877* (Baton Rouge: Louisiana State University Press, 1967).

3. General Field Orders No. 28, Headquarters, Army and Division of West Mississippi, Mobile, 19 April 1865, *The War of the Rebellion: A Compilation of the Official Records of the Union and Confederate Armies* (Washington, D.C.: Government Printing Office, 1897), ser. I, vol. XLIX, pt. II, pp. 410-411 (hereafter cited as OR).

4. See Bell I. Wiley, *Southern Negroes: 1861-1865* (New Haven: Yale University Press, 1938), chap. XIII; on Union treatment of blacks in occupied Louisiana during the war, see William Messner's Ph.D. dissertation "The Federal Army and Blacks in the Gulf Department, 1862-1865" (University of Wisconsin, 1972).

5. Lieutenant Colonel C. T. Christensen, General Field Orders No. 28, Headquarters, Army and Division of West Mississippi, Mobile, 19 April 1865, OR, ser. I, vol. XLIX, pt. II, pp. 410-411.

6. Circular, Headquarters, District of North Alabama, 17 July 1865, in the Huntsville *Advocate*, 19 July 1865.

7. Conway to Lieutenant Colonel Christensen, New Orleans, 3 June 1865, OR, ser. I, vol. XLIX, pt. II, p. 954.

8. See, for example, James Mallory, diary, 24 June 1865, Southern Historical Collection, University of North Carolina; John H. Parrish to Henry Watson, Greensboro, 30 July 1865, Watson Papers, Duke University Library; Samuel S. Gardner, Sub-Assistant Commissioner to Swayne, Selma, 10 August 1865, FBP, Alabama Operations Reports.

9. John Parrish to Henry Watson, Greensboro, 30 July 1865, Watson papers.

10. M. D. Sterrett to Governor Parsons, Columbiana, Shelby County, 11 December 1865, Parsons Papers, Alabama State Department of Archives and History.

11. See the New York *Daily Tribune*, 4 December 1865, which reported that a "party of negroes from plantations near Mobile, armed with rifles and sabers, attacked some white men on a neighboring farm. The leading negroes were killed: the others escaped."

12. Parrish to Watson, Greensboro, 19, 25 June 1865; J. A. Wemyss to Watson, Mobile, 14 July 1865; contract, 26 June 1865: Watson Papers.

13. Watson to his daughter Julia, Greensboro, 16 December 1865, Watson Papers. See the agreement between Hagin and freedman W. L. Camp, 1 February 1866, Watson Papers.

14. J. B. Moore, diary, 30 April 1862, Alabama State Department of Archives and History.

15. See, for example, Henry Watson to his daughter Julia, Greensboro, 16 December 1865, Watson Papers.

16. John A. Winston to Governor Parsons, Gainsville, Sumter Co., 1 August 1865, Parsons Papers.

17. A. Geddis to Swayne, 7 September 1865, FBP, Alabama Operations Reports.

18. Howard to Charles Nordhoff, Washington, D.C., 19 March 1866, FBP, Assistant Adjutant General's Office, Letters Sent. For a recent study which concludes that the Bureau failed significantly to benefit the Negroes and frequently acted in concert with planter interests, see William S. McFeely, *Yankee Stepfather: General O. O. Howard and the Freedmen* (New Haven: Yale University Press, 1968).

19. Brigadier General J. McArthur to Lieutenant Colonel J. Hough, Selma, 9 June 1865, OR, ser. I, vol. XLIX, pt. II, pp. 975-976; Charles W. Buckley to Conway, Montgomery, 11 June 1865, FBP, Assistant Adjutant General's Office, Letters Received.

20. Charles W. Buckley to Carl Schurz, Montgomery, 19 August 1865, Schurz Papers, Library of Congress.

21. Montgomery *Daily Advertiser*, 29 October 1865.

22. *Daily Selma Times*, 16 November 1865.

23. Charles W. Buckley, Assistant Superintendent, to Swayne, Montgomery, 1 August 1865, FBP, Alabama Operations Reports; Statement of F. W. Kellogg, Collector of Internal Revenue, Mobile, 9 September 1865, Andrew Johnson Papers, Library of Congress; Charles A. Miller, Acting Assistant Adjutant General, to Howard, Montgomery, 25 September 1865, FBP, Assistant Adjutant General's Office, Letters Received.

24. Captain D. W. Whittle to Howard, Union Springs, 8 June 1865, FBP, Assistant Adjutant General's Office, Letters Received. See the letter of Mrs. J. M. Miles to President Johnson advocating a policy of gradual emancipation. Autauga, 19 June 1865, Johnson Papers.

25. Conway to Howard, Mobile, 25 May 1865, FBP, Assistant Adjutant General's Office, Letters Received.

26. Sarah Espy, diary, 3 July 1865, typed copy, Alabama State Department of Archives and History.

27. See, for example, the contract between Benjamin Blasingame and thirteen former slaves, Chambers County, 24 July 1865, FBP, Alabama Letters Received. For an example of a report, see Chaplain J. W. Davis to Swayne, Sparta, 9 September 1865, FBP, Alabama Letters Received.

28. Cogswell to Swayne, Columbia, 25 September 1865, FBP, Alabama Letters Received.

29. Richard W. Griffin, "Problems of the Southern Cotton Planters after the Civil War," *Georgia Historical Quarterly* 39 (1955): 103-104.

30. Wager Swayne to Howard, 4 September 1865, FBP, Alabama Weekly Reports.

31. William H. Peck, Assistant Superintendent, Tuscaloosa, 20 October 1866, FBP, Alabama Operations Reports.

32. Contract, Autauga County, 1 June 1865, FBP, Alabama Letters Received; Contract, 26 June 1865, Watson Papers. They "will be greatly disappointed when they get their portion of the crop," predicted Watson's friend J. A. Wemyss to Watson, Mobile, 14 July 1865, Watson Papers. Charles A. Miller, Acting Assistant Adjutant General, to Howard, Montgomery, 25 September 1865, FBP, Assistant Adjutant General's Office, Letters Received.

33. J. B. Moore, diary, 3 June 1865.

34. Contract, 26 June 1865, Watson Papers.

35. Huntsville *Advocate*, 19 October 1865.

36. Swayne to Howard, 9 October 1865, FBP, Alabama Weekly Reports; William A. Poillon, Assistant Superintendent, to Swayne, Monroe County, November 1865, FBP, Alabama Letters Received; Spencer Smith, Assistant Superintendent, Tuskegee, 2 December 1865, FBP, Alabama Operations Reports.

37. Oscar Zeichner, "The Transition from Slave to Free Agricultural Labor in the Southern States," *Agricultural History* 13 (1939): 23.

38. Martin Abbott, "Free Land, Free Labor, and the Freedmen's Bureau," *Agricultural History* 30 (1956): 151-152.

39. See, for example, "Facts for Freedmen," by Assistant Superintendent Samuel S. Gardner, in the *Alabama Beacon*, 24 November 1865.

40. M. D. Sterrett, commander of the militia in Shelby County, to Governor Parsons, Columbiana, 11 December 1865, Parsons Papers; John G. Bannes and E. F. Boke to Governor Robert M. Patton, Notasulga, 17 December 1865, Patton Papers, Alabama State Department of Archives and History.

41. Schurz to President Johnson, New Orleans, 15 September 1865, Johnson Papers.

42. Swayne to Howard, 31 January 1866, FBP, Alabama Weekly Reports.

43. Selma *Morning Times*, 24 January 1866. See also Swayne to Howard, 2 January 1866, FBP, Alabama Weekly Reports; the Livingston *Journal*, quoted in the Montgomery *Daily Advertiser*, 6 January 1866; and the Eufaula *News*, quoted in the Mobile *Advertiser and Register*, 9 January 1866.

44. J. B. Moore, diary, 11 March 1866. See also the Union Springs *Times*, 21 March 1866, and the Livingston *Journal*, quoted in the Mobile *Advertiser and Register*, 25 January 1866.

45. Spencer Smith, Assistant Superintendent, to Col. Cadle, 20 January 1866, FBP, Alabama Operations Reports.

46. George S. Houston to his wife, Washington, D.C., 22 February 1866, George S. Houston Papers, Duke University Library.

47. For a discussion of the "general strike" of Southern blacks during the war, see W. E. B. Du Bois, *Black Reconstruction in America* (New York: Harcourt, Brace and Co., 1935), chap. 4.

48. See, for example, the *Alabama Beacon*, 19 January 1866; John G. Harris to Governor Patton, Chambers County, 21 April 1866, Patton Papers.

49. Montgomery *Daily Advertiser*, quoted in the Mobile *Advertiser and Register*, 22 June 1866.

50. William H. Peck, Assistant Superintendent, Tuscaloosa, 20 October 1866, FBP, Alabama Operations Reports; C. W. Pierce, Superintendent, Demopolis, 24 October 1866, FBP, Alabama Operations Reports; *Alabama Beacon*, 5 January 1866.

51. James Mallory, diary, 5 January 1866.

52. Swayne to Howard, 2 January 1866, FBP, Alabama Weekly Reports; *Alabama Beacon*, 5 January 1866; William H. Peck, Assistant Superintendent, Tuscaloosa, 20 October 1866, FBP, Alabama Operations Reports; C. W. Pierce,

Superintendent, Demopolis, 24 October 1866, FBP, Alabama Operations Reports; Swayne to Howard, Montgomery, 31 October 1866, FBP, Annual Report; F. D. Sewell, Inspector General, to Howard, Washington, D.C., 30 October 1866, FBP, Assistant Adjutant General's Office, Letters Received.

53. Mobile *Advertiser and Register*, 12 July 1866; Swayne to Howard, Montgomery, 1 September 1866, FBP, Assistant Adjutant General's Office, Letters Received; George H. Tracy, Superintendent, to Swayne, Mobile, 31 October 1866, FBP, Alabama Operations Reports.

54. *Clarke County Journal*, 26 July 1866.

55. David B. Smedley to Swayne, Troy, Pike County, 9 November 1866, FBP, Alabama Letters Recieved.

56. The same practice had occurred in 1865. See W. A. Poillon, Assistant Superintendent, to Swayne, Mobile, 24 August 1865, FBP, Alabama Letters Received; Captain J. W. Cogswell to Swayne, Columbia. 25 September 1865, FBP, Alabama Letters Received; George D. Robinson, Superintendent, to Col. Cadle, Mobile, 17 January 1866, FBP, Alabama Operations Reports.

57. William H. Peck, Assistant Superintendent, Tuscaloosa, 10 October 1866, FBP, Alabama Operations Reports.

58. A. C. Tyrce to Howard, Eutaw, Greene County, 12 November 1866, FBP, Alabama Letters Received. See also Swayne to Howard, Montgomery, 1 September 1866, FBP, Assistant Adjutant General's Office, Letters Received; J. F. McGogy, Agent, Greenville, 31 October 1866, FBP, Alabama Operations Reports.

59. In one case, a justice of the peace agreed to the expulsion from their plantation of two freedmen who had been absent without the planter's permission for four hours, but overruled the forfeiture of their wages. *B. F. Blow* vs. *Jerry Marrast and Abram Marrast*, J. A. Pruitt, Justice of the Peace, Hayneville Beat, Lowndes County, 13 September 1865, FBP, Alabama Letters Received.

60. James Mallory, diary, 1 January 1867; "Letter from the Country," Mobile *Advertiser and Register*, 4 January 1867; *Daily Selma Messenger*, 4 January 1867.

61. *Daily Selma Messenger*, 5 January 1867; *Clarke County Democrat*, 10 January 1867.

62. *Alabama Beacon*, 6 April 1867; Elmore *Standard*, 5 July 1867; J. Callis, Superintendent, to Swayne, Huntsville, 1 May 1867, FBP, Alabama Operations Reports; C. W. Pierce, Sub-Assistant Commissioner, Demopolis, 11 June 1867, FBP, Alabama Operations Reports.

63. *Daily Selma Messenger*, 9 May 1867.

64. In such cases, wages of between $7 and $12 per month were most common. Athens *Post*, 29 December 1867. See also the contract between Jacob McGavock and twenty-three heads of families, December 1866. George S. Houston

Papers. McGavock paid annual wages ranging from $96 to $268, with most of his hands receiving between $130 and $145. The contract also gave McGavock the right to dismiss "disorderly or disrespectful" laborers without compensation, and stipulated that the employees were not "to have any gatherings or to entertain any visitor without the knowledge & consent of said McGavock."

65. William E. Connelly, Sub-Assistant Commissioner, Eufaula, 31 October 1867, FBP, Alabama Operations Reports; Selma *Daily Messenger*, 1 November 1867.

66. *Alabama Beacon*, 12 January 1867; Samuel S. Gardner, Sub-Assistant Commissioner, Greenville, 18 June 1867, FBP, Alabama Operations Reports; C. W. Pierce, Sub-Assistant Commissioner, Demopolis, 11 June 1867, FBP, Alabama Operations Reports.

67. Swayne to Howard, 30 September 1867, FBP, Assistant Adjutant General's Office, Annual Report.

68. Some whites opposed the share system for this reason. See, for example, the Athens *Post*, 29 December 1866.

69. Bernard Houston to George S. Houston, Athens, 3 August 1867, George S. Houston Papers.

70. George Hagin to Henry Watson, Greensboro, 8 September 1867, Watson Papers.

71. Union Springs *Times*, 9 November 1867.

72. George Shorkley, Selma, 5 August 1867; R. Blair. Sub-Assistant Commissioner, Tuscaloosa, 30 August 1867; C. W. Pierce, Sub-Assistant Commissioner, Demopolis, 1 September 1867; J. C. Hendrix, Acting Sub-Assistant Commissioner, Montgomery, 5 October 1867: FBP, Alabama Operations Reports.

73. John Parrish to Henry Watson, Greensboro, 14 October 1867, Watson Papers.

74. H. B. Slater, President, Colored Lodge No. 1, et al., Tuscumbia, 19 October 1867, FBP, Alabama Letters Received.

75. Bernard Houston, Athens, 3 August 1867; George S. Houston to Sub-Assistant Commissioner John Callis, Athens, 13 August 1867; Houston to Swayne, 16 September 1867: George S. Houston Papers.

76. R. Blair, Sub-Assistant Commissioner, to Major O. D. Kinsman, Tuscaloosa, 30 August 1867, FBP, Alabama Operations Reports.

77. John B. Callis, Sub-Assistant Commissioner, to O. D. Kinsman, Huntsville, 31 August 1867, FBP, Alabama Operations Reports.

78. C. W. Pierce to O. D. Kinsman, Demopolis, 1 September 1867, FBP, Alabama Operations Reports.

79. Mobile *Advertiser and Register*, 27 December 1867.

80. See the reports to the Freedmen's Bureau of J. B. McClellan, Probate Judge, Union Springs, 8 January 1868, FBP, Alabama Letters Received; D. A. McCall, Probate Judge, Union Springs, 10 January 1868, FBP, Alabama Letters Received; R. Blair, Agent, Tuscaloosa, 1 February 1868, FBP, Alabama Operations Reports; Charles C. Bartlett, Selma, 6 February 1868, FBP, Alabama Operations Reports.

81. I. Wright and others to Swayne, Russell County, 30 December 1867, FBP, Alabama Letters Received.

82. See, for example, the *Alabama Beacon,* 7 December 1867. The paper agreed with planters that "the *labor,* upon which the planter has to rely, *must be subject to his control."*

83. Selma *Daily Messenger,* 20 December 1867.

84. *Daily State Sentinel,* 8 April 1868; R. Blair, Tuscaloosa, 31 May 1868, FBP, Alabama Operations Reports; G. Hagin to Henry Watson, Greensboro, 5 June 1868, Watson Papers; Tuscaloosa *Independent Monitor,* 16 June 1868; O. L. Shepherd, Assistant Commissioner, to Howard, Montgomery, 11 April 1868, FBP, Assistant Adjutant General's Office, Letters Received. See also John Barrister, Sub-Assistant Commissioner, Opelika, 31 July 1868; G. W. Kingsboro [?], Opelika, 30 September 1868; J. F. McGogy, Greenville, 2 October 1868: FBP, Alabama Operations Reports.

85. James Curtis, Sub-Assistant Commissioner, to O. L. Shepherd, Selma, 6 July 1868, FBP, Alabama Operations Reports.

86. J. Hayden, Assistant Commissioner, to Howard, Montgomery, 7 March 1868, FBP, Assistant Adjutant General's Office, Letters Received.

87. Edwin Beecher, Assistant Commissioner, to Howard, Montgomery, 10 November 1868, FBP, Assistant Adjutant General's Office, Letters Received.

88. Mobile *Daily Register,* 3 January 1869.

89. I. Wright and others to Swayne, Russell County, 30 December 1867, FBP, Alabama Letters Received.

90. Josiah Gorgas, diary, 9 January 1869, University of Alabama Library.

91. William E. Connelly, Sub-Assistant Commissioner, Eufaula, 1 August 1867, FBP, Alabama Operations Reports.

92. Montgomery *Daily Advertiser,* 14 May 1867.

93. On white tenancy, see Robert Gilmour, "The Other Emancipation: Studies in the Society and Economy of Alabama Whites during Reconstruction" (Ph.D. diss., Johns Hopkins University, 1972), pp. 123-141.

94. James Mallory, diary, 16 March 1869.

95. William E. Connelly, Sub-Assistant Commissioner, Eufaula, 1 August, 1 October 1867, FBP, Alabama Operations Reports.

96. A. S. Bennett, Sub-Assistant Commissioner, to G. H. Shorkley, Acting Assistant Adjutant General, Demopolis, 31 January 1868, FBP, Alabama Operations Reports. See also Robert Blair, Agent, to Swayne, Tuscaloosa, 27 December 1868, FBP, Alabama Operations Reports, and *Alabama Beacon*, 4 January 1868.

97. Mobile *Daily Register*, 30 May 1869.

98. See chap. 6.

99. James Mallory, diary, 30 December 1867.

3

Strengthening the Black Family

I

Although conditions varied from area to area and from plantation to plantation, slavery was not generally conducive to strong
family ties. For many Negroes before the war, the family was not
a basic unit of either life or labor. Indeed, the peculiar institution
fostered a family structure among blacks that was often radically
different from the dominant white pattern and at odds with the
social ideals upon which white family relations were based. As
W. E. B. Du Bois noted, the three "essential features of Negro
slavery in America" were the absence of legal marriage, family,
and control over children.[1]

The absence of legal recognition of the slave family weakened
permanent relations both between black males and females and
between black parents and children. Changing "marriage" partners was neither difficult nor generally condemned; the real
source of authority over slave children lay not in their own parents, but in their white owners. The absence of legal support need

not in itself have been an insuperable barrier to stable family relations, but the slave family also faced the constant threat of forcible separation of husband from wife and child from parent. Although separation may not have occurred in the majority of slave families, it always remained a possibility, and, equally important, slaves knew that it was a possibility.[2]

The combination of weak family ties and the demands that slavery placed on both men and women produced a slave family that frequently tended to be matrifocal. The mother-child relationship, at least during the early years of childhood, was essential. Slavery often placed the male, however, in an anomalous position. Not only was he unnecessary within the family, but he was forced to play a servile role that was usually regarded as unmasculine without as well.[3] As Du Bois wrote, "[h]is wife could be made his master's concubine, his daughter could be outraged, his son whipped, or he himself sold away without his being able to protest or lift a preventing finger. . . . [H]e easily sank to a position of male guest in the house, without respect or responsibility."[4]

II

The overthrow of slavery initially appeared to many to weaken further the already precarious bonds that held members of black families together. In the excitement of emancipation, old relationships were broken and new ones formed. The wartime dislocation in the north, followed by the exodus from the plantations in 1865 throughout the state, put many blacks in contact with numerous others for the first time. Weak ties, which had meant little in the first place, were sometimes altogether broken in the confusion.[5]

The aged and infirm presented a serious new problem. Before the war, slaves who had been too old to work had been supported by their owners. With the end of slavery, however, such paternalistic planter responsibilities also came to an end. Thousands of old freedmen with no known families had nowhere to turn. Occasionally there were touching scenes in which whites expressed concern for their former slaves. One such ex-slave owner wrote to a Freedmen's Bureau official about an "old man[,] 80 large odd years old, who serve'ed me faithfully for 40 odd years, who" was now too old to earn a living. He continued, "as long as I have a crust of bread I will dived [*sic*] it with him," and explained that "as I am very much attached to my former slaves, the most of them being born my property, I am desirous of doing the best I can for them."[6] Many planters, however, felt that emancipation freed them from supporting useless property and others simply could not bear the added financial burden. As a result, evictions of aged freedmen from plantations on which they had spent years were common.[7]

Some of the very young posed a similar problem. Under slavery, they too had been supported by their masters until they were old enough to work. Children without parents were now homeless. Freedmen's Bureau officials and other interested persons found "many little black children . . . roving about through the Country" in need of assistance.[8] Swayne reported that there were also many large families headed by women, some of whom were "widows, some have had their husbands sold before we came here, and some were deserted by their husbands."[9] Such women often found it difficult to secure employment.[10]

The dominant impression among most whites after the war — especially among Freedmen's Bureau officials and other Northerners who had never before had contact with Southern Negroes — was that there was a shocking increase of black promiscuity and immorality, and that white moral supervision was desperately needed. "I am pained, daily, at the connubial relations of the colored people," wrote an assistant superintendent from Montgomery in September 1865. "Husbands and wifes are separating at a fearful rate: and 'taking up' with other persons. Not unfrequently a man is living with two or three wifes." He added that "[t]hough this has been the custom of the race and habits of the country for years, yet it cannot be looked upon in any light than a huge system of prostitution, by sane persons. It ought to be stopped."[11] What horrified Northern whites often amused Southern ones. Newspapers delighted in printing mocking case histories of Negro infidelity, such as that of "Erastus Letour, a very 'patriotic' darkey," who ran away to fight in the Union army and returned to Mobile to find "his wife living in a very respectable family with her 'second husband.'"[12]

III

Although such promiscuity certainly existed, there is little evidence that it heralded a decline in Negro mores, or more than a temporary celebration of freedom. In some instances, it may have been connected with peculiar problems of overcoming the legacy of slavery. Slaves who had been forcibly separated from their spouses were now able to rejoin them. Others who had been forbidden to marry each other because they had different owners were now able to do so.

The abolition of slavery could not fail to produce significant changes in the black family. Now, instead of fostering a weak and impermanent family structure, the force of the law and of white public opinion supported black conformity to family patterns commonly accepted by whites. Most Northern whites who had contact with Negroes — whether Freedmen's Bureau officials, missionaries, teachers, or army officers — had strong ideas about family morality, which they constantly held up to the freedmen as standards of free behavior.

Probably the most important immediate manifestation of this change in the condition of the Negro family was the result of the legalization of marriages. Now marriage was not only expected but required of freedmen, and those who persisted in living together in an unmarried state would feel the full weight of the law. The problems involved in so rapid a change were legion. Many blacks had been living together as man and wife for years. Would it be necessary for them to undergo formal marriages? Were their children to be considered legitimate? Other Negroes had been forcibly separated from their spouses and had subsequently lived with other partners. In such cases, who was to be regarded as whose husband or wife? Who should have custody of the children?

Legal provisions for all of these contingencies — as well as the actual solutions to them — were arrived at only over a period of several years. Late in the summer of 1865, General Swayne issued a circular stating the Freedmen's Bureau's initial position. He deplored the ambiguity of black marriages, and in order that "the outgrowth of a bygone system should now cease" he directed that a "general re-marriage (for the sake of the record) of all persons married without license, or living together without marriage, should be insisted upon by employers and urged by all who have any connection with, or knowledge of such persons." The circular continued, "[t]hey should know that if after ample facilities have been for some time afforded, they have not conformed to this necessity of social life, they will be prosecuted and punished," and requested officials to refuse to marry two freedmen when one of them had been living with a third person.[13] Swayne's circular was soon recognized as impractical as well as harsh, and it was quickly superseded. The Alabama Constitutional Convention of 1865 passed an ordinance declaring Negroes who had been living together before the war to be man and wife, and their children to be legitimate.[14] The Radical Constitutional Convention of 1867 adopted a similar ordinance.[15]

Although both state conventions legitimized preemanciaption "marriages," some couples persisted in formalizing the marriage relationship. "At a church in the lower part of Russell county, Ala. . . . twenty-six colored couples, who had been living together for a series of years, were married," reported a correspondent of the Columbus *Sun* in November 1865. "The minister told them that the State Convention had legalized their former marriages," but they insisted on the new ceremony anyway.[16]

The desire of some freedmen to have a formal wedding may in part have been the result of widespread confusion among them about the marriage laws — confusion that was also shared by many whites. One white wrote to a Freedmen's Bureau offiical that he was "requested by a number of Freedmen & White persons to ask you if there is any *law*, military or civil, compelling freedpersons to *marry*, who have been living together as Husband and Wife for years?"[17] In another instance, a black man who failed to procure a marriage license after being told that it was unnecessary was indicted for adultery.[18] Given the confusion, the safest course for freedmen seemed to be official marriage.

But the efforts of blacks to formalize what was already recognized by law as legitimate also demonstrated their desire to accept prevailing values. Although frequently bewildered by their new condition, Negroes desperately wanted to do what was "right" and behave as they thought free men did. Often they turned to the Freedmen's Bureau for advice. One freedman, who caught his wife in the act of adultery, begged Swayne for assistance. "My object[,] therefore, in writing is to ask what I must do," he explained. "Can I not by *moderate* chastisement compel her to obey me? If she insists on leaving me can I not keep the children? I wish Gen[era]l you would write to me and direct me. I do not want to do anything wrong."[19]

Similar confusion, once again accompanied by the desire to avoid doing "anything wrong," also existed among blacks concerning the acceptability of sexual relations between the races. The prewar regime had allowed widespread if illicit relations between slave women and white men. After the war, some Negroes — and apparently some whites as well — were perplexed by the social code which prescribed rigid sexual separation of the races. Alabama newspapers occasionally reported liaisons between whites and blacks. In one small town, the marriage of a white man to a Negro "was not at all approved by the good people of the village, who seized the happy bridegroom, tore him from the gentle arms and tender bosom of his dark Alabama bride, and treated his venerable person to a souze in dirty pondwater, afterwards applying some gentle touches of raw hide to his rear. The Miscegenator was then put on the train, and sent off without Madame M."[20] Interracial sexual relations were not always between white men and black women. The Athens *Post,* for example, told of a white woman and a black man who were arrested for living together. The paper noted approvingly that they were provided with separate prison cells.[21] In Montgomery, a white woman was arrested for strangling "a colored infant, to which she gave birth."[22]

Although both whites and blacks were reluctant to talk or write about interracial sex, and the evidence is necessarily meager, the few such incidents that did come to public attention suggest that sexual relations between Negroes and whites — especially poor whites who were often thrown into contact with blacks following emancipation — were more common than has often been assumed. Occasionally whites expressed their fears concerning this new contact. The editor of the Selma *Messenger* observed that the changing agricultural patterns in the "upper counties" were leading to closer relations between freedmen and poor whites. Because of the rise of white tenancy, he explained, "many families who never owned a negro now have from one to five gathered around them. This connection must of course be degrading to the whites and corrupting to the negro."[23]

Blacks occasionally appealed to the Freedmen's Bureau for advice on the ticklish problem of interracial sex. One desperate, semiliterate freedman wrote Swayne that he had been arrested for living with a white female employee of his. He was sentenced to a fine of two hundred dollars and thirty days in jail. Thinking to rectify the situation, he explained: "I proposed to mary hir but the Judge woodent suffer me. I shal loose my crop if you dont do something for me. . . . ," he implored. "I am ignoant of the laws of the Country. I will try to do write in the future."[24]

Conformity to dominant white values was also evident in the new self-assertion of Negro men. Almost immediately after the end of the war, there were signs of a fundamental alteration of the matrifocal structure that had previously prevailed under the slave regime. Before the war, slave women had usually labored in the fields beside the men, but now freedwomen increasingly stayed home as housewives. Despite an acute shortage of labor in the early postwar years, many blacks insisted that the men should be the breadwinners for their entire families.[25]

Planters did not find this development to their liking. One planter complained that "[t]he women say they never mean to do any more outdoor work, that white men support their wives and they mean that their husbands shall support them."[26] The following year he was still upset because "[t]he female laborers are almost invariably idle — [they] do not go to the field but desire to play the lady & be supported by their husbands 'like the white folk do.'"[27]

The striking disparity in the number of young black men and women may have made it easier for men to assert themselves.

The Manuscript Census Returns for the state census of 1866 reveal in every county an excess of Negro women between the ages of twenty and twenty-nine.[28] This difference was probably in part the result of wartime deaths of young blacks, since in 1860 there were actually more black men than women between the ages of twenty and twenty-nine.[29] Whatever the cause, however, the effect was to place men at a premium and ensure them a "buyer's market" for women.

IV

Relationships between black parents and children were affected almost as much as those between men and women. The establishment of a school system for Negroes, in which blacks and Northern whites constituted the bulk of the teaching force, was one of the most important factors in bringing about the rearing of the black child in an environment over which the planter had relatively little influence. For this reason, black education came under special attack from Alabama whites. Schoolhouses were burned and teachers were advised to leave town. The objection was not so much to Negro education per se — although that too existed — as to Negro education in the wrong hands.[30]

In order for planters to maintain control of the black population, it was essential for them to have full authority over Negro children, to bring them up to know their place and fear to step out of it. Immediately after the war, planters and state authorities launched a campaign to ensure that the major source of influence over black children would remain with them rather than with black parents. No doubt many planters thought of themselves as benevolently looking out for the interests of their unfortunate ex-slaves, but in effect their effort amounted to an attempt to reestablish *de facto* slavery within the confines set by the Thirteenth Amendment.

Late in 1865, the state legislature gave probate judges the power to apprentice all Negro orphans or minors whose parents were unable to support them adequately. The intent of this seemingly innocuous act was made clear by two key provisions. One was that the probate judge would "be entitled to a compensation of one dollar to be paid by the master or mistress" to whom the child was apprenticed. (One dollar, when compounded by the apprenticing of numerous children, was not a negligible fee in the impoverished Alabama of 1865.) The other was "that the former owner of said minor shall have the preference when proof shall be made that he or she shall be a suitable person for the purpose."[31]

In parts of the state — especially the blackbelt, where the demand for Negro labor was great — this act was the signal for the wholesale apprenticing of children to their former owners. Some probate judges used practically any excuse to bind out black children. Although in some cases the children were in fact orphans, many others not only had parents, but had parents who vigorously objected to the confiscation of their children.[32] Complaints from distressed parents and relatives poured into Freedmen's Bureau offices.

The death of one or both parents frequently resulted in the apprenticing of children even if other relatives insisted they were able to provide for them. One black woman, for example, wrote to Swayne telling how her granddaughter had been apprenticed immediately following the death of the child's father. "[T]here was to[o] much hurry to get her," the desperate woman explained. "Her father was hardly cold." The writer maintained that she was able to support her grandchild. "General," she added plaintively, "I dont know the way to apply to you in because I dont know your rules. I have got a white friend to write this for me."[33] Occasionally requests for help transcended state boundaries. A man in Marietta, Georgia, wrote President Johnson, explaining that "I have drop you a few lines to in formin you of my childrond in decal [Dekalb] County[,] Alabama that I am not abel get them home. . . . Please give me transportation for them to get them home," he begged. "The man that have my childrond says that if I come after them he will kill me."[34]

In Russell County, a blackbelt county in the eastern part of the state, Probate Judge J. F. Waddell created a reign of terror among black parents by readily apprenticing their children to former owners.[35] A typical case there was related by a Negro woman to a Freedmen's Bureau official, who reported her story.

She told him

> that she lived on the plantation of Frank Boyken, Russell County, Ala.
> with her two children, Mary and Joseph, until last Christmas. When
> she left [the plantation] Mr. Boyken refused to give up the children,
> saying that they were duly bound to him by Judge F. A. Waddell. . . .
> When she protested against her children being bound without her con-
> sent, she was driven off the place. She then stole her children, but the
> Sheriff of the County pursued her and took the children back. A week
> ago she went to Judge Waddell, and asked to have the children re-
> stored to her, he would not listen to her, saying the children were
> bound, no matter with or without her consent. He threatened to put
> her in jail if she would come again.[36]

Some probate judges were as confused as freedmen over the
proper course to follow with respect to apprenticing. "Can I apprentice children without the consent of a mother?" enquired
one probate judge of Swayne.[37] Although few judges questioned
the justice or humanity of the apprenticing policy, some began —
after persistent complaints from blacks — to doubt its feasibility.
A probate judge reported to Swayne that although he had apprenticed some children and had many more applications for ap-
prentices, he was constantly annoyed by parents who objected to
the practice. He noted that few parents were "willing to bind
their children whether they can support them or not," and finally
decided that to save himself the trouble of "double trials" and
"having every freedman in the County annoying me by explana-
tions," he would only bind out children after asking their parents
to "show cause if any they have why they should not be bound
out & if they are unable to do that, then to consult their wishes as
to whom they desire them bound to."[38]

Whites were often truly surprised at the extent of Negroes'
opposition to the apprenticing of their children. Accustomed to
believe that blacks were incapable of forming lasting ties of affection for their offspring, some planters and probate judges
found it difficult to explain the black indignation over apprenticing. "Freedwomen I find have a great antipathy to their children being apprenticed," wrote one puzzled judge to Swayne. He

explained that "I think however it is the result of ignorance of the contract and a want of confidence in the faithful performance of the guardian."[39]

Some Freedmen's Bureau officials tried to protect freedmen from indiscriminate apprenticing. One sub-assistant commissioner wrote Judge Waddell questioning his right to apprentice children whose parents were still living. The Bureau official declared that he "very much doubt[ed] the legality of such proceedings" and warned that he would "consider them null and void."[40] Waddell explained to Swayne, who had so far not publicly objected to the widespread apprenticing of black children, that he was acting under a state law that had never been challenged by the Freedmen's Bureau, and would continue his apprenticing.[41] The Bureau sub-assistant commissioner then determined to act on his own. He wrote that there were continuous reports of children being bound out despite the objections of their parents, and announced, "I consider such a course illegal and have sent some of the minors so apprenticed [back] to their parrents."[42]

Despite such efforts by individual Bureau officials, there were too few of them to limit apprenticing effectively without the full support of Swayne. The assistant commissioner, however, at first seemed to accept the system fully. Although the apprenticing law specifically mentioned Negroes, in a circular of December 1865 which won the praise of the conservative Mobile *Advertiser and Register,* Swayne informed the state's probate judges that "[n]othing in the tenor of these [apprenticing] laws or their present channel of administration forbids application to colored orphans, or other children, where humanity plainly requires such interposition, the same as if they were white persons."[43]

Eventually, however, complaints became so numerous and the abuses of the apprenticing law so obvious that Swayne was led to reconsider. The assistant commissioner, who throughout 1865 and 1866 had been repeatedly praised by Alabama whites for his moderation, was becoming increasingly Radical as he sensed the change of the political climate. On 16 April 1867, he issued a general order which noted that "[c]omplaints of hardship in the needless apprenticing of minors, particularly in pursuance of the preference given to the 'former owner' in the law, have become almost incessant," and instructed probate judges to revoke indentures in all cases where children could be adequately supported by themselves or their parents.[44] This order, combined with the increasingly prevalent Radicalism produced by the passage of the congressional Reconstruction Acts, put an end to the widespread apprenticing of black children to their former masters. "[T]he Probate Judges have respected General Orders No. 3, and indentures have been revoked upon all applications by the parents of apprenticed children," reported one Freedmen's Bureau official in June. "The number of these applications is large."[45] The coming to power of the new Republican government in 1868 insured that the indiscriminate apprenticing of Negro children would not be resumed.

V

The state of the Negro family in 1870 is made clear by a comparison of white and black family structures as revealed by an examination of nine sample districts in the Manuscript Census Returns of that year.[46] The samples I selected consist of Beat No. 1 in Lowndes County and Hills Beat in Marengo County, both typical rural, blackbelt regions; Township 3, Range 2 West and Township 3, Range 1 West in Madison County, both plantation and farming regions of the Tennessee Valley; Beat No. 2 in Shelby County, in the piedmont; Demopolis, a rapidly growing blackbelt town with a Negro majority; Ward 1 of Tuscaloosa, Ward 2 of Huntsville, and Ward 2 of Mobile. These nine beats, townships, and wards contained 9,681 inhabitants. or slightly less than 1 percent of the state's population.

I classified all residents of these nine units as members of all-black households, all-white households, or mixed households.[47] In the rural areas, most blacks lived in all-black households,[48] but in the towns and cities a substantial minority of them lived with whites.[49] A large proportion of whites in both town and country lived in mixed households.[50] With very few exceptions, the Negroes who lived with whites were in subordinate positions; either, as in the vast majority of cases, they were domestic servants, or else they were employed by the whites in some other capacity, such as farm laborers.[51]

There were differences between the black families and the white. The most obvious of these was that the vast majority of white women stayed at home, while many black women — despite the trend of some to stay home as housewives — worked (Table 6). But the most significant fact to emerge from a comparison of white and black families is their essential similarity.

Table 6 *Female Residents of All-Black Households over Eighteen Years Old Working and at Home in Sample Districts, 1870*

	WORKING	AT HOME
Lowndes County, Beat 1	65.9%	34.1%
Marengo County, Hills Beat	79.2%	20.8%
Madison County, Township 3, Range 2 West	27.8%	72.2%
Madison County, Township 3, Range 1 West	65.4%	34.6%
Shelby County, Beat 2	4.3%	95.7%
Demopolis	19.6%	80.4%
Tuscaloosa, Ward 1	40.0%	60.0%
Huntsville, Ward 2	29.0%	71.0%
Mobile, Ward 2	68.2%	31.8%

Source: Manuscript Census Returns of 1870.

Perhaps most interesting, in light of persistent comments by contemporaries on Negro marital instability, the percentage of unmarried adults in all-black households was strikingly close to that in all-white ones. Regional variations in the proportion of single adults were greater than the differences between the proportion of unmarried blacks and the proportion of unmarried whites within the same region. With the exception of Mobile, where there lived an unusually large number of single persons — both black and white — the proportion of unmarried Negro and white adults generally varied from one-fifth to one-third, with urban areas having the highest incidence of singles. While such figures are entirely static, and do not reveal how long couples remained married, they do show that in 1870 about the same number of black and white families were headed by both a husband and a wife (Table 7).[52]

Table 7 *Residents of All-Black and All-White Households over Eighteen Years Old Unmarried in Sample Districts, 1870*

	BLACK	WHITE
Lowndes County, Beat 1	26.6%	37.4%
Marengo County, Hills Beat	16.9%	26.0%
Madison County, Township 3, Range 2 West	29.4%	28.8%
Madison County, Township 3, Range 1 West	29.5%	23.1%
Shelby County, Beat 2	21.7%	34.8%
Demopolis	19.2%	35.6%
Tuscaloosa, Ward 1	36.4%	27.8%
Huntsville, Ward 2	39.5%	36.8%
Mobile, Ward 2	47.2%	56.9%

SOURCE: Manuscript Census Returns of 1870.

The pattern was very different among the much smaller number of blacks who lived in mixed households. Although sometimes Negro families did live in mixed households, much more often the servants who made up the bulk of black residents in such houses were unrelated to each other. A large proportion of house servants were women and children (Table 8).[53] Such circumstances were not conducive to normal family relations, and the proportion of single adults among Negroes in mixed households was uniformly high (Table 9).[54]

Negro and white couples had about the same number of children as well. Once again, regional variations were as great as differences between white and black families. The number of children per married couple within the same regions was remarkably consistent — usually between two and three — for white and black couples (Table 10).[55]

Table 8 *Black Men and Women over Eighteen Years Old in Mixed Households in Sample Districts, 1870*

	MEN	WOMEN
Lowndes County, Beat 1	19	44
Marengo County, Hills Beat	2	4
Madison County, Township 3, Range 2 West	1	2
Madison County, Township 3, Range 1 West	0	0
Shelby County, Beat 2	8	8
Demopolis	17	33
Tuscaloosa, Ward 1	6	17
Huntsville, Ward 2	61	116
Mobile, Ward 2	52	60
Total	166	284

SOURCE: Manuscript Census Returns of 1870.

Table 9 *Black and White Residents of Mixed Households over Eighteen Years Old Unmarried in Sample Districts, 1870*

	BLACKS	WHITES
Lowndes County, Beat 1	66.7%	38.9%
Marengo County, Hills Beat	66.7%	9.1%
Madison County, Township 3, Range 2 West	33.3%	14.3%
Madison County, Township 3, Range 1 West	—	—
Shelby County, Beat 2	56.3%	32.6%
Demopolis	72.0%	43.3%
Tuscaloosa, Ward 1	78.2%	38.9%
Huntsville, Ward 2	68.3%	42.9%
Mobile, Ward 2	73.2%	59.7%

SOURCE: Manuscript Census Returns of 1870.

It was fairly common for both all-white and all-black households to contain more than one family. Occasionally two or more families shared a home, but more often one or two single persons lived either with families or with other single persons. Frequently, several generations of one family — including grandparents, aunts, uncles, and cousins — lived together. Once again, however, the number of residents per household was very close for whites and blacks. If the size of the black family was near to that of the white one, so too was the size of the black household near to that of the white. (Table 11).

Most black families, then, were structured similarly to most white ones in 1870. The minority of blacks who lived with whites as servants did not, it is true, have stable family lives. Women greatly outnumbered men among them, and only a minority of these adults were married. But among the vast majority of freed-

Table 10 *Average Number of Children per Married Couple in All-Black and All-White Households in Sample Districts, 1870*

	BLACKS	WHITES
Lowndes County, Beat 1	2.3	2.1
Marengo County, Hills Beat	2.1	2.4
Madison County, Township 3, Range 2 West	3.2	2.4
Madison County, Township 3, Range 1 West	2.5	2.0
Shelby County, Beat 2	3.2	3.3
Demopolis	1.2	2.1
Tuscaloosa, Ward 1	2.3	2.2
Huntsville, Ward 2	2.3	2.2
Mobile, Ward 2	2.1	2.2

SOURCE: Manuscript Census Returns of 1870.

Table 11 *Average Number of Residents in All-Black and All-White Households in Sample Districts, 1870*

	BLACKS	WHITES
Lowndes County, Beat 1	4.6	4.5
Marengo County, Hills Beat	4.3	4.9
Madison County, Township 3, Range 2 West	4.9	4.8
Madison County, Township 3, Range 1 West	4.4	3.8
Shelby County, Beat 2	4.7	5.3
Demopolis	5.5	4.4
Tuscaloosa, Ward 1	3.6	5.5
Huntsville, Ward 2	5.3	5.2
Mobile, Ward 2	3.0	4.2

SOURCE: Manuscript Census Returns of 1870.

men who lived in all-black households, there was little to distinguish the outward structure of the family from that of whites. Black families were about the same size as white ones. Approximately the same number of Negroes lived in the average black household as whites in the average white one. The proportion of single adults was similar among blacks and whites, or, conversely, about the same percentage of black as of white families were headed by two parents.

VI

It would be imprudent to suggest that because the Manuscript Census Returns of 1870 reveal striking similarities between white and black family structures that the average Negro family was as stable after five years of freedom as the average white one, or that there were no differences between them. The census figures are entirely static: they tell us what the family looked like at one instant, but not how well it was able to endure over a period of time. It is conceivable, for example — although by no means certain given the high proportion of unmarried whites — that many more blacks than whites had been only briefly or temporarily married in 1870, or that many more blacks subsequently left their spouses.

But the evidence does suggest that the early Reconstruction period in Alabama witnessed a fundamental change in the life of the black family. Relations between men and women were altered by the legalization of marriages, the removal of the threat of forced separations, and the introduction of penalties — both legal and moral — for promiscuity or adultery. At the same time, a readjustment of the traditional Negro matriarchy occurred, with men often assuming the responsibility of supporting their families and women frequently staying home as housewives. Relations between parents and children were also affected. After a desperate and often tragic struggle, freedmen gained control over their own children, at the same time dispelling the planter-fostered myth that Negroes were too childlike and irresponsible to show real affection for or take care of their children. The introduction of education for Negro children was a development of major significance; its impact on the black family could not fail to be momentous.

Blacks themselves played a major role in bringing about almost all of these changes through their defense of the black family, and through their conscious imitation of patterns commonly accepted by whites. Negroes saw the behavior of whites as the behavior of free men, and they were determined now that they were free to act in the same way, whether this meant insisting on a formal marriage, having their women play a more subordinate role, or teaching their children to read and write.

NOTES

1. W. E. B. Du Bois, *The Negro American Family*, The Atlanta University Publications, No. 13 (Atlanta: Atlanta University Press, 1908), p. 21.

2. Sellers maintains that there was "a general intention of planters to keep slave families together" but he concedes that there were frequent separations. James B. Sellers, *Slavery in Alabama* (University, Alabama: University of Alabama Press, 1950), pp. 168-169.

3. For an analysis of the denigration of the twentieth-century Negro male, who has also been forced, under very different conditions. to play an "unmasculine" role, see Thomas F. Pettigrew, *A Profile of the Negro American* (Princeton, New Jersey: D. Van Nostrand Company, Inc., 1964), pp. 2-25; Abram Kardiner and Lionel Ovesey, *The Mark of Oppression: A Psychological Study of the American Negro* (New York: W. W. Norton and Company, Inc., 1951), pp. 44-47; and Andrew Billingsley, *Black Families in White America* (Englewood Cliffs, New Jersey: Prentice-Hall, Inc., 1968), passim. See also Lee Rainwater and William L. Yancey, eds., *The Moynihan Report and the Politics of Controversy* (Cambridge, Mass.: The M.I.T. Press, 1967).

4. Du Bois, *The Negro American Family*, p. 49. But see also Bobby Frank Jones, "A Cultural Middle Passage: Slave Marriage and Family in the Ante-Bellum South" (Ph.D. diss., University of North Carolina, 1965). Jones claims that the matrifocal nature of the slave family has been exaggerated, and that black families were stronger under slavery than most historians have believed. Not all of his evidence supports his thesis; he admits that "sexual laxity became a trait of even the best slave families" (p. 168), that liaisons between planters and slave women were common (pp. 176-188), and that "[s]eparation from parents . . . surely must have contributed to a tendency not to commit oneself too deeply in any relationship" (p. 105). Perhaps the best appraisal is that of Billingsley in his *Black Families in White America*, p. 65. He writes that "[t]he Negro family existed during slavery in the United States, but it was a most pre-

carious existence, dependent wholly on the economic and personal interests of the white man, and the grim determination and bravery of the black man."

5. See E. Franklin Frazier, *The Negro Family in the United States* (Chicago: University of Chicago Press, 1939), pp. 96-97, 106-109.

6. James Parker, Uniontown, 8 January 1867, FBP, Alabama Letters Received.

7. See, for example, the letter from W. H. T. Randall asking on behalf of himself and other planters for Swayne's permission to remove old Negroes from their plantations. Selma, 20 December 1865, FBP, Alabama Letters Received.

8. Hiram Read to General Pope, Auburn, 10 August 1867, FBP, Alabama Letters Received; see also John B. Callis, Sub-Assistant Commissioner, to Swayne, Huntsville, 31 January 1867, FBP, Alabama Operations Reports.

9. Swayne to Howard, Montgomery, 18 September 1865, FBP, Assistant Adjutant General's Office, Letters Received.

10. David Read, Probate Judge, to O. D. Kinsman, Sub-Assistant Commissioner, Opelika, 18 January 1868; W. H. Thornton, Probate Judge, to Kinsman, Talladega, 16 January 1868: FBP, Alabama Letters Received.

11. C. W. Buckley to Swayne, 1 September 1865, FBP, Alabama Operations Reports.

12. Mobile *Advertiser and Register*, 14 August 1866.

13. Circular, 7 September 1865, in the Montgomery *Daily Advertiser*, 9 September 1865.

14. See U.S., Congress, House, "State Laws Regarding Freedmen," Ex. Doc. No. 118, 39th Cong., 1st sess., pp. 30-32.

15. *Official Journal of the Constitutional Convention of the State of Alabama* (Montgomery: Barrett and Brown, 1868), pp. 262-263.

16. Quoted in the Montgomery *Daily Advertiser*, 23 November 1865.

17. M. C. Osborn to O. D. Kinsman, Clarke County, 28 February 1867, FBP, Alabama Letters Received.

18. B. T. Falkner, Probate Judge, to Swayne, Jones County, 20 April 1867, FBP, Alabama Letters Received.

19. William Bird to Swayne, Chambers County, 28 August 1867, FBP, Alabama Letters Received.

20. Montgomery *Daily Advertiser*, 6 February 1867, quoting the Huntsville *Independent*. The incident occurred in Courtland.

21. Athens *Post*, 21 July 1866.

22. Montgomery *Daily Advertiser*, 16 May 1867.

23. *Clarke County Journal,* 28 September 1865, quoting the editor of the Selma *Messenger.*

24. Bill Wyrosdick to Swayne, Crenshaw County, 22 May 1867, FBP, Alabama Letters Received.

25. Selma *Daily Messenger,* 13 March 1866; George Shorkley, Sub-Assistant Commissioner, to O. D. Kinsman, Selma, 4 June 1867, FBP, Alabama Operations Reports; Thomas J. Wolfe, Probate Judge, to Captain S. C. Green, Linden, Marengo County, 10 January 1868, FBP, Alabama Letters Received. A survey of selected beats and townships in the Manuscript Census Returns, 1870, reveals widely varying patterns of labor among black women. See Table 6. The Manuscript Census Returns are in the National Archives.

26. Henry Watson to his daughter Julia, Greensboro, 16 December 1865, Watson Papers, Duke University Library.

27. Watson to W. A. & G. Maxwell & Co., Northampton, Mass., 11 July 1866, Watson Papers. Male assertion among freedmen also took other forms. A Mobile newspaper noted an alarming increase of wife beating among blacks. It observed with surprise that when blacks were arrested for wife beating, the women usually "begged the Mayor to let their husbands off." The paper noted that "the negro women seem to labor under the impression that their husbands have a perfect right to beat them on all and every occasion." Mobile *Daily Register,* 2 July 1868.

28. In Lowndes County, for example, a typical blackbelt region, there were 1,535 black men and 1,896 black women between twenty and twenty-nine. In Talladega, in the piedmont, there were 850 black men and 1,119 black women between twenty and twenty-nine. In Limestone County, in the Tennessee Valley, the corresponding figures were 580 and 743, and in the mountain county of Walker they were 24 and 38. The disparity was less marked among blacks between thirty and thirty-nine, and nonexistent for very young and very old Negroes. Manuscript Census Returns, 1866, Alabama State Department of Archives and History.

29. In 1860, there were 40,363 black men between twenty and twenty-nine, and 39,180 women in the same age group. U.S. Census Office, *Eighth Census: Population* (Washington, D.C.: Government Printing Office, 1864), pp. 2-7. In 1870, the census did not break down the population by race, sex, and age, but, in 1880, the disparity was once again evident. There were 25,150 black males and 32,124 black females between the ages of thirty and thirty-nine in Alabama. U.S. Department of the Interior, Census Office, *Tenth Census: Population* (Washington, D.C.: Government Printing Office, 1883), pp. 552-553. Other states had fewer black males than females, as well. In 1870, there were 407,558 black males between twenty and twenty-nine in the United States and 470,344 black females. U.S. Department of Commerce, Bureau of the Census, *Negro Population, 1790-1915* (Washington, D.C.: Government Printing Office, 1918), p. 166.

30. See chap. 4 for the establishment of the freedmen's schools.

31. Montgomery *Daily Advertiser,* Supplement, 14 December 1865.

32. See the reports of Charles Merwine, Montgomery County, 3 May 1866, and Spencer Smith, Tuskegee, 1 January 1866, FBP, Alabama Letters Received.

33. Lucy Abney to Swayne, sworn to before Robert Anngton, Jr., Livingston, 9 April 1867, FBP, Alabama Letters Received. Mrs. Abney was not aware that the Freedmen's Bureau sub-assistant commissioner for the area was cooperating with the probate judge, and had requested the ex-owner to raise the child against the grandmother's wishes. The Bureau agent later reported that the girl was well cared for by the planter, and recommended that no change was necessary. C. V. Pierce to Col. Cadle, Demopolis, 1 May 1867, FBP, Alabama Letters Received.

34. Jackson Easly to President Johnson, 24 September 1866, FBP, Alabama Letters Received. The letter was referred to the Freedmen's Bureau, and on 6 November Commissioner Howard did send transportation orders for the children.

35. See Fred Mashibah, Sub-Assistant Commissioner, to O. D. Kinsman, Columbus, Georgia, 1 August 1866, and Thomas D. Fears, M.D., to Swayne, Chambers County, 5 January 1866, FBP, Alabama Letters Received.

36. Laura Taylor, sworn and subscribed to Fred Mashibah, Sub-Assistant Commissioner, Columbus, Georgia, 31 July 1866, FBP, Alabama Letters Received.

37. J. M. Henderson to Swayne, Conecuh County, 25 January 1866, FBP, Alabama Letters Received.

38. B. W. Starke to Swayne, Elba, 15 January 1866, FBP, Alabama Letters Received.

39. J. M. Henderson to Swayne, Conecuh County, 25 January 1866, FBP, Alabama Letters Received. See also his letter to Swayne. 26 November 1867, FBP, Alabama Letters Received, in which he wrote that blacks "have a great hor[r]or to being apprenticed." He complained that even when their children were well treated "not one of them would suffer their children for any am[oun]t, to stand in the relation an apprentice does to the master."

40. Spencer Smith to Waddell, Tuskegee, 27 December 1865, FBP, Alabama Letters Received.

41. Waddell to Swayne, Crawford, Russell County, 4 January 1866, FBP, Alabama Letters Received.

42. Spencer Smith to Col. Cadle, 1 January 1866, FBP, Alabama Letters Received.

43. Circular No. 4, 29 December 1865, in the Mobile *Advertiser and Register,* 4 January 1866.

44. General Order No. 3, in the Montgomery *Weekly Advertiser*, 23 April 1867.

45. Robert Smith, Sub-Assistant Commissioner, Opelika, 29 June 1867, FBP, Alabama Operations Reports. See also the reports of J. F. McGogy, Sub-Assistant Commissioner, to O. D. Kinsman, Talladega, 5 June 1867, FBP, Alabama Operations Reports; S. S. Gardner, Sub-Assistant Commissioner, to Kinsman, Greenville, 18 June 1867, FBP, Alabama Operations Reports; and Swayne to Howard, Montgomery, 1 October 1867, FBP, Alabama Annual Reports.

46. The Manuscript Census Returns are not, of course, entirely accurate. There were occasional errors of omission, resulting in the failure to list individuals without homes or in transit at the time of the census. Errors of commission were probably even more numerous, because the answers to some of the census questions (for example, the value of real property) depended primarily on the judgment of the census taker or resident. For the purposes of this study, however, in which I am interested in broad statistical categorization, such individual errors do not vitiate the general usefulness of the Manuscript Census Returns, which provide the best overall picture of the state's population.

47. Households are distinguished from families, two or more of which could and frequently did occupy the same household.

48. In Lowndes County, Beat No. 1, for example, 2,788 blacks lived in all-black households and 116 in mixed ones; in Marengo County, Hills Beat, 434 Negroes lived in all-black households and 7 in mixed ones.

49. In Tuscaloosa's Ward 1, there were 58 blacks in all-black households and 39 in mixed ones; in Mobile's Ward 2, there were 228 Negroes in all-black households and 150 in mixed ones.

50. For example, in Lowndes County, Beat No. 1, 238 whites lived in all-white households and 248 in mixed ones; in Mobile's Ward 2, 401 whites lived in all-white households and 307 in mixed ones.

51. In Lowndes County, Beat No. 1, 73 Negroes living in mixed households were servants, 9 were farm laborers, and 2 were "day laborers"; in Huntsville's Ward 2,125 were servants, 27 were "general laborers," 4 were artisans or skilled laborers, and 3 were field hands.

52. In fact, as the figures show, slightly more blacks than whites were married. It is not always clear from the Manuscript Census Returns whether a man and a woman with the same last name in the same household were married, brother and sister, or even father and daughter. Since I have assumed whenever possible that a man and a woman were married, my figures may underrate the number of single persons. This error is relatively slight, however, and is consistent for both black and white families.

53. In almost all of the beats, townships, and wards sampled the number of Negro women over eighteen years old in mixed households exceeded that of Negro men over eighteen.

54. In Madison County, Township 3, Range 2 West, the sample — 8 blacks and 13 whites, including children — was too small to yield significant statistics.

55. Since not all children lived with their parents, the figures are not an entirely accurate guide to family size. They are, however, a rough approximation. It should also be realized that since young couples with no children are included in the survey, the number of children that most couples *eventually* had was greater than the figures shown in Table 10.

4

The Coming of Black Education

I

Before the Civil War, virtually none of Alabama's blacks had received any formal education. Realizing that a literate servile class would imperil the very basis of slavery, in 1832 the state legislature prohibited the education of any Negro.[1] The only exceptions were a small number of free Creoles in Mobile, descendants of the French and Spaniards who once ruled the area. These Creoles were guaranteed all the rights of American citizens by the Louisiana Purchase Treaty. In 1860, 114 of them attended school in Mobile.[2]

Indeed, there was little schooling for white Alabamians either. Although the state legislature provided for the creation of a public-school system in 1854, under which some schools were opened, "not much was accomplished before the trouble preceding the Civil War, and the call to arms silenced all effort in that direction."[3] Mobile did establish an effective public-school system in 1852, which continued to operate after the war. and upper-class white children were often educated in private academies.[4] Most white children, however, like most black ones, did not regularly attend school until after the Radical Republicans established a new public-school system in 1868.

The absence of formal education did not necessarily mean that all Negroes were kept in total ignorance. A few slaves received special treatment from masters more lenient than the law, and others managed to absorb the rudiments of reading and writing by themselves. Planters encouraged slaves to learn technical skills.[5] Those who did receive some education, however, whether on their own or illegally from whites, never represented more than an insignificant percentage of Alabama's Negroes. In 1860, with a few scattered exceptions, the state's black population was illiterate and uneducated.

II

Most Northerners believed that free blacks, in order to be good, sober citizens, should be provided with a modicum of education. To insure that the freed slaves learn to read and write, master simple arithmetic, and perhaps most important of all, learn to pray the right way, numerous benevolent associations were formed during and immediately after the war. Religious in affiliation and humanitarian in purpose, they sent hundreds of men and women south to bring learning to the ignorant. The benevolent societies cooperated closely with the Freedmen's Bureau, the former sending teachers to the South and paying their salaries, the latter providing school buildings, transportation for teachers, and general educational supervision.[6]

Alabama was less fortunate than most of the other Southern states in securing assistance from the Northern benevolent societies. They extended most of their aid either to states that were less distant, such as Virginia and North Carolina, or to states where large areas were liberated early in the war, such as Louisiana and South Carolina.[7] One society, however, the American Missionary Association, played a major educational role in Alabama during the Reconstruction period.[8]

During the war it was only in the northern, Tennessee Valley section of Alabama, occupied by Union forces from 1862, that any educational work was possible. A few schools for Negroes were established, although a small number compared with those in other occupied areas of the South.[9] The Pennsylvania Freedmen's Aid Association set up schools in Huntsville and Stevenson, and others were started in Florence and near Huntsville on the plantation of ex-Governor Chapman.[10] Early in 1864, a Huntsville resident wrote in her diary of the opening of a local school for blacks, and complained that her maid Corinne was sending her son Jim to it "against my positive commands."[11]

These wartime beginnings gave the northern section of Alabama a substantial head start over the rest of the state. During the first few months after the war, progress throughout most of Alabama was extremely limited. In September 1865 Swayne complained, "I do not think a single teacher has come into the State since I did."[12] As late as November of that year, there were only two schools for blacks in Alabama south of the Tennessee Valley, one in Montgomery and one in Mobile.[13] In the northern part of the state, the situation was more promising. In July 1865, there were eleven schools with an average attendance of 803.[14] Most of these were in Huntsville, where schools supported by the Pennsylvania Freedmen's Aid Society were "in a very flourishing and prosperous condition,"[15] but several were scattered in other locations as well. In Athens, a village with a total Negro population of only 338, the chaplain of the Forty-sixth Wisconsin Volunteers and his wife opened a school in May, and within a month its attendance had shot up from 93 to 198. "The scholars learn *very fast*," he reported; "faster than any I have ever seen at the North."[16]

The winter and spring of 1865-1866 continued to be a time of very slow progress for black education in Alabama. At the end of his first year's work, Charles W. Buckley, state superintendent of education for the Freedmen's Bureau and future congressman, knew of only 35 schools for Negroes in Alabama, with 55 teachers and 3,338 students.[17] These freedmen's schools were not evenly distributed throughout the state. Buckley explained that "[c]ities and larger towns have been selected, being the centre of influence, as places in which first to locate schools." Small towns and rural areas were generally neglected, and more than half the counties still lacked schools.[18]

Substantial results were achieved in three areas. In the northern counties, where black education was already a going concern at the end of the war, the freedmen's schools continued to flourish.[19] They were scattered among five towns and cities, with only slightly more than one-third of their pupils attending the Huntsville school.[20] At the opposite end of the state, in Mobile, one large school and six smaller ones boasted of almost as many students as those in the Tennessee Valley.[21] The school system was most widely organized in a rural environment in Montgomery County, where in January 1866, exclusive of the capital city, 578 pupils attended 13 schools.[22] The rest of the state, however, was virtually ignored, and in February 1866 there was still no school in Selma or Tuscaloosa.[23]

The following year was one of marked improvement for black education in Alabama. The congressional act of 16 July 1866 that provided for the continuation of the Freedmen's Bureau specifically directed it to cooperate with Northern societies in bringing education to the freedmen, and from that time the Bureau played a much more active role than previously in stimulating education. During the year 1866-1867, for example, the Freedmen's Bureau paid the salaries of all sixteen AMA teachers in Alabama.[24]

The year was also one of great progress in terms of the number of students attending the freedmen's schools.[25] The three areas where schools had been firmly established previously continued to lead the way.[26] Other areas of the state, however, also saw the introduction of freedmen's schools. The AMA opened three schools in Selma and by February had 348 students there. Similar progress occurred in Tuscaloosa and numerous smaller towns.[27]

III

At first, Negro students of all ages were at basically the same level of learning: the most elementary. Teachers concentrated on reading and writing, and what was known as "mental arithmetic," which meant arithmetic simple enough to do in one's head. Geography was also a common subject.

Teachers were impressed — and some evidently surprised — at the rapidity with which the children learned. "[S]o far as I have had opportunity to observe, their progress is about an average of white children under far more favorable circumstances," wrote an army chaplain in 1865. Other teachers and travelers made similar observations.[28] One teacher noted that "it is not always the lightest or 'brightest' skinned ones that are the best scholars. . . . [T]he only really *black* scholar I have has, I think, the best intellect in school." Her impression was confirmed by another teacher who noted that "[t]he very dark ones [learn] as rapidly as the ligh[t] colored."[29]

After a short period, differences of ability and the entrance of new students necessitated the introduction of different levels of instruction. Gradations appeared most rapidly in reading, for which a series of progressively more difficult readers — usually McGuffey's — was used. One teacher wrote from a small black-belt town in 1868 that she had a class of only the advanced students, "about thirty-six in number. They read very well," she continued, "the first class in McGuffy's Fourth Reader, the others in the Third and Second. All can write — some quite well."[30] By March 1866, Buckley reported that less than half the students were still at the lowest, or "alphabet and primer," stage of reading.[31] In arithmetic, on the other hand, which "seems to be the one big mountain of all to these people," progress was less marked.[32] In March 1866 only twenty-two black students in Alabama had entered the second or third level, and not one was enrolled in "higher" arithmetic, algebra, or geometry.[33] Many of the smaller schools were devoted entirely to the most elementary studies. One teacher in the blackbelt town of Greensboro reported that all of his forty-five pupils were at the alphabet and primer level.[34]

Gradually the spread between the most elementary and the more advanced students widened. A few large institutions in major cities developed into graded schools. Most notable of these were the Emerson Institute in Mobile and the Swayne School in Montgomery, each of which had eleven teachers in January

1871.[35] Graded schools also developed in Huntsville, Talladega, Selma, and Marion.

Having the students recite out loud, in concert, was the most common form of instruction. One of the more ambitious teachers described her day as follows:

> We teach four hours per day without room recess, varying the exercise with concert repetition and singing, and then dismiss for the day. Besides Reading and Spelling, they are paying great attention to Penmanship, and I give them Bible lessons, teach them the Geography of their own State, the tables of Arithmetic in concert, something of the proceedings of a court of justice, many particulars of good manners; and I design giving them oral lessons upon United States History and Physiology.[36]

The wide variety of her curriculum was somewhat unusual, but not the inclusion of Bible study. Most teachers, especially the Congregationalist AMA envoys, considered religious instruction to be an integral part of the education they were providing. "My first work was to try to build up a conscience — to teach them of their personal responsibility to God," explained the principal of a school in Selma. "Each teacher devotes half an hour every morning in religious exercises and it makes me so happy to see the spirit of devotion which I have been able to cultivate in them — even the smallest."[37] Not all teachers, however, were so satisfied with the religious environment. A teacher at the Emerson Institute in Mobile complained that most of the other teachers were not religious enough, and the school itself was deficient for lack of "moral and religious influences."[38]

IV

Teachers and observers, in Alabama as in other Southern states, were struck with the ardent desire of the freedmen for education. "Too much cannot be said of the desire to learn among this people," declared Swayne of Alabama's blacks. "Everywhere, to open a school has been to have it filled."[39] A witness before the Joint Congressional Committee on Reconstruction testified that the Alabama Negroes "have scarcely a leisure moment that you cannot see them with a book in their hand learning to read."[40] Contrary to the expectations of many, most observers found that the desire of the freedmen for learning continued unabated through the 1860s. In June 1868, R. D. Harper, who had replaced Buckley as Bureau superintendent of education when the latter was elected to Congress earlier in the year, reported, "[t]he interest on the part of the col'd people in the cause of education is increasing."[41] The following year Edward Beecher, who occupied both the positions of assistant commissioner and superintendent of education after the Freedmen's Bureau had begun to curtail its activities, wrote that the yearning of blacks for education remained high.[42] Even Walter L. Fleming, historian and critic of Alabama Reconstruction, admitted that "[t]he whole [black] race wanted to go to school; none were too old, few too young."[43]

Fleming's view of the cause of the black enthusiasm for education was less perceptive. He explained that the "seeming thirst for education was not rightly understood in the North; it was, in fact, more a desire to imitate the white master and obtain formerly forbidden privileges than any real desire due to an understanding of the value of an education."[44] John W. Alvord, the Freedmen's Bureau general superintendent of education, who analyzed the causes of the black passion for education in an early report, showed a more profound understanding of the psychology of the freedmen. After passing quickly over the "natural thirst for knowledge common to all men," Alvord came to the crux of the matter. Negroes had "seen power and influence among white people always coupled with *learning* — it is the sign of that elevation to which they now aspire."[45] As he recognized, blacks did indeed imitate whites, for the behavior of whites was to them the behavior of free men, and now that they were no longer slaves they too could act like free men. Rather than indicating that freedmen did not understand the real value of education, this imitation showed that Negroes clearly grasped the role of education in American society. It was that understanding that led the first convention of blacks in Alabama, meeting in Mobile in December 1865, to declare, "we regard the education of our children and youth as vital to the preservation of our liberties."[46] It had been the same understanding that had led Alabama whites to forbid their slaves to learn to read and write.

Blacks went to considerable effort to provide education for their children, bearing much of the cost of the new schooling themselves. Many parents paid tuition fees of from 50¢ to $1.50 — or about one-tenth the wages of an agricultural laborer — every month. Swayne explained that "the principle has been enforced that while all should be made welcome, those who could must pay."[47] In general, those who could not afford to pay were admitted free.[48] Negroes also sometimes raised money to pay teachers' salaries or purchase school buildings. They held meetings to promote education and occasionally petitioned to have schools continued or established.[49] One freedman, for example, wrote to the head of the AMA begging for assistance. "As there is no person here that will teach a freeman Shool we desire you to send us two teachers," he explained. "Mis Lucy M. Peck now liveing Deansville Oneida Co. N.Y. taught School for us in 1867 & we want her a gain if she will come she shall have Board fee of charge plese send her soon there is a bout 75 childern wanting to go to School. Plese rite soon."[50]

Children, too, often made substantial sacrifices for the sake of education. Many students had to walk two or three miles or farther to attend school. Others attended irregularly, "being hired out by their parents to assist in making their living."[51]

Although most of the students in the freedmen's schools were children, adults also sought education. In some cases, parents received instruction from their children who attended school, while others attended school with their children.[52] In February 1867, more than one-tenth of the black students were over eighteen years of age.[53] In some areas, the proportion of adults in the schools was much higher. "[A]bout one half of my pupils are adults, & almost without exception in part or wholly, dependent on their own exertions for a livelihood," wrote one enthusiastic teacher in explaining the discrepancy between the number of students enrolled in her school and the average daily attendance. "Some of them are regularly irregular, losing two days in the week from school, which are spent in washing & ironing. Nothing trivial keeps them from school, and when absent they do their utmost by study at home, to keep pace with their classes & generally succeed in doing so."[54] In some instances, the establishment of special night schools for adults enabled persistent freedmen to attend school without cutting down on their daily labors.

V

Negro teachers made a major contribution to black education. Throughout the Reconstruction (and post-Reconstruction) period, black teachers played an increasingly important role, but they were active from the very introduction of the freedmen's schools in 1865. At first, they were frequently used as assistants to white teachers in the large schools of Mobile and Montgomery.[55] In the capital city, the only school in existence in 1865 was run by a Northern white man, who was assisted "merely by inexperienced and very poorly educated colored young men." The white teacher added that "[t]hese young men, however, are very energetic and promising persons." He spent a portion of each day giving them pedagogical instructions, and as a result concluded, "I have, I think, brought on my school of beginners nearly as well as though I had had more experienced help."[56]

Other Negroes served as the primary or only teachers in schools. In the little blackbelt village of Gainsville, Richard Burke, a black minister sixty years old — and a future state legislator — conducted a school attended by twenty-two pupils. All of them paid tuition, and all were at the alphabet and primer level.[57] In Wetumpka, a blackbelt town not far from Montgomery, William V. Turner, also a future state legislator, taught both a day and a night school.[58] At first, black teachers were especially numerous during the summer, when Northern whites often went home for vacation. In June 1866 in Mobile, for example, ten of thirteen teachers were Negroes.[59]

Black teachers were especially prevalent in the Sunday schools — usually referred to as Sabbath schools — that sprang up across the state. These schools gave instruction in elementary education as well as religious subjects, and many Negroes who could not afford the time to go to school every day did attend Sunday school.[60] Although numerous children received their only formal education in these schools, because the instruction was often on a very elementary level and the teachers were usually black, white teachers tended to look down on the Sabbath schools. Superintendent Buckley, for example, wrote in 1866 that in Montgomery there were "two very large colored Sabbath schools, but the teachers are ignorant, mostly colored, or entirely so now."[61]

It is difficult to estimate the precise number of black teachers because many of them were not included in the Freedmen's Bureau school reports. According to Bureau statistics, the number of Negro teachers between October 1866 and May 1868 ranged from 7 to 24 and the number of white teachers varied from 39 to 126, with blacks thus constituting approximately one-fifth of the teaching force.[62] Throughout this period, however, there were schools that either did not report to the Freedmen's Bureau, or were totally independent of the Bureau. The latter were designated "private schools" by Bureau officials, although schools under the control of the Bureau or Northern benevolent societies were also in fact semiprivate. "We hear, constantly, that 'paying schools' are springing up all over the South," complained the *Freedmen's Record,* the organ of the New England Freedmen's Aid Society, "and that the wealthier colored people prefer sending [their children] to 'private schools' to supporting free ones."[63] Black teachers were especially prevalent in the private and nonreporting schools.

In both cities and smaller towns, these private schools flourished. In 1866 the superintendent of schools in Mobile noted that "[f]amily and private schools are quite numerous, [and] as nearly as we can estimate about 250 scholars are attending these schools."[64] In Tuscaloosa, a teacher guessed that in addition to the two schools that had reported to the Bureau there were three other nonreporting schools with one white and two black teachers. "There is a school of 25 wholly sustained by Freedmen," he added.[65] The existence of these schools meant that from 1865 to 1868 Bureau statistics consistently underestimated the number of black teachers and students.[66]

Most white observers considered the Negro teachers less well qualified than the Northern missionaries, although it was frequently added that their qualifications were rapidly improving.[67] Although Northerners sometimes noted that most freedmen preferred black teachers to white ones, it did not occur to Freedmen's Bureau officials or other whites that relatively uncultured black teachers might be just as effective as learned whites in imparting the rudimentary skills emphasized in the freedmen's schools. Nor did many whites consider that black students might be able to relate better to Negro teachers who were familiar with their customs and culture. Usually whites merely noted that black teachers were themselves uneducated, but occasionally there were more specific criticisms. "This school is on the decline," reported one white of Negro teacher Richard Burke's institution in the blackbelt community of Gainsville. "[H]e has them read all the time, commencing with 'one' he continues till all have read, then No. 1 again & so on till the hour is up. One pupil forms a class & for recreation he reads to them out of the Bible or NewsPapers."[68]

It is not easy to determine the origins of the first black teachers. Many of them apparently came from backgrounds which offered them unusual opportunities even before the war. Either they had been free, or else they had received preferential treatment from their masters and acquired at least the rudiments of an education. Prince Murrell, for example, who taught school in Tuscaloosa and for several years was that city's only black Baptist preacher, was born in Savannah in 1817, the grandson of an Englishman. He learned to read while still a slave, became a Baptist preacher, and in 1855 was able to purchase his freedom.[69]

After 1868, however, most black teachers were graduates of normal schools established with the specific aim of providing more Negro teachers. From the beginning, it was the policy of both the Freedmen's Bureau and the benevolent societies to encourage the training of black instructors. "It is evident that the Freedmen are to have teachers of their own color," wrote Bureau General Superintendent of Education John Alvord in 1866. "Many such . . . are already employed. The rural districts and plantations give them the preference, though inferior in their qualifications." He advised the speedy establishment of teacher training schools for Negroes.[70]

By 1870 several such institutions were in existence. The graded schools in Mobile, Montgomery, Selma, and Marion all provided pedagogical training in addition to their traditional programs.[71] Much of the lower level instruction in these schools was carried out by the normal students.[72] In Huntsville, the Freedmen's Aid Society of the Methodist Episcopal church established the Rust Institute to train black teachers.[73]

The largest, earliest, and most successful normal school was set up by the American Missionary Association in Talladega in 1867. Henry E. Brown, the white, Oberlin-educated director of the school, first met with Negroes in their log churches to explain the purposes of the new institution and recruit students for it.[74] "Pick out the best specimen of a young man you have for a teacher, and bring to church with you next Sunday all the corn and bacon you can spare for his living," he told them, "and I will take him into my school and make him a teacher." That first November only eight or nine were chosen. During the summer vacation they all taught "bush schools" before returning in October 1868 to resume their studies.[75] Brown explained that although all but two of the students had been slaves, "on account of some previous practice in thinking [they] are able to do service as teachers, long before they are thoroughly educated in all common branches." Because of the urgency of educating the freedmen and the shortage of teachers, he continued, "we encourage young people . . . to master the elements of a few most needed branches, as arith[metic], writing, & music, & then go out to teach a few months; thus beginning the primary schools, & getting a little money with which to return to school."[76]

The second year, the same program was repeated with about fifty students. By then Talladega Normal had begun to influence Negroes over a wide area, and as the news of its program spread it became "the ambition of many young men, one hundred and fifty and two hundred miles away . . . to some how make their way to the 'Colored people's College' in Talladega." Two years later, the school boasted eight teachers and one hundred and thirty students, eighty of whom boarded on campus. Candidates for admission had to be at least twelve years old, and were required pass a test in "Reading, Writing, Spelling, Elements of English Grammar, General Geography, [and] Arithmetic through Fractions."[77]

Observers were struck with the successful results of Talladega's program. One wrote Reverend Brown that in every community where his students established schools, the impact on blacks was remarkable. "The benefits resulting from the establishment of this school is by no means confined to 'book learning,'" he added, "but extends to the development of a higher standard of morality, than has hitherto been attained by colored people."[78] The superintendent of education of Talladega County agreed that the school resulted in "a marked difference in the course of the colored population," not only in Talladega, but "also in the adjoining counties." He added that, as a consequence, crime among blacks had been drastically reduced.[79] An early student of Talladega Normal later remembered Swayne Hall, the school's first building, as "the center of the life of colored people. . . . This was true of both town and country people."[80]

VI

Most historians have argued that Southern whites were sympathetic to the idea of Negro education immediately after the war, and that this initial receptivity changed to hostility only when whites saw Northern abolitionist teachers spreading envy of whites among the freedmen. It was not so much the education of the blacks that Southern whites objected to as the way in which they were being educated.[81] Walter L. Fleming denied that schools were burned just because they were schools. "As a rule the schoolhouses (and churches also) were burned because they were the headquarters of the Union League and the general meeting places for Radical politicians," he explained, "or because of the character of the teacher and the results of his or her teachings."[82] Southern whites, too, claimed that they had no objection to teaching blacks (what else was slavery but a school for savages?) but only to the spreading of hatred among them. The Elmore *Standard* explained that Southerners must undertake the education of Negroes, "for if it is not done by them it will be done by strangers coming from the North, who will infuse into them wrong notions and prejudices in regard to the feelings of the Southern people towards them."[83]

There is, in fact, some truth to this argument. Northerners did not ignore the opportunity to inculcate among the freedmen their own social and moral ideals. Some white Alabamians did support the education of Negroes in the proper hands, and a few helped establish schools for freedmen. An AMA official noted that whites in several Alabama cities were helping with Negro education.[84] A few planters built schools on their plantations, and in 1867 the Montgomery *Advertiser* called on citizens to contribute toward the purchasing of a lot upon which blacks planned to build a schoolhouse. It added, "[o]ur people have not been as prompt to teach the colored people themselves as they should be, trusting it to those who do not have very kind feelings for the South."[85] That year, in something of an overstatement, Buckley claimed, "[n]o difficulty is now experienced in getting competent Southern persons who are willing to teach colored schools."[86]

There is little evidence to suggest, however, that white sentiment toward black education in Alabama followed a simple course of initial receptivity followed by increasing opposition. In 1866 and early 1867, almost every teacher or Freedmen's Bureau official who commented upon the subject reported that, although Alabama whites had at first been strongly opposed to Negro schools, they were gradually becoming reconciled to the idea as it became apparent that schools would be introduced with or without their support.[87] Typical was Buckley's optimistic report in the spring of 1866 that "[o]ur cause is meeting with less opposition, prejudice is giving way, and colored schools are bringing to their aid the moral support of many right minded men in various parts of the State."[88]

Late in 1867 and early in 1868, there was once again a sharp increase in white hostility to black education, coinciding with the meeting of the Radical Constitutional Convention and the subsequent bitter struggle over the ratification of the new constitution. Although a few teachers continued to report generally favorable white sentiment, more typical was the observation of a

Bureau sub-assistant commissioner that "the spirit of Rebellion is more violent and intollerent than ever it has been since the surrender."[89] Throughout the state, in the blackbelt as well as the predominantly white areas, native white opposition to the freedmen's schools mounted. In one blackbelt town, a Bureau official noted that public sentiment was "generally adverse" to black education, while in another a teacher reported white sentiment toward education "averse to colored and indifferent to poor white."[90] In a small mountain town, a Bureau sub-assistant commissioner wrote that although the freedmen were anxious for a school, "it would be very doubtful if a suitable white person could be obtained as teacher, the prejudice is so great against persons serving in that capacity."[91] In Mobile, black education declined in 1867, explained another agent, because "the principal school and church buildings had been destroyed by incendiarism."[92]

Once the political struggles of 1867-1868 were over, however, the bitter white opposition to Negro education began to subside. In 1869, the new superintendent of education of Lauderdale County in the Tennessee Valley reported that "there has not been manifested any very bitter opposition" to the establishment of schools for blacks in his area, and superintendents from other counties agreed that, while white sentiment had been distinctly unfriendly during the first half of 1868, conditions had improved since then. Almost every school report from teachers in early 1869 contained the same message.[93] While most Alabama whites may not have especially liked the idea of educating their ex-slaves, they went along peacefully when it appeared that they had no alternative.

VII

The cause of education was buttressed by the Radical constitution that came out of the state Constitutional Convention in late 1867 and was ratified in February 1868. It provided for the establishment of free public schools for children between the ages of five and twenty-one. Although the constitution was discreetly silent on whether the schools were to be integrated and the dele-

Table 12 *Freedmen's Bureau Statistics of Students in Freedmen's Schools in Alabama, 1866-1870*

	REGULARLY REPORTING	NOT REGULARLY REPORTING
November 1866	3,220	
February 1867	5,352	
May 1867	8,822	
November 1867	1,692	
February 1868	3,072	38
May 1868	3,859	
November 1868	2,881	
February 1869	3,690	3,000
May 1869	4,088	6,000
August 1869	1,417	10,000
November 1869	2,110	5,000
February 1870	3,474	12,000

SOURCE: FBP, Educational Division, Consolidated School Reports; FBP, Alabama Educational Division, Reports of the Superintendent of Education.

Table 13 *Freedmen's Bureau Statistics of Teachers in Freedmen's Bureau Schools in Alabama, 1866-1870*

	REGULARLY REPORTING		NOT REGULARLY REPORTING	
	White	*Black*	*White*	*Black*
October 1866	39	7		
February 1867	75	20		
June 1867	126	24		
January 1868	41	15		
May 1868	67	24	10	
October 1868	36	7		2
January 1869	40	1	9	11
May 1869	65	6	55	20
August 1869	24	6	200	100
October 1869	25	2	200	100
January 1870	58	12	150	50

SOURCE: FBP, Educational Division, Consolidated School Reports.

gates defeated a motion requiring the establishment of segregated schools, it was understood that separate school systems would be created.[94] On 11 August 1868, the new state board of education confirmed these expectations with a resolution that "in no case shall it be lawful to unite in one school both colored and white children, unless it be by the unanimous consent of the parents and guardians of such children; but said trustees shall in all other cases provide separate schools for both white and colored children."[95]

Despite the prospects for the establishment of free and universal public education, the year 1867-1868 witnessed stagnation among the freedmen's schools and an actual decline in the number of children attending them.[96] (See Table 12.) Education was most drastically cut back in many of the smaller rural communities. "There are no Freedmen's schools within this sub dist [rict], to my knowledge," reported a sub-assistant commissioner from the blackbelt town of Opelika, "and the closing of those formerly maintained by the Bureau is bitterly lamented by the freedmen."[97] In Tuscaloosa, there was only one school with fifty pupils in December 1867.[98] Black Freedmen's Bureau agent John Mercer Langston, after a special inspection tour of Alabama's schools, concluded sadly that a "great many of the counties of the State — and some of these counties are among those especially densely populated by the freed people — are without schools."[99]

The reasons for this decline in school attendance are not hard to discover. It corresponded directly with the period of most intense white oppostion. In addition, the period was a transitional one. Few black teachers had graduated from the normal schools. The new public-school system was not yet organized; indeed, the newly created state board of education did not even meet until July 1868. The Freedmen's Bureau was beginning to curtail its operations. Finally, as Northern interest in the freedmen declined, less aid was forthcoming from the benevolent societies. The Freedmen's Bureau sent them urgent requests, but as Superintendent of Education Harper wrote Howard, "the prospect of securing teachers from the Benevolent and Christian associations of the north is by no means promising."[100]

The outlook for the following year appeared equally bleak. In August 1868 Harper informed Howard that he did not expect any financial help from the state in 1868-1869. and so far only 26 teachers had been hired for the entire state. His modest estimate was that 133 more were needed. He noted that there were 91 focal points in the state where 145 schools could be set up if only teachers and financial aid were provided.[101]

Upon first glance it would appear that the grim prophesies for 1868-1869 were more than fulfilled, and at least one historian has concluded that the freedmen's schools reached their peak of development in Alabama in 1866-1867 and subsequently declined.[102] Indeed, the number of students listed in the Bureau reports remained pitifully low — well below the level of 1866-1867. (See Tables 12 and 13.)

Nevertheless, upon closer examination it is clear that the year was one of broad recovery for black education in Alabama. By the summer of 1869, more blacks were attending school than ever before. Most of the schools operating after January 1869 were simply not included in the Bureau reports. Although some teachers stopped sending in reports, the problem lay mainly in the several district headquarters of the Freedmen's Bureau, where reports, which agents commonly neglected to forward to Montgomery, piled up. Occasionally the assistant commissioner would find out about some of these schools, and not realizing that the Bureau agents rather than the teachers were remiss, would list the schools as nonreporting. "In going through one county in November last month I found twelve colored schools in operation that I knew nothing of before," wrote Beecher in 1870.[103] Although sometimes these schools were listed in Bureau reports as nonreporting, the figures represented crude estimates rather than precise statistics. Numerous schools were ignored altogether. By August 1869, the Bureau figures for students attending nonreporting schools stood at ten thousand. The assistant commissioner estimated that they were being instructed by two hundred white and one hundred black teachers.[104]

VIII

From 1868 to 1871, the new public-school system gradually developed. During the summer of 1868, the state board of education met for the first time and urged that wherever possible county superintendents of education should arrange for the opening of public schools in October.[105] Although at first it appeared that no money would be appropriated for the schools that year, at the last minute the state legislature adopted a bill drawn up by Harper himself, providing $200,000 for the academic year 1868-1869.[106] During that year most of the freedmen's schools received state or county assistance for the first time. In many cases, the Freedmen's Bureau continued to pay the rent of school buildings, and the AMA maintained its support of several of the larger institutions, such as the Emerson Institute in Mobile and Talladega Normal School.[107]

From the summer of 1869 to January 1870 most schools were closed, as the board of education reorganized the system and began the new term in January instead of October. Some schools, especially the private ones, continued to function without state aid. When the schools reopened in January, they were still suffering from a shortage of funds and administrative confusion. Some teachers continued to report to the Freedmen's Bureau, but most did not.[108]

It was not until the following year that the new school system was prepared to handle massive numbers of children. That year 41,308 blacks and 75,760 whites attended school, and in the fall of 1871 the figures jumped to 54,336 Negroes and 86,976 whites. Although none of the schools was integrated, the days of blatant discrimination were still to come. In 1871, the 973 teachers in black schools received an average monthly salary of $43.06, or 91¢ more than the 2,497 teachers of white children, who received an average of $42.15.[109]

IX

The freedmen's schools that existed prior to the establishment of the public-school system have received little acclaim. Fleming considered them to have been an unqualified failure. George Bentley, the historian of the Freedmen's Bureau, judged their most important achievement to have been that "the idea of Negro schools had become established in Southern thinking,

white and black." Almost as modest was Bureau Superintendent
of Education R. D. Harper. "What has been done has been well
done," he concluded in August 1868; "but after all, but little
has been accomplished compared with the magnitude of the un-
dertaking. It is safe to say that there are 100,000 children in the
State who have never learned the alphabet nor been inside of a
schoolhouse."[110]

Harper was right, of course. Illiteracy had not been wiped out
in three years; the majority of black children had not attended
school. But for the time, the effort had been unique in the annals
of history. Between October 1865 and January 1869, the Freedmen's Bureau had spent $113,452 on education in Alabama. The
money was devoted to the renting and construction of school buildings, the transportation of teachers, school books, and in some
cases teachers' salaries.[111] Benevolent societies and the freedmen
themselves had provided more. If a whole people had not been
taught to read, surely the yield was greater than merely implant-
ing the idea of education, an idea that was evidently already
alive in the minds of most Negroes in 1865.

It is impossible to state with precision the number of freedmen
who received some education. In 1860, there were 173,204
blacks between the ages of five and nineteen in Alabama.[112]
Although some adults did attend school, that figure will serve as
a good approximation of the potential black school-age population. According to Bureau statistics, at no time prior to the establishment of the public-school system were there more than
9,799 pupils in regularly reporting schools, and at many times
the number was as low as 3,000 or 4,000. Such figures, however,
must be supplemented. Some children attended schools that
either did not report regularly or were totally unknown to the
Bureau; others attended Sunday schools. Alvord estimated that
when night schools, nonreporting schools, and Sunday schools
were added to the regularly reporting schools, there were in
Alabama 18,159 black students in January 1868, representing
about one-ninth of the potential school-age population.[113] There
was no doubt a considerable turnover of students from 1865 to
1869, so the total number of blacks who received at least some
schooling during the period must have been somewhat greater

than one-ninth. Even then, one is in danger of underestimating the spread of education. One teacher noted that parents frequently received instruction during the evenings from their children who attended school by day.[114]

The impact of the freedmen's schools cannot be measured, however, only by the number of Negroes who attended school. Less tangible but perhaps equally important results ensued. The schools became one of the prime vehicles for the introduction of new values — frequently Northern, middle-class values — among the freedmen. These included first and foremost religion, temperance, and "conventional" behavior in all walks of life. The desire of blacks to prove their freedom by behaving like whites — and especially like their Northern white benefactors — proved to be an important source of social change among Negroes. A Northern teacher sent into Alabama by the AMA was struck by the implicit faith the freedmen placed in their teachers. "I am surprised every day at the readiness which is manifested in complying with my advice, even when it is most against their natural feelings," he wrote.[115]

At the same time, blacks demonstrated their independence and self-reliance in educational matters. They enthusiastically supported the idea of sending their children to school. They held meetings to raise money for buildings and teachers and paid tuition so their children could learn. Black teachers played a major role in the education of the freedmen. Tens of black instructors were already teaching by 1866; in the next few years they were joined by hundreds more.

Finally, the freedmen's schools served as the precursors of the new public schools that were in operation by 1870. If the public-school system had not been set up, one might perhaps be justified in regarding the earlier schools for blacks as a hopeful but insufficient temporary measure. In fact, they laid the groundwork for black education in the following decades. In education, as in other areas of life, most of the basic patterns of the new order were well established within a few years after the end of the war.

Notes

1. James B. Sellers, *Slavery in Alabama* (University, Alabama: University of Alabama Press, 1950), p. 117.

2. Horace Mann Bond, *Negro Education in Alabama: A Study in Cotton and Steel* (Washington, D.C.: The Associated Publishers, Inc., 1939), p. 15.

3. Willis G. Clark, *History of Education in Alabama: 1702-1889* (Washington: Government Printing Office, 1889), p. 7.

4. Ibid., pp. 203-239.

5. Sellers, *Slavery in Alabama*, pp. 117-120.

6. See Henry Lee Swint, *The Northern Teacher in the South: 1862-1870* (Nashville, Tennessee: Vanderbilt University Press, 1941).

7. In January 1866, for example, the New England Freedmen's Aid Society had teachers in the following states, in descending numerical order: South Carolina, Virginia, Maryland, North Carolina, Georgia, and the District of Columbia. *Freedmen's Record* 2, no. 1 (January 1866): 14. The *Freedmen's Record* was the monthly organ of the New England Freedmen's Aid Society.

8. See the American Missionary Association Papers (hereafter cited as AMAP) at Fisk University, and the *American Missionary*, the monthly journal of the AMA, for the story of that body's Southern endeavors.

9. See John W. Blassingame, "The Union Army as an Educational Institution for Negroes, 1862-1865," *Journal of Negro Education* 34 (1965): 152-159, for an important side of black education during the war.

10. Robert Stanley Bahney, "Generals and Negroes: Education of Negroes by the Union Army, 1861-1865" (Ph.D. diss., University of Michigan, 1965), pp. 191-192; Walter L. Fleming, *Civil War and Reconstruction in Alabama* (New York: Columbia University Press, 1905), p. 456.

11. Mrs. W. D. Chadick, diary, 8 February 1864, Alabama State Department of Archives and History.

12. Swayne to Howard, Montgomery, 11 September 1865, FBP, Assistant Adjutant General's Office, Letters Received.

13. Their combined attendance was 817. Swayne to Howard, telegram, Montogmery, 28 November 1865, FBP, Assistant Adjutant General's Office, Letters Received.

14. Bahney, "Generals and Negroes," p. 198.

15. *National Freedman* 1, no. 6. (15 July 1865): 183. The *National Freedman* was the monthly journal of the National Freedman's Relief Association.

16. Charles Anderson to Howard, Athens, 26 June 1865, FBP, Alabama Letters Received.

17. Buckley to Swayne, Montgomery, 24 October 1866, FBP, Alabama Educational Division, Annual Report of the Superintendent of Education.

18. Ibid.

19. In February 1866, 1,113 students attended 6 schools in the Tennessee Valley region of Alabama and were taught by 15 teachers. J. B. Callis, Sub-Assistant Commissioner, Huntsville, February 1866, FBP, Alabama Educational Division, Monthly School Report.

20. Ibid.

21. In March 1866, the Lincoln Institute had 763 pupils and 7 teachers. The other 6 schools had 235 Negro students. Elijah C. Branch, Superintendent of Schools in Mobile, March 1866, FBP, Alabama Educational Division, Monthly School Report.

22. Montgomery, January 1866, FBP, Alabama Educational Division, Monthly School Report. An additional 230 students were recorded in Montgomery City. J. Silsby to Rev. E. P. Smith, Montgomery, 26 March 1866, AMAP.

23. J. Silsby to Rev. W. Fisk, Mobile, 17 February 1866, AMAP.

24. Buckley to E. P. Smith, Montgomery, 15 August 1867, AMAP.

25. In November 1866, Buckley reported 3,220 students enrolled. In February 1867, the figure was 5,352, and by May it had reached 8,822. During the same period, the number of teachers rose from 68 to 132. November 1866, February 1867, May 1867, FBP, Alabama Educational Division, Monthly Reports of the Superintendent of Education. See Tables 12 and 13.

26. In February, for example, 3,539 of the state's 5,352 black school children were in the Tennessee Valley, Montgomery County, or Mobile. February, 1867, FBP, Alabama Educational Division, Monthly Report of the Superintendent of Education.

27. J. Silsby, Selma, December 1866, FBP, Alabama Educational Division, Monthly School Report; February, 1867, FBP, Alabama Educational Division, Monthly Report of the Superintendent of Education. Charles C. Aems, Tuscaloosa, February 1867, FBP, Alabama Educational Division, Monthly School Report.

28. W. G. Kephart, Chaplain, 10th Iowa Veterans, to Lewis Tappan, Decatur, 9 May 1865, AMAP. See also Charles Anderson, Chaplain, 46th Wisconsin Volunteers, to Howard, Athens, 26 June 1865, FBP, Alabama Letters Received; J. Silsby to Elliott Whipple, Montgomery, 14 September 1866, AMAP; E. L. Benton to Rev. E. P. Smith, Tuscaloosa, 22 May 1867, AMAP; Elliott Whipple, LaFayette, August 1867, FBP, Alabama Educational Division, Teacher's Report.

29. Emeline M. Wright to Rev. E. P. Smith, Eufaula, 30 December 1868, AMAP; Miss J. E. Beigle to Rev. Cravath, Oswichee, 29 October 1870, AMAP.

30. Emeline M. Wright to Rev. E. P. Smith, Eufaula, 30 December 1868, AMAP.

31. According to Buckley, 790 students were in alphabet and primer, 536 in the first reader, 294 in the second, 241 in the third, 106 in the fourth, and 28 in the fifth. March 1866, FBP, Alabama Educational Division, Monthly Report of the Superintendent of Education.

32. Emeline M. Wright to Rev. Smith, Eufaula, 30 December 1868, AMAP.

33. Charles Buckley, Montgomery, March 1866, FBP, Alabama Educational Division, Monthly Report of the Superintendent of Education.

34. Thomas Martin, Greensboro, March 1866, FBP, Alabama Educational Division, Teacher's Report.

35. *American Missionary* 15, no. 1 (January 1871): 2-3. Of the 514 students at the Emerson Institute in 1868, only 203 were in alphabet and primer. Mathematics still seemed to present more of a problem, but 114 students had progressed beyond mental arithmetic, and 2 were studying higher arithmetic and algebra. Report of the Emerson Institute, Mobile, 8 December 1868, AMAP.

36. Mary Atwater to Howard, Haynesville, 25 April 1868, FBP, Assistant Adjutant General's Office, Letters Received.

37. E. Wheeler to Rev. E. P. Smith, Selma, 4 June 1870 [?], AMAP.

38. Henry J. Kelsey to Messrs. Whipple and Strieby, Mobile, 18 February 1869, AMAP.

39. Report of Wager Swayne, 31 October 1866, U.S., Congress, Senate, Ex. Doc. No. 6, 39th Cong., 2d sess., p. 13.

40. Testimony of General B. H. Grierson, 2 March 1866, U.S., Congress, *Report of the Joint Committee on Reconstruction* (Washington: Government Printing Office, 1866), pt. 3, p. 122.

41. R. D. Harper to Howard, Montgomery, 22 June 1868. FBP, Alabama Book Records, Superintendent of Education, Letters Sent.

42. Edward Beecher to John W. Alvord, Montgomery, 13 July 1869, FBP, Alabama Educational Division, Report of the Superintendent of Education.

43. Fleming, *Civil War and Reconstruction,* p. 458.

44. Ibid.

45. 1 January 1866, U.S., Congress, House, Ex. Doc. No. 70, 39th Cong., 1st sess., p. 334. Alvord concluded with an interesting observation: "Their freedom has given wonderful stimulus to *all effort.*"

46. New York *Daily Tribune,* 12 December 1865, p. 4. For more on black conventions, see chap. 7.

47. U.S., Congress, Senate, Ex. Doc. No. 6, 39th Cong., 2d sess., p. 12. In the white public schools set up in the 1850s, "more than one half of the cost of the schools was paid by the parents of pupils attending the schools." Clark, *History of Education in Alabama,* p. 241. There was evidently little white education in the 1860s.

48. In February 1867, for example, of 5,325 black students, only 1,075 paid tuition. FBP, Alabama Educational Division, Consolidated School Reports. At the Lincoln Institute in Mobile, in March 1866, 341 students were admitted free while 184 paid tuition. Elijah C. Branch, March 1866, FBP, Alabama Educational Division, Monthly School Report.

49. See, for example, Elliott Whipple to Rev. E. P. Smith, LaFayette, 5 August 1867, AMAP, and the *Alabama Beacon's* report on the proceedings of a freedmen's educational meeting in Marion, 16 June 1866.

50. C. L. Johnson to Rev. E. P. Smith, Union Springs, 14 March 1869, AMAP.

51. LaFayette, Chambers County, August 1867; John Wiley, Troy, October 1866: FBP, Alabama Educational Division, Teachers' Reports.

52. Mary Atwater to Professor John Ogden, Benton, 4 December 1867, AMAP.

53. Of 5,352 students, 578 were adults. FBP, Alabama Educational Division, Consolidated School Reports.

54. Cynthia M. Copson, Talladega, January 1867, FBP, Alabama Educational Division, Teacher's Report.

55. Swayne to Howard, Montgomery, 31 October 1866, FBP, Assistant Adjutant General's Office, Annual Report.

56. J. Silsby to Rev. George Whipple, Montgomery, 2 November 1865, AMAP.

57. Thomas E. Lynn, Gainsville, May 1866, FBP, Alabama Educational Division, Teacher's Report.

58. William V. Turner, Wetumpka, March 1866, FBP, Alabama Educational Division, Teacher's Report.

59. E. C. Branch, Superintendent of Schools for Mobile, June 1866, FBP, Alabama Educational Division, Monthly School Report.

60. In February 1867, for example, there were 4,268 Negroes in 50 reporting Sunday schools. FBP, Alabama Educational Division, Consolidated School Reports.

61. Buckley to Whipple, 13 March 1866, AMAP.

62. FBP, Alabama Educational Division, Consolidated School Reports.

63. *Freedmen's Record 3*, no. 7 (July 1867): 113. Although most private schools charged tuition, this was not their defining characteristic, since most Bureau run schools also charged at least some of their pupils.

64. E. C. Branch, June 1866, FBP, Alabama Educational Division, Monthly School Report.

65. Charles C. Aems, Tuscaloosa, February 1867, FBP, Alabama Educational Division, Monthly School Report.

66. It is likely that the actual number of black teachers was twice the figures reported by the Bureau, while the number of black students was one-third

higher. Bureau statistics did sometimes include nonreporting schools under a separate column, but these figures were fragmentary and incomplete. See Tables 12 and 13.

67. See, for example, Beecher to Alvord, Montogomery, 1 July 1870, FBP, Alabama Educational Division, Report of the Superintendent of Education.

68. Thomas E. Lynn, Gainsville, May 1866, FBP, Alabama Educational Division, Teacher's Report.

69. Charles Octavius Boothe, *The Cyclopedia of the Colored Baptists of Alabama: Their Leaders and Their Work* (Birmingham: Alabama Publishing Co., 1895), pp. 174-176; Nancy Claiborne Roberson, "The Negro and the Baptists of Antebellum Alabama" (Master's thesis, University of Alabama, 1954), p. 143.

70. John Alvord to Howard, Washington, D.C., 18 December 1866, Abstract of School Reports, FBP, Assistant Adjutant General's Office, Letters Received.

71. *American Missionary* 15, no. 1 (January 1871): 2-3.

72. Henry J. Kelsey to the Secretaries of the AMA, Mobile, 6 May 1869, AMAP.

73. "Fourth Annual Report of the Freedmen's Aid Society of the Methodist Episcopal Church," *Reports of the Freedmen's Aid Society of the Methodist Episcopal Church, 1866-1873* (Cincinnati: Western Methodist Book Concern, 1873 [?]), p. 9.

74. William Leonard Hawkins, "The History of the Administration of Talladega College from 1867-1947" (Senior project, Talladega College, 1949), p. 9.

75. *American Missionary* 12, no. 10 (October 1868): 217-218.

76. Brown to Captain Bush, n.d. [probably 1868], FBP, Alabama Educational Division, Special Report of the Talladega Normal Class.

77. Brown to Rev. Taylor, Talladega, 18 February 1868, AMAP; *American Missionary* 13, no. 3 (March 1869): 61-63, 15, no. 7 (January 1871): 2-3; Talladega Normal School, circular, 1870-1, p. 7, Talladega College Archives.

78. Charles Pelham to Rev. Brown, Talladega, 30 October 1869, AMAP.

79. J. G. Chandron to Rev. Brown, Talladega, 30 October 1869, AMAP.

80. F. G. Ragland to Rev. Charles A. Jaquith, Birmingham, 12 September 1927, in folder marked "History, 1869-1899 (Talladega)." Talladega College Archives.

81. Swint, *The Northern Teacher in the South*, pp. 94-109, 116-140; George R. Bentley, *A History of the Freedmen's Bureau* (Philadelphia: University of Pennsylvania Press, 1955), pp. 178-183.

82.. Fleming, *Civil War and Reconstruction*, p. 628.

83. Elmore *Stardard*, 26 July 1867.

84. J. Silsby to Rev. Whipple, Montgomery, 14 September 1866, AMAP.

85. Montgomery *Weekly Advertiser*, 14 May, 30 July 1867.

86. Buckley to Alvord, Montgomery, 1 July 1867, FBP, Alabama Educational Division, Report of the Superintendent of Education.

87. See Alvord to Howard, 18 December 1866, FBP, Assistant Adjutant General's Office, Letters Received; L. M. Peck to Rev. E. P. Smith, Union Springs, 21 June 1867, AMAP; Buckley to Swayne, 1 October 1867, FBP, Alabama Educational Division, Annual Report of the Superintendent of Education.

88. Buckley to Swayne, Montgomery, 30 April 1866, FBP, Alabama Letters Received.

89. R. Blair, Tuscaloosa, January 1868, FBP, Alabama Educational Division, Monthly School Report. For an example of a report showing whites favorably inclined toward black education, see that of Robert Harrison, Sub-Assistant Commissioner, Jacksonville, 4 June 1868, FBP, Alabama Educational Division, Superintendent of Education, Letters Received.

90. R. T. Smith, Opelika, April 1868; Eufaula, February 1868: FBP Alabama Educational Division, Monthly School Reports.

91. C. C. Bartlett, Elyton, 4 June 1868, FBP, Alabama Educational Division, Superintendent of Education, Letters Received.

92. Extract from report of James Gillette, 15 July 1868, Frederick G. Bromberg Papers, Southern Historical Collection, University of North Carolina.

93. Alabama Department of Education, *Report of the Superintendent of Public Instruction . . . for . . . 1869* (Montgomery: J. G. Stokes and Co., 1870), pp. 7-11. See also the reports in the FBP, Alabama Educational Division, Teachers' Reports.

94. *Official Journal of the Constitutional Convention of the State of Alabama* (Montgomery: Barrett and Brown, 1868), pp. 152-153.

95. *School Laws of the State of Alabama* (Montgomery: J. G. Stokes and Co., 1870), p. 15.

96. In February 1867, there were 5,352 freedmen in regularly reporting schools; one year later there were 3,072. FBP, Alabama Educational Division, Consolidated School Reports. There does not seem to have been a significant increase in the number of schools not reporting at this time. Later there was.

97. Robert Smith, 1 November 1867, FBP, Alabama Operations Reports.

98. R. Blair, December 1867, FBP, Alabama Operations Reports.

99. John Mercer Langston to Howard, Washington, D.C., 3 March 1868, FBP, Assistant Adjutant General's Office, Letters Received.

100. For an example of a request for financial assistance, see Harper to Rev. James S. Waville, Secretary of the Pennsylvania Freedmen's Aid Committee,

Montgomery, 1 April 1868, FBP, Alabama Book Records, Superintendent of Education, Letters Sent. Harper to Howard, Montgomery, 22 June 1868, FBP, Alabama Book Records, Superintendent of Education, Letters Sent.

101. Harper to Howard, Montgomery, 11 August 1868, FBP, Alabama Book Records, Superintendent of Education, Letters Sent; ibid., August 1868, FBP, Assistant Adjutant General's Office, Letters Received.

102. See Elizabeth Bethel, "The Freedmen's Bureau in Alabama," *Journal of Southern History* 14 (1948): 89.

103. Beecher to Alvord, Montgomery, 5 January 1870, FBP, Alabama Educational Division, Report of the Superintendent of Education.

104. FBP, Alabama Educational Division, Consolidated School Reports.

105. *School Laws of the State of Alabama*, p. 10.

106. Harper to Howard, Montgomery, 9 October 1868, FBP, Alabama Book Records, Superintendent of Education, Letters Sent.

107. See teachers' reports, FBP, Alabama Educational Division.

108. In February 1870, the assistant commissioner wrote that 41 schools with 3,474 pupils, 63 white and 16 black teachers had reported to him. He estimated that there were 120 other schools for freedmen, with 12,000 students, 100 white and 50 black teachers. FBP, Alabama Educational Division, Report of the Superintendent of Education. His guess proved to be fairly accurate: the state superintendent reported that in 1869-1870, 16,097 Negroes had attended school. Alabama, Department of Education, *Report of Joseph Hodgson, Superintendent of Public Instruction . . . for . . . 1871* (Montgomery: W. W. Screws, 1871). In 1870, 25,963 whites attended school.

109. Ibid.; U.S., Bureau of Education, *Report of the Commissioner of Education for the Year 1872*, p. 5.

110. Fleming, *Civil War and Reconstruction*, pp. 467-468; Bentley, *A History of the Freedmen's Bureau*, p. 182; Report of J. D. Harper, FBP, Assistant Adjutant General's Office, Letters Received.

111. Beecher to Howard, Montgomery, January 1869, FBP, Alabama, Annual Report of the Assistant Commissioner.

112. U.S. Census Office, *Eighth Census: Population* (Washington, D.C.: Government Printing Office, 1864), pp. 552-553.

113. U.S. Bureau of Refugees, Freedmen, and Abandoned Lands, *Fifth Semi-Annual Report on Schools for Freedmen* (Washington: Government Printing Office, 1868), p. 47.

114. Mary Atwater to Professor John Ogden, Benton, 4 December 1867, AMAP.

115. Elliott Whipple to Rev. E. P. Smith, LaFayette, 17 June 1867, AMAP.

5

The Establishment of
the Black Churches

I

The establishment of black churches was one of the most important developments in the emergence of a new black community. In the few years following the Civil War, almost all the black members of the Southern white churches withdrew from them, frequently over the strenuous protests of their white members, and established black churches of their own. The new Negro churches quickly became central institutions within the black communities, and the black ministers emerged as community leaders. The process was a remarkably rapid one; by 1870 there were practically no Negro members in the white Southern Baptist or Methodist churches.

II

Before the war, Negro religion, although frequently intense, was a marginal activity dependent upon the variable and varying whims of slave owners. Throughout the antebellum period, Southern whites held ambivalent attitudes toward slave religion. On the one hand, some feared that an immersion in Christian doctrine was likely to impress slaves with the equality of all souls before God and make them less subservient. The 1831 insurrection led by slave preacher Nat Turner appeared to confirm the worst fears of slave owners that education, even religious education, tended to make slaves less content in their servitude. On the other hand, many Southerners saw religious indoctrination as a useful method of social control. The biblical injunction of obedience to one's master seemed clear, and the promise of reward in the life after death could be useful in keeping an oppressed class docile.

Despite an 1833 state law forbidding blacks to preach except in the presence of five slaveowners, the latter viewpoint generally came to predominate among slaveowners in Alabama. During the prewar years, whites became increasingly concerned with the religious indoctrination of their slaves. White missionaries of the Southern Baptist and Methodist Churches converted many blacks. The number of Methodist slave missions in Alabama increased from two in 1837 to forty in 1860. A typical notice in the *South Western Baptist* that "Rev. T. W. Tobey, of Sumterville, has baptized eleven negroes within the last few months, into the fellowship of the Sumterville Baptist Church," testified to similar efforts on the part of the Baptists.[1]

Most slaves who attended church went to the white churches of their masters, where they sat in segregated slave galleries and listened to white preachers.[2] The all-black churches that had been founded in the North in the early nineteenth century — the African Methodist Episcopal and the African Methodist Episcopal Zion Churches — were entirely excluded from Alabama before the war by a planter class suspicious that any sort of black organization presaged trouble.[3]

Although independent black church organizations were prohibited, there were some situations in which Negroes were allowed to attend their own churches and listen to black preachers. Urban Negroes, especially free ones, often enjoyed this privilege. In Mobile, black Baptists had their own church from 1839. Even in rural areas, as the number of Negro churchgoers came to exceed the number of white ones in many areas during the 1840s and 1850s, it became increasingly common to establish branch churches for the blacks. In 1859 in Tuskegee, for example, although slaves had traditionally worshipped with their masters, the white Baptists built a new church and gave the old one to the slaves. From then on, led by Dock Phillips, a "converted slave," the blacks conducted their own services. Similarly, in the Tennessee Valley town of Decatur, the white members of a church who were outnumbered by Negro members forty to seven abandoned the building to the blacks just before the war.[4]

Thus, a small group of Negro preachers emerged before the war. Although looked up to by many blacks, they were of necessity subservient to the whites who had trained, ordained, and now allowed them to preach. Indeed, it was this subservience that was the most essential feature of black religion before the war. Whether Alabama's slaves worshipped with their masters or in their own churches, the cardinal principle of white control was never relaxed. Antebellum black religion was never an independent concern, but was supervised and controlled, allowed or not allowed, by the white slave owners.

III

White Alabamians saw little reason, at first, why these established church relations should be at all changed by war or emancipation.[5] At a meeting of the Baptist State Convention in 1865, the Committee on the Religious Instruction of the Colored People reported that "the changed political status of our late slaves does not necessitate any change in their relation to our churches," and advised "that their highest good will be subserved by their maintaining their present relation to those who know them, who love them, and who will labor for the promotion of their welfare." The Methodists made similar recommendations.[6] Many whites apparently expected the Negro galleries to be maintained as well. When a black woman tried to sit with whites in a Montgomery church, she was "very politely told that accommodations were prepared for her in another part of the building, and she moved off quickly and took her place in the gallery."[7]

Most freedmen, however, did not share the white views on the maintenance of church relations. Now that they were free, they saw little reason to remain in a subservient position in the churches of their ex-masters. Leaving the white churches and establishing their own black ones was as much a part of the new freedom as leaving the old plantations.

The process of separation was most easily carried out among the Baptists, a relatively unstructured sect which had traditionally maintained much greater local church autonomy than the Methodists. Freedmen spontaneously formed numerous local black Baptist churches across the state following the war.[8] In 1866, for example, Tuscaloosa's Negroes, who had previously worshipped with their masters in the white Baptist church, founded the First African Baptist Church of that city. Secessions continued during the following year, in little communities such as Water Valley,[9] and in cities such as Montgomery. Nathan Ashby, the black minister of the new First Baptist Church of Montgomery, had before the war preached to Negroes in the basement of the white Baptist church.[10] Only in December 1868, after a substantial number of black Baptist churches had already been formed on the local level, did they combine to organize a Colored Baptist State Convention, with Ashby the first president and Holland Thompson, who would soon make a name for himself as a state legislator, the first secretary. During the next few years, the Convention sponsored the formation of numerous regional Baptist associations across the state.[11]

Unlike the Baptist churches, which were formed on the local level first, the black Methodist churches were built from the top down. Because there already existed two Negro Methodist churches in the North, black Methodists were from the start much more highly organized than the Baptists, and received considerable direction and assistance from outside the state. The African Methodist Episcopal Zion Church had the greatest initial success because of its early activities in Montgomery and Mobile.[12] As early as November 1865, ten preachers and five exhorters from the Montgomery area held a convention in that city. J. J. Clinton, a bishop from the North sent to Alabama to organize the Church, instructed them on their duties. In April 1867, when he presided over the first statewide convention of the AME Zion Church in Mobile, there were already 71 ministers representing 6,698 members across the state. By April 1870, at the time of the fourth annual convention, there were 137 ministers and 13,752 church members.[13]

The organization of the AME Church was similar. The Louisiana Conference, which when formed in 1865 included the states of Alabama, Arkansas, Mississippi, and Texas along with Louisiana, supervised the early establishment of the AME churches in Alabama.[14] During the next few years, numerous local groups of black Methodists joined the AME Church. In April 1867, for example, the Negro members of the Methodist church in the blackbelt community of Union Springs voted unanimously to dissolve all connection with the white Methodists and join the AME Church. The action was taken at the urging of Henry Stubbs, an aged black minister sent from Georgia to Alabama as a missionary.[15]

Because of its relatively slow start and the need to compete with the AME Zion Church, the AME Church relied heavily on out-of-state assistance in its formative years. When it first met in Selma in December 1868, the Church's Alabama Annual Conference contained only six churches with 5,616 members. All five of the traveling elders and all ten of the deacons had been transferred from the earlier established Georgia or Louisiana conferences. Seven local preachers were Alabamians. Progress was somewhat more rapid thereafter and by 1872 there were 10,558 church members in sixty-six churches throughout the state.[16]

IV

As freedmen made clear their determination not to remain passive members of white churches, many whites began to reconsider their own position. By 1867 most white church bodies were actively advocating the secession of blacks.[17] One reason for this change was that in many regions of the blackbelt and Tennessee Valley the black churchgoers greatly outnumbered the white. If the freed Negroes were to remain in the white churches, there would be a very real danger that they might gain control of them.[18] To meet this threat, the Coosa River Baptist Association recommended at its annual session in 1866 that churches with only a few Negroes permit them to remain, but those with many freedmen encourage them to separate.[19] As early as 1865, whites supported the formation of separate black churches in some areas of the Tennessee Valley where, as one white pastor later explained, blacks had been in the majority and "if they saw proper to exercise their rights as [church] members, now being free, they could control those churches and call whom they pleased as pastor."[20]

Although encouraging the secession of blacks, white churches often sought to maintain some influence over them. Unwilling to accommodate the Negroes who still remained in the white church, but also reluctant to concede them to the independent black churches, in 1866 the Southern Methodists sponsored the formation of a separate Colored Methodist Episcopal Church under white supervision. Despite, or perhaps because of, the support of the Southern Methodists, the Colored Methodists were never able to attract more than a small number of "loyal" Negroes.[21]

More successful were white efforts to establish friendly relations with the new black churches. Whites conducted programs of religious education for freedmen and attempted to train black preachers who would be sympathetic to the interests of the Southern white churches.[22] They also sometimes helped the new black churches establish themselves. As early as 1866, the *Nationalist* noted the new white attitude: "[t]he ministers of the M.E. Church South were at first disposed to object to the loss of so large a portion of their flocks, but finding that their opposition was useless, they now *co-operate* with the colored congregations; turn over the colored members of their congregations; help them to erect churches, and, in short, generally manifest a liberal Christian spirit in their dealings with them."[23] The formation of the black First Baptist Church of Montgomery was a model of this sort of cooperation. At the time of the separation, there were over 700 blacks and only 300 whites in the white church. When the Negro members voted to form their own church, the whites approved the decision and helped them erect a new building, which was formally dedicated on 30 May 1867.[24]

The break was not always so harmonious. In 1868 and 1869, the attitude of whites toward the black churches hardened as it became clear that Negroes intended their churches to be fully independent.[25] By 1869, some regional white Baptist associations were bitterly recommending the severing of all relations with black churches.[26] When white church bodies supported the exodus of Negro members, there was now less talk of cooperation and more evidence of hostility and resentment. One Baptist association, for example, recommended that Negroes, "[o]wing to their excessive want of confidence in the white people, produced by the evil influence of designing men," be encouraged to secede.[27]

As a result of the black desire for independence and the white fear of Negro domination, the process of separation accelerated in the late 1860s. By 1870, only a few blacks remained in the white Southern churches.[28] In the Mobile district, of 10,763 Negro members of the Southern Methodist Church in 1865, only 752 remained in 1870. In the Montgomery district, only 188 remained out of 7,494. In Tuscaloosa, there was not one Negro member of the Southern Methodist Church by 1870.[29]

V

The new black churches were not without competition. The freedmen appeared to offer a fertile new field for the Northern churches that had long protested the immorality of slavery. One of the least likely but most persistent efforts to recruit Alabama Negroes was made by the Congregational Church. There were few if any Congregationalists in Alabama before the war, and the reasoned, self-controlled nature of Congregationalism contrasted strongly with the emotional character of most Southern black religion. Nevertheless, the AMA was determined to spread — along with education — its version of the word of God. Talladega Normal School provided the perfect springboard for the effort.

In 1868, shortly after the opening of Talladega Normal, the school's white director founded the Congregational Church of Talladega, with seventeen members.[30] Under AMA guidance, churches were also established during the next three years at Montgomery and Marion.[31] Teachers and students at Talladega Normal labored unflaggingly for their church. A white supervisor reported proudly that "[p]reaching services and Sabbath Schools are sustained in mountains and plains for miles on every side. Sunday is no day of rest for teachers or pious students at this institution."[32]

Despite such efforts, the Congregationalists attracted only a small number of Negroes. There were exceptions, including such prominent persons as Yancey B. Sims, who served as a registrar of elections while still a student at Talladega Normal and later became a leading minister in Alabama, Georgia, and finally Arkansas.[33] But in 1876 there were only 607 Congregationalists in the whole state of Alabama.[34] Seven years earlier, a Northern missionary had reported sadly that "there is much suspicion on the part of the colored preachers & churches concerning us, and . . . it will not meet with their approval if we attempt to establish churches of our order."[35] The slight success of Congregationalism in Alabama confirmed his analysis.

A more widespread effort was that of the Northern Methodists.[36] They were quick to recognize that the freeing of the slaves presented them with a prime opportunity for undercutting the influence of the Southern Methodists, as well as for gaining new recruits of their own. The *Methodist Quarterly Review* proclaimed that Negroes presented "a great obligatory mission field in the South, which the North must speedily fill," and warned that blacks must not be "left to depend upon the Southern Church hereafter to supply them with the Gospel."[37]

According to many Alabama whites, the Northern Methodist missionaries were more interested in teaching hatred and mistrust of Southern Methodists and in disrupting established church relations, than in providing religious instruction to the blacks.[38] J. G. Wilson, secretary of the Southern Methodist Church in Alabama, bitterly denounced the new rival to his church as an "enemy . . . employed in vilifying & misrepresenting through the columns of Northern papers our Southern people and Southern churches."[39] At least some missionaries did engage in extra-curricular activities. One of the most active of these was A.S. Lakin, a Radical who was instrumental in helping to organize the Union Leagues in the Tennessee Valley. "We have a perfect organization in this city and can carry this country almost to a man (col'd)," he exulted from Huntsville in 1867.[40]

The Northern Methodists were consequently the objects of considerable persecution by native Alabama whites. Missionaries told repeatedly in their reports of the hostility they encountered and the physical violence that freedmen interested in their church faced.[41] In addition, the Northern Methodists often faced the opposition of the black churches. "There seems to be some sort of *understood* collusion between the [AME] Zion agent or Bishop and the Southern Church, to operate against my success," complained one missionary.[42]

Although such collusion may have existed, it was not the primary ingredient in the failure of the Northern Methodists among Alabama blacks. The Northern Methodists were hindered by the same essential problem that the Congregationalists were: they were a white church, with mostly white ministers. As such, they were always ambivalent about the direction of their efforts in Alabama. They were most successful among whites in the northern part of the state, and even in the piedmont their work was directed mainly at whites.[43] Only in selected areas of the black-belt and Tennessee Valley did they labor seriously among the blacks, and there their success was spotty at best. Despite grandiose predictions by missionaries, most blacks were reluctant to trade the tutelage of white Southerners for that of white Northerners.[44] A few black clergymen were attracted to the Northern Methodists, among them Benjamin Inge, a delegate to the Constitutional Convention of 1867, and Howell Echols of Huntsville, who explained that he chose the Northern Methodists over the AME church because, although he "believed in 'birds of a feather flocking together,'" he "did not believe in children trying to eat before they got teeth."[45] But the membership of the Northern Methodists continued to lag well behind that of the black churches. By 1874, the Northern Methodists claimed only 9,052 members in Alabama, most of whom were probably white.[46]

VI

Alabama's black clergymen came from varied backgrounds. A few of them, such as Dock Phillips, a Baptist preacher in Tuskegee since 1859, had been slave preachers before the war. Others had begun their preaching careers before the war as free Negroes in the South. Nathan Ashby, minister of the black First Baptist Church in Montgomery, was an invalid carpenter who purchased his freedom in 1842 and began preaching in 1845. Prince Murrell, whose paternal grandfather was an Englishman, bought his freedom in 1855. He had already learned to read as a slave, and had been baptized in 1842. Licensed by the white Baptist church in Tuscaloosa to preach to blacks, after the war he taught in Tuscaloosa's first freedmen's school and for many years was that town's only black Baptist minister.[47]

Other black clergymen came either from the North or from neighboring Southern states to aid in the organization of the new churches. There were very few Baptist outsiders, since the formation of the black Baptist churches was a spontaneous local movement and there was no national Negro Baptist organization to engage in missionary activities among the freedmen. The two black Methodist denominations, however, took an active role in the organization of churches throughout the South. In Alabama, the AME Church was especially dependent during the early postwar years on out-of-state assistance. Although the AME Zion Church was established earlier in much of the state, and consequently had to rely less on outside missionaries, J. J. Clinton, the presiding bishop of Alabama for the first five postwar years, was born in Philadelphia, where he had attended school and been licensed as an AME Zion preacher in 1840 at the age of seventeen. Before the war he had climbed through the ranks as deacon, elder, superintendent, and finally in 1864, bishop, and was sent to Montgomery to organize the Church in Alabama.[48]

Most black ministers, however, had little or no experience in the pulpit before the war. The great majority had been slaves until 1865 and were ordained in the late 1860s after relatively little religious training. Indeed, white Alabamians often complained of "self-called" preachers who, unlike the slave preachers ordained by white Southerners, were superstitious, "often incompetent, and often immoral."[49] These new black ministers did differ somewhat from the few who were holdovers from the days of slavery. They tended to be less educated. While not so ignorant as whites charged, many of them were only semiliterate and some were totally illiterate. Typical was Adam Gachet, a slave until 1865, who was ordained a Baptist minister in 1869. The historian of Alabama's black Baptists explained that although "Gachet has had no educational advantages, he reads intelligently and writes some."[50] Ministers in the cities were usually better educated than those in rural areas, but an illiterate urban preacher was by no means a curiosity.[51]

In general, the Negro preachers, although extremely influential in their local communities, were not men who achieved great prominence or notoriety on a state or regional level. While a few of them went on to careers in politics, the vast majority lived relatively obscure lives. They were men of slave backgrounds and little education; they were also, for the most part, men of little wealth. True, a few of them — especially those who had preached before the war — accumulated a modest amount of property by 1870. But the $3,000 farm owned by AME Zion minister Allan Hannon in Montgomery County was quite exceptional. Most black clergymen owned little or no property, and those who did were rarely wealthy men.[52] With some exceptions, the new black clergymen were a group close to the black masses.

VII

The sudden organization of the black churches created numerous problems. Impoverished freedmen often could not afford to purchase or construct church buildings. Sometimes they received assistance from the white churches in putting up new buildings or were given old ones when white churches moved to new locations. But more often the blacks had to cope with extremely primitive surroundings and found it necessary to hold "their services under bush arbors or in some private home." Frequently black congregations worshipped "in an old log cabin," or "in sheds and groves without the aid of church buildings."[53]

Whites, whether Alabamians or Northerners, were more disturbed by what they considered the primitive nature of black religion than by the buildings in which freedmen worshipped. Negroes just did not seem to have a correct understanding of Christian doctrine, especially of the New Testament. "There is no part of the Bible with which they are so familiar as the story of the deliverance of the children of Israel," noted one Northern army chaplain upon his arrival in Alabama in 1865. "Moses is their *ideal* of all that is high, and noble, and perfect, in man." He found, however, that blacks "have been accustomed to regard Christ not so much in the light of a *spiritual* Deliverer, as that of a second Moses. . . . I have talked with some of the old men, and some who were *preachers*," he concluded with dismay, "and I have never found one who seemed to have an *intelligent* notion of the atonement."[54] Other whites were certain that the freedmen, in choosing to listen to the preachers "springing up among them . . . without ordination, and claiming to receive their ministerial commissions and biblical information directly from the mouth of God," were "falling back into their native superstition and idolatry as fast as the wheels of time can carry them."[55] In 1868, the Alabama Baptist State Convention's Committee on the Religious Instruction of the Colored People reported that the religious condition of the freedmen was rapidly deteriorating. "Naturally superstitious and credulous," the report stated, "no delusions are too absurd to find entrance into their minds."[56]

If the word of numerous whites is accepted, much of black religion was little more than paganism with the trappings of Christianity tacked on. An Alabama white who left the Southern Methodists to become a Northern Methodist missionary predicted that the freedmen "if left to themselves . . . will lapse into some of the forms of heathenism. Large numbers of them now, on some of our plantations are not far removed from that state."[57] A county newspaper complained that black preachers "travel about and preach funerals of persons who died many years ago in some instances," and the Baptist State Convention's Committee on the Religious Instruction of the Colored People

observed that "[i]n some places, the Bible is practically repudi-
ated and denounced as the 'white man's book,' and they [blacks]
have surrendered themselves to the guidance of 'prophets' and
'prophetesses,' who are leading them into every abominable and
revolting excess of idolatry."[58]

Equally unnerving to whites — especially to Northerners unused to the Southern revival tradition, but to many Southern
whites as well — was the emotionalism prevalent in much of black
religion. A Congregationalist minister later recalled sadly that
the church "member, whether male or female, who could shout
the loudest in meeting, was at a premium."[59] Another North-
erner noted "an excessive effervescence of emotional feeling,
with very little intelligent understanding of even the first elementary principles of the Gospel."[60] A small planter in Talladega
complained of "Negro religious exercises night and day" in
which "the wildest excitement continues, screams, yells and
distressing cries rend the air for hours." He was disturbed that
the freedmen "think to become happy in feeling is all the effects
necessary." A few days later, he wrote that "religious excitement among the freedmen has become alarming."[61]

What was most alarming to whites, however, and what was
probably at the root of many of their comments about black
superstition, paganism, and emotionalism, was that Negroes
were no longer willing to accept white religious supervision and
control. To whites who believed freedmen desperately needed
white guidance, it seemed logical that the natural outcome of
black religious independence must be religious and moral degen-
eration. Almost every white observation of the shortcomings of
black religion was coupled with a complaint that "they will not
receive instruction from the whites," or that the black "masses
believe . . . [the] statements [of the Negro ministers] and prefer
their preaching to that of the whites."[62] A white Alabamian
concluded sadly that since "the negroes have nearly all forsaken
their old churches and teachers . . . [t]hey are as sheep without
the care of the shepherds."[63] To Alabama's white shepherds,
the independence of her sheep — black sheep, one might add
— seemed an ominous development.

VIII

Despite the widespread conviction on the part of whites that Negro religion was excessive, degenerate, and superstitious, in most ways the black churches performed very much the same functions that the white ones did, and black religion served the same purposes as did white religion. The black churches acted as defenders of public morality, supporting the principles of hard work, honesty, and marital fidelity. It was the black minister who now married Negro couples, baptized their children, and was the community arbiter of what was and what was not morally acceptable. Because the churches were the only major organizations actually controlled by blacks, and because the lives of most freedmen were barren of other social activities, the churches quickly became central institutions in the black communities. On the most basic level, black religion acted as an important stabilizing agent — or, as E. Franklin Frazier has written, "a refuge in a hostile white world" — providing hope and comfort for the poor and ignorant and a social outlet for those long denied outside attachments or means of identification.[64]

The black churches also performed certain secular functions. In the field of education, they provided a major supplement to the work of the Freedmen's Bureau and the Northern benevolent societies. Churches frequently made their buildings available to schools for classrooms.[65] Black preachers taught thousands of children reading and writing — along with the word of the Lord — in the Sunday schools that sprang up across the state following the war. Often, too, early black preachers doubled as teachers in freedmen's schools, especially before the normal schools began to turn out an annual supply of more professional teachers.

Many of the black ministers also played significant political roles. As influential and respected community figures whose remarks were assured good publicity, preachers were in an ideal position to engage in local political leadership. "[H]is influence among his People is far above any man of his color in the County," noted one white of black Baptist minister Alfred Peters.[66] Although relatively few ministers became prominent or full-time politicians, many of them took the opportunity provided by their pulpits to mobilize freedmen behind a party or candidate — usually Republican.

The political activities of black preachers, more than anything else, called down upon them the wrath of white Alabamians. Shandy W. Jones, for example, was an AME Zion preacher in Tuscaloosa who had been a free barber before the war. In 1868, after an abortive campaign for Congress as an independent black candidate, he was denounced by the conservative Tuscaloosa *Independent Monitor* as "the greatest rascal among the negroes of Tuskaloosa," who "ought to have been Ku-Kluxed, and negro ambition squelched in its incipiency."[67]

Negro ministers who were too active politically were often beaten, lynched, or killed. Americus Tramblies, for example, in addition to his political activities, committed the indiscretion of boarding a white woman schoolteacher with his family. Whites soon came to feel that "he was exerting an influence upon the colored population in his preaching that was deleterious"; in 1870 he was murdered by several white men. Henry Giles, a deacon of the black Baptist Church in piedmont Coosa County, was forced to flee to Montgomery when whites burned his church because, as he explained, "we were too strong Republicans." Richard Burke, who had been a Baptist preacher in the black-belt county of Sumter since antebellum days, "made himself obnoxious to a certain class of young [white] men by having been a leader in the Loyal League and by having acquired a great influence over people of his color." He also taught a freedmen's school and served briefly in the state legislature. In 1870, he was shot and killed in his home.[68]

Not all black ministers were ardent Republicans, although most of them were. Alfred Hall, an AME Zion minister in Montgomery, opposed the ratification of the constitution of 1867 at a Conservative rally.[69] Sometimes preachers who refrained from Republican politics risked almost as much as those who engaged in it. Charles Powell, a black Baptist minister, was whipped by several white Republicans who charged he was a Democrat.[70] Black ministers, in short, paid a price for their prominence. They were frequently so influential that they were likely to antagonize some group, and endanger their own safety, no matter what political stand they took.

The primary significance of the new black churches, however, lay less in the persecution of Negro preachers or in their deviation from white church practices than in the voluntary black separatism that underlay their establishment. By the late 1860s, the essentials of postwar black religious life had been made clear. Blacks had demonstrated that they would not exchange slavery for some other form of subservience. If whites were unwilling to contemplate Negro equality within existing institutions, then blacks would not hesitate to form parallel institutions of their own.

Notes

1. Carter G. Woodson, *The History of the Negro Church* (Washington, D.C.: The Associated Publishers, 1921), p. 116; James B. Sellers, *Slavery in Alabama* (University, Alabama: University of Alabama Press, 1950). p. 294; Nancy Claiborne Roberson, "The Negro and the Baptists of Antebellum Alabama" (Master's thesis, University of Alabama, 1954), p. 157; W. P. Harrison, *The Gospel Among the Slaves: A Short Account of Missionary Operations Among the African Slaves of the Southern States* (Nashville: Publishing House of the M.E. Church, South, 1893), pp. 151, 182, 323; *South Western Baptist*, 30 June 1859, p. 2. The *South Western Baptist* was published weekly in Tuskegee and was later known as the *Alabama Baptist*.

2. Roberson, "The Negro and the Baptists of Antebellum Alabama," p. 173; Charles Hays Rankin, "The Rise of Negro Baptist Churches in the South through the Reconstruction Period" (Master's essay, New Orleans Baptist Theological Seminary, 1955), pp. 26-28; W. Harrison Daniel, "Southern Protestantism and the Negro, 1860-1865," *North Carolina Historical Review* 41 (1964): 339-340.

3. On the development of these two Churches in the North before the war and in the South after the war, see David Henry Bradley, Sr., *A History of the A.M.E. Zion Church* (Nashville: The Parthenon Press, 1956); J. W. Hood, *One Hundred Years of the African Methodist Episcopal Zion Church; or the Centennial of African Methodism* (New York: A.M.E. Zion Book Concern, 1895); John Jamison Moore, *History of the A.M.E. Zion Church, in America* (York, Pennsylvania: Teachers' Journal Office, 1884); Grant S. Shockley and Leonard L. Haynes, "The A.M.E. and A.M.E. Zion Churches," in Emory Stevens Bucke, ed., *The History of American Methodism* (New York: Abingdon Press, 1964), II, 526-582; Daniel A. Payne, *History of the African Methodist Episcopal Church* (Nashville: Publishing House of the A.M.E. Sunday-School Union, 1891); George A. Singleton, *The Romance of African Methodism: A Study of the African Methodist Epis-*

copal Church (New York: Exposition Press, 1952); Charles Spencer Smith, *A History of the African Methodist Episcopal Church* (Philadelphia: Book Concern of the A.M.E. Church, 1922).

4. Roberson, "The Negro and the Baptists of Antebellum Alabama," p. 104; Woodson, *The History of the Negro Church*, p. 103; Bond, *Negro Education in Alabama*, p. 19; E. Franklin Frazier, *The Negro Church in America* (New York: Schocken Books, 1964), pp. 25-26; Works Projects Administration, Survey of State and Local Historical Records: Church Records (1936; located in the Alabama State Department of Archives and History; hereafter cited as WPA Church Inventory), Mount Olive Baptist Church, Tuskegee, Macon County; Josephus Shackelford, *History of the Muscle Shoals Baptist Association* (Trinity, Alabama: published by the author, 1891), p. 155.

5. Rankin, "The Rise of the Negro Baptist Churches," pp. 57-59; Owen Hunter Draper, "Southern Negro Religious Adjustments to Freedom, 1865-1867" (Master's thesis, University of Alabama, 1966), pp. 18-19.

6. *Minutes of the Forty-third Annual Session of the Alabama Baptist State Convention, 1865* (Atlanta: Franklin Steam Printing House, 1866), p. 10; Walter L. Fleming, *Civil War and Reconstruction in Alabama* (New York: Columbia University Press, 1905), p. 647.

7. Montgomery *Daily Advertiser*, 22 August 1865. "The old woman was hardly to blame," added the paper. "She knew no better, and probably had been told that she was as good as the whites, and entitled to as many privileges."

8. Stevenson Nathaniel Reid, *History of the Colored Baptists in Alabama* (n.p., 1949), pp. 50-51.

9. WPA Church Inventory, Tuscaloosa, Tuscaloosa County; Mt. Moriah Missionary Baptist Church, Water Valley, Choctaw County.

10. Charles Octavius Boothe, *The Cyclopedia of the Colored Baptists of Alabama: Their Leaders and Their Work* (Birmingham: Alabama Publishing Co., 1895), pp. 111-113; Alfred Louis Bratcher, *Eighty-three Years: The Moving Story of Church Growth* (Montgomery: The Paragon Press, 1950), p. 10.

11. Boothe, *The Cyclopedia of the Colored Baptists*, p. 37; Reid, *History of the Colored Baptists*, p. 51.

12. Hood, *One Hundred Years*, pp. 365-366.

13. Montgomery *Daily Advertiser*, 26 November 1865; Moore, *History of the A.M.E. Zion Church*, pp. 362, 179, 180; *Nationalist*, 2 May 1867.

14. Shockley and Haynes, "The A.M.E. and A.M.E. Zion Churches," p. 537.

15. Union Springs *Times*, 24 April 1867; Singleton, *The Romance of African Methodism*, p. 129; Alexander W. Wayman, *Cyclopaedia of African Methodism* (Baltimore: Methodist Episcopal Book Depository, 1882), p. 159.

16. Wesley J. Gaines, *African Methodism in the South: or Twenty-five Years of Freedom* (Atlanta: Franklin Publishing House, 1890), p. 226; W. H. Mixon,

History of the African Methodist Episcopal Church in Alabama with Biographical Sketches (Nashville: A.M.E. Church Sunday School Union, 1902), p. 30.

17. Draper, "Southern Negro Religious Adjustments to Freedom," p. 79; Reid, *History of the Colored Baptists*, p. 103.

18. Fleming, *Civil War and Reconstruction*, pp. 639, 642-643.

19. *Minutes of the Thirty-third Annual Session of the Coosa River Baptist Association* (September 1866).

20. Shackelford, *History of the Muscle Shoals Baptist Association*, p. 84.

21. Charles T. Thrift, Jr., "Rebuilding the Southern Church," in Bucke, ed., *The History of American Methodism*, II, pp. 284-288; C. H. Phillips, *The History of the Colored Methodist Episcopal Church in America* (Jackson, Tennessee: Publishing House C.M.E. Church, 1925), pp. 25-26.

22. Draper, "Southern Negro Religious Adjustments to Freedom," pp. 40-49.

23. *Nationalist*, 12 July 1866.

24. Draper, "Southern Negro Religious Adjustments to Freedom," p. 84; Bratcher, *Eighty-three Years*, pp. 7-10; Spingeon Davis, "The Colored Baptists of Montgomery," in Charles A. Stakely, ed., *History of the First Baptist Church of Montgomery, Alabama* (Montgomery: Paragon Press, 1930), p. 68; Montgomery *Daily Advertiser*, 31 May 1867.

25. Draper, "Southern Negro Religious Adjustments to Freedom," pp. 87-92.

26. For example, the Coosa River Baptist Association. See the *Minutes of the Thirty-sixth Annual Session of the Coosa River Baptist Association* (1869).

27. *Minutes of the Seventeenth Annual Session of the Bigbee Baptist Association* (October, 1869), pp. 6-7.

28. Although I have confined my analysis to the Baptists and Methodists, which were by far the largest denominations in Alabama, smaller sects were equally unsuccessful in their attempts to continue working with the freedmen. Because "the ex-slaves would take neither their politics nor their religion from their former owners," the Episcopal Church, for example, "yielded . . . to necessity in abandoning for a time her efforts to evangelize the Negro." Walter C. Whitaker, *History of the Protestant Episcopal Church in Alabama, 1763-1891* (Birmingham: Roberts & Son, 1898), pp. 197-198.

29. Draper, "Southern Negro Religious Adjustments to Freedom," p. 100; James E. Elliott, "A History of Methodism in Western Alabama, 1818-1870" (Master's thesis, University of Alabama, 1947), p. 151.

30. Christine Robinson, "The Founding and Chartering of Talladega College" (Senior project, Talladega College, 1949), p. 8; E. C. Silsby, "Congregationalism in Alabama" (read before the Twenty-fifth Annual Meeting of the Congregational Association of Alabama, Florence, 3 April 1900, printed copy in the Talladega College Archives), pp. 1-2.

31. *American Missionary* 15, no. 1 (January 1871): 1.

32. Rev. G. D. Pike, District Secretary, *American Missionary* 15, no. 3 (March 1871): 54.

33. See "Recollections of Yancey B. Sims," Scrapbook 16, Talladega College Archives.

34. Silsby, "Congregationalism in Alabama," p. 2.

35. Henry S. Kelsey, Principal of the Emerson Institute in Mobile, to Rev. Smith, 15 March 1869, AMAP.

36. See the Freedmen's Aid Society Papers for Western Georgia and Alabama of the Methodist Episcopal Church (hereafter cited as FASP), consisting primarily of letters and reports from Northern Methodist missionaries to James F. Chalfant, superintendent of the West Georgia and Alabama District of the Methodist Episcopal Church, in the Interdenominational Theological Seminary Library, Atlanta. For a general treatment of the Northern Methodists and Reconstruction, see Ralph E. Morrow, *Northern Methodism and Reconstruction* (East Lansing, Michigan: Michigan State University Press, 1956).

37. Editorial, *Methodist Quarterly Review* 47 (October 1865): 632; John H. Caldwell, "Relations of the Colored People to the Methodist Episcopal Church, South," *Methodist Quarterly Review* 48 (July 1866): 433-434.

38. Fleming, *Civil War and Reconstruction*, pp. 636-639; *Ku Klux Conspiracy*, testimony of Governor Robert B. Lindsay, VIII, 208.

39. Wilson to Chalfant, Huntsville, 3 June 1866, FASP.

40. Lakin to Chalfant, 29 March 1867, FASP.

41. See, for example, W. Handy to Chalfant, Franklin County, 15 December 1866; J. A. McCutchin to Chalfant, Eutaw, 24 June 1867; and McCutchin to Chalfant, Spring Field, 30 July 1867, FASP.

42. Isaac Parker to Chalfant, Wetumpka, 19 September 1867, FASP.

43. See, for example, the report of John J. Brasher, whose circuit in St. Clair County contained 204 white members and 1 Negro. 1 April 1867, FASP.

44. For example, that of J. B. T. Hill to Chalfant, Eutaw, 8 March 1867, FASP.

45. Echols to Chalfant, Huntsville, 22 August 1867, FASP.

46. Rev. Henry J. Fox, "Our Work at the South," *Methodist Quarterly Review* 56 (January 1876): 35.

47. Boothe, *Cyclopedia of the Colored Baptists*, pp. 111-113, 174-176, 187; WPA Church Inventory, Mt. Olive Baptist Church, Tuskegee, Macon County; Bratcher, *Eighty-three Years*, p. 10; Roberson, "The Negro and the Baptists of Antebellum Alabama," p. 143.

48. Moore, *History of the A.M.E. Zion Church*, p. 362.

49. Fleming, *Civil War and Reconstruction*, p. 644.

50. Boothe, *The Cyclopedia of the Colored Baptists*, p. 146.

51. In a study of the Manuscript Census Returns of 1870 for selected counties, I found that while most black preachers listed could read and write, a substantial minority could not. In Montgomery County, two of the eight black ministers listed were illiterate. In Dallas County, which includes the city of Selma, four were literate and two could read but not write. The two black preachers in Macon County, both of whom lived in Tuskegee, could read and write, while in the rural blackbelt county of Marengo, three were literate and three could read but not write. In Talladega County, in the piedmont, two ministers could read and write, one could read but not write, and one was totally illiterate. In the Tennessee Valley county of Madison, which includes Huntsville, two out of five Negro ministers were illiterate.

52. Manuscript Census Returns of 1870, Montgomery County, Township 16. Hannon also owned $150 of personal property. According to the Manuscript Census Returns of 1870, eighteen of the thirty-one black ministers in Montgomery, Macon, Dallas, Marengo, Talladega, and Madison counties did not own any real or personal property at all. Of the remaining thirteen, seven were worth less than $500, three between $500 and $1,000, and only three over $1,000.

53. Reid, *History of the Colored Baptists*, pp. 50-51; WPA Church Inventory, Mt. Moriah Missionary Baptist Church, Water Valley, Choctaw County; Elliott, "A History of Methodism in Western Alabama," p. 138.

54. W. G. Kephart, Chaplain, 10th Iowa Veterans, to Lewis Tappan, Decatur, 9 May 1865, AMAP.

55. *Clarke County Journal*, 18 October 1866.

56. *Minutes of the Forty-sixth Annual Session of the Alabama Baptist State Convention* (Atlanta: Franklin Steam Printing House, 1869), p. 11.

57. J. B. F. Hill to Rev. J. P. Durbin, Eutaw, 2 August 1866, FASP.

58. Clarke *County Journal*, 18 October 1866; *Minutes of the Forty-sixth Annual Session*, p. 11.

59. W. M. P. Gilbert. "Some Experiences in Alabama Twenty-Four Years Ago," IV, 1891, Scrapbook No. 16, Talladega College Archives.

60. W. G. Kephart, Chaplain, 10th Iowa Veterans, to Tappan, Decatur, 9 May 1865, AMAP.

61. Mallory, diary, 15, 26 August 1868, Southern Historical Collection, University of North Carolina. In part, Mallory's alarm may have been dictated by economic interest. He complained (15 August) that because of the "religious exercises," "all work by the freedmen have been suspended this week."

62. Ibid., 26 August 1868; *Clarke County Journal*, 18 October 1866.

63. J. B. F. Hill to Rev. J. P. Durbin, Eutaw, 2 August 1866, FASP.

64. Frazier, *The Negro Church in America*, p. 45.

65. See, for example, J. Silsby to Rev. George Whipple. Mobile, 2 December 1865, AMAP; and Silsby to Rev. E. P. Smith, Montgomery 26 March 1866, AMAP.

66. Thomas M. Peters to Swayne, Moulton, Lawrence County, 29 May 1867, Swayne Papers, Alabama State Department of Archives and History.

67. *Alabama Beacon*, 18 January, 1 February 1868; Tuscaloosa *Independent Monitor*, 11 August 1868.

68. *Ku Klux Conspiracy*, testimony of Judge Jefferson Falkner, IX, 1119. On Tramblies, see *Ku Klux Conspiracy;* IX, 1042-1048, 1114-1125; on Giles, ibid., IX, 1110; on Burke, ibid., VIII, 331-355, IX, 997-1004, X, 1662-1734, 1771-1785.

69. Montgomery *Daily Advertiser*, 12 January 1868.

70. *Ku Klux Conspiracy*, testimony of Powell, X, 1845-1846. Powell later denied that he was a Democrat and explained that he was apolitical, had once voted Republican, but no longer bothered to vote.

6

Black Social Structure

I

Within a few years of the end of the Civil War, a wide degree of social stratification had developed among Alabama's Negroes. There had always been some variations in occupation, education, status, and wealth among blacks. If before the war the vast majority had been field hands who toiled for their masters from sunup to sundown, there had also been house servants, artisans, preachers, urban slaves, and free blacks. But the overthrow of slavery greatly accentuated the process of social differentiation, especially at the top of the black social hierarchy. Freedom brought with it new opportunities and new occupations. It changed the relationships and attitudes not only of blacks to whites, but also of blacks to each other.

II

Most Alabama blacks — approximately nine out of ten — remained unskilled laborers during the Reconstruction years, performing heavy physical labor for their livelihoods. They were generally illiterate and accumulated little or no money. The greatest portion of this lower class had been field hands before the war and remained such as freedmen. Whether on large plantations or small farms, they continued to cultivate cotton and other agricultural products. Now, however, they were sharecroppers or hired laborers rather than slaves, and their changed legal condition fostered among them a growing consciousness of independence.

A much smaller number of unskilled laborers resided in cities and towns. By 1870, there were some twenty-five thousand blacks in the state's four major cities and sixteen thousand more in towns of over five hundred persons, together constituting about 9 percent of the black population. Some of these urban blacks were migrants who had arrived following emancipation; most had lived there before the war. Most lived, like their rural counterparts, by physical labor. Like agricultural laborers, black urban workers performed the same kinds of jobs they had before the war. Most of the working women and some of the men were servants of whites. They worked as cooks, maids, porters, washers, gardeners, and general servants in hotels, restaurants, and private homes.[1] Other blacks hired themselves out as day laborers. In Mobile, there was a sizable number of Negro dock workers, and in other areas blacks worked on railroads, in sawmills, in turpentine plants, and in mines.[2]

There were also some urban Negroes with at best very periodic employment. Despite the general shortage of labor on the plantations, the lure of the city was strong enough to keep some freedmen idle on the streets. Immediately after the war, when numerous blacks poured into the cities, unemployment was especially widespread. Whites complained of Negro "vagrancy," and many cities took stringent measures to meet the situation. Late December and early January of each year was usually a time of widespread temporary unemployment, when rural freedmen, having completed their year's labor, were in the habit of coming into nearby towns and cities to celebrate the Christmas holidays and seek new employment.[3] Some of the unemployment was more permanent, however, and occasional listings of "no occupation" appear next to the names of urban blacks in the Manuscript Census Returns of 1870.

Living conditions for most urban blacks were primitive. The influx of freedmen immediately following the war forced many Negroes to live in "cellars, shelters, stables & vacant lots," "out-houses and sheds," or "in shanties, old furnaces, boilers, &c."[4] Domestic servants — especially women — were frequently able to escape the prevalent dilapidated housing by living with white families for whom they worked, as they had before the war. Other Negroes, however, usually lived in segregated housing in predominantly black areas of the city.

If lower-class urban Negroes performed much the same labor they had under slavery, they did not always perform it in the same manner. They were as conscious of their freedom as rural freedmen, and when they thought they were being treated un-fairly they sometimes acted to protect their interests. In Selma, a group of blacks formed an association "to enforce the pay of $20 a month 'and found' by employers." When six restaurant waiters actually struck for the twenty dollar wage, however, they were fired and placed "in the service of the city, pressing brick on the pavement."[5] Semiskilled workers were in a better position to protest grievances than were servants. In March 1867, the black dock workers of Mobile struck for an increase of their hourly wage from twenty-five to fifty cents. They also declared "that no white men shall be employed in the work of discharg-ing and loading steamboats until the present difficulty is ar-ranged." The strike was unsuccessful, in part because some of the workers refused to go along with it, but before it ended "a grow-ing feeling of dissatisfaction and discontent" spread to "the entire negro laboring population, including alike those engaged on the levee, those employed in saw-mills, and those who seek odd jobs and day's-work generally."[6]

While such strikes were rarely successful, they indicated a heightened assertiveness on the part of the black urban popula-tion. Freedmen were no longer willing to be subject to abuse without protesting. After a meeting in December 1865, the blacks of Tuscaloosa petitioned Swayne "to grant to us the appoint

ment of sume man to the freedmen beauro" to "give us our just
rights as we are denied of them by our [white] sitizens." The
Negroes complained that "our polies gard searches our houses
for arms and takes what little money we have." After reciting
other grievances, they concluded in understatement that "this
is not the persuit of happiness."[7]

Whites expressed considerable annoyance over the behavior of
urban blacks. "The negroes in the city," wrote an ex-Confederate officer who would soon become a prominent iron manufacturer, "are growing troublesome."[8] The *Daily Selma Times*
agreed, complaining that "the negroes of the city are becoming
too impudent and noisy as a general thing," and the Montgomery
Daily Advertiser denounced the "outrageous conduct of . . . negro
servants," noting that "[t]he negro girls as a general thing
are worthless." The paper found just as much to blame in the
"younger portion of the masculine negro population of the city,"
who tended to be "disorderly if not riotous."[9]

III

About 10 percent of the black population of Alabama constituted
a group that could be described as the black middle class. It
was a diverse class, consisting of both old and new elements,
many of whose members catered to whites and at the same
time fancied themselves the most respected and respectable
members of black society. In fact, it was hardly a class at all,
except that it consisted of several groups who considered themselves — and were usually considered by others — to be a notch
above the mass of freedmen, but who were also clearly not part
of the much smaller new Negro upper class.

Domestic servants of wealthy white families — the house
Negroes on the large plantations and the personal servants of
rich whites, both rural and urban — were part of this middle
class.[10] Such servants were not a new group; they had been "at
the top of the slave hierarchy" before the war. Often they had
identified more closely with their white masters, with whom they
lived and to whom they owed their privileged status, than with
the field hands whom they saw only occasionally.[11] After the

war, this formerly privileged group of Negroes felt the conflicting pressures of freedom as acutely as any other freedmen. They were often conscious of being apart from most blacks and sometimes felt real affection for their white masters. On the other hand, because they lived in close proximity to whites, they were more likely than most freedmen to feel intense personal hatred for and jealousy of their former owners. Finally, as blacks they frequently found it difficult to avoid identifying with the goals and aspirations of an oppressed race.

Some servants remained faithfully with their old masters as if little had changed. The wife of one prominent planter wrote with pleasure that despite other hardships "Aunt Maria still cooks for us" and "Clement & Willie take care of our domicile."[12] She was grateful that "the servants are kind and attentive. . . . They are infinitely better than strangers." She personally brought up Matt, a mulatto child on the plantation. "I wish he was all white," she confided. "I don't think it right to rear a little darkey quite so much like white folks."[13]

The small number of servants who stood loyally by their old masters were probably the most alienated of any blacks from the mass of freedmen. The few black Democrats in the 1860s often came from servant backgrounds. Typical of this group was Caesar Shorter, who before the war was the body servant of Governor John Gill Shorter and after the war became the servant of Robert Lindsay, the Democrat who was elected governor in 1870. As early as December 1867, Caesar Shorter addressed a Conservative meeting in Montgomery.[14] Later, he testified before a congressional committee that he did not think Negroes were qualified to vote or hold office. When asked if he was afraid of other blacks, he replied "Yes, sir: I don't go out in the country."[15]

But such behavior was not typical of most blacks who had been servants before the war. They too were subject to the lure of freedom and the desire to be treated as equals rather than subordinates, and many left their masters as soon as they could. During the war, a Huntsville woman reported of the federal occupation that "Corinne and Jim seized this opportunity for leaving. She has gone to the Hotel in the capacity of chambermaid." She noted sadly that all her servants but one had left.[16] After the war, complaints by whites about the insubordinate behavior of house servants were common. One newspaper declared that since emancipation "Negro girls have been worthless as house servants," and another suggested that the only solution was to fill domestic positions with white European immigrants.[17] A decade and a half later, one white commented that "[m]y wife says she would not have felt so bad about the results of the war if it had only left her her negro house servants."[18]

Artisans and skilled workers were a second component of the black middle class. When one Freedmen's Bureau official arrived in Montgomery, he was impressed by the "vast mechanical skill" among the freedmen. "Many planters whose plantations I have visited have pointed to one of the negroes and said 'that man built this house; he framed it all alone,' 'that man is my blacksmith; he makes all my plows and plantation tools,'" he wrote.[19] Scattered throughout the state, concentrated in the towns and cities but also occasionally located in the countryside, were Negro shoemakers, blacksmiths, wheelwrights, carpenters, mechanics, barbers, and small merchants.[20] Although a few of them had been free before the war, the vast majority had been trained as slaves. Like the black servants, then, they were not a new group. These black artisans, who were among the most solid and respected members of the Negro community, were at the same time not far removed from the mass of freedmen. The majority of them were illiterate, and few of them were wealthy, although many managed to accumulate a small amount of property — perhaps one or two hundred dollars.[21]

Negro artisans were generally able to be considerably more independent than most servants. True, like the servants, they were frequently dependent upon whites for employment and consequently under constant pressure to behave in a subservient manner. Sometimes the change from slavery to freedom created real hardships for them. Fourteen Mobile barbers, for example, wrote to Swayne protesting the license fees they were required to pay. "[B]efore the war," they explained, "[we] never paid any License or ever was required to do so on account of us being recognized as Property."[22] But artisans did not usually live with their employers as servants did, and were therefore not so subject to constant supervision. Artisans often accumulated enough property so that they were not entirely dependent on the goodwill of the white community. In the towns and cities, there was a Negro market for their services, as well as a white one. Indeed, the *Nationalist* called upon Negroes to patronize only other blacks. "Every colored man who gets to doing a large business helps to give respectability to his whole race,"[23] it declared.

IV

The third major element of the black middle class consisted of those who somehow managed to acquire a small parcel of land. The expectation that land would be distributed among the freedmen had originally been stimulated by the Freedmen's Bureau. Commissioner Howard, in an effort to make land available to blacks, had intended to pursue a policy of selling or renting confiscated and abandoned land to them in lots of forty acres for a nominal fee. Only after the direct intervention of President Johnson did Howard reverse this policy and begin restoring land to the old owners. Little or no land in Alabama was actually given to the freedmen, and by the end of 1865 the restoration process was essentially completed.[24]

Despite the frequent denials of Freedmen's Bureau officials, many blacks continued to believe that land would be given to them. To meet the desire of Southern Negroes and poor whites for land, in 1866 Congress passed the Southern Homestead Act, providing for the homesteading of public lands in Alabama, Arkansas, Florida, Louisiana, and Mississippi. Under the original act, homesteading was limited until 1867 to citizens who had been loyal during the war.[25]

From the point of view of Alabama's freedmen, the Southern Homestead Act was an almost total failure. Despite their ardent desire for land, relatively few blacks were able to take advantage of the act. In the northern portion of the state, where one of Alabama's three land offices was located in Huntsville, there were only sixty-three Negro homestead entries between April 1867 and June 1869.[26] The Mobile and Montgomery land offices did not list homesteaders by race, but the complaints and comments of freedmen and their friends suggest there is no reason to believe that a substantially greater number of Negroes was able to secure homesteads there than in the northern part of the state.

There were several reasons for the failure of blacks to enter claims. Only marginal land was available for homesteading in most instances, and very little of it was in the blackbelt or other regions of Negro concentration. Administrative complications and the greed of white officials were also important factors. Persons desiring to enter claims had to go to the nearest land office — in Mobile, Montgomery, or Huntsville — which was often a considerable distance away. Illiterate Negroes anxious for land were easily taken advantage of by men posing as their friends or advisers who were out to make a profit for themselves. Those freedmen who were aware of the existence of the Homestead Act — and many were not — were often "misled as to the preliminaries necessary to establish a claim."[27] Freedmen found that the fees involved in homesteading spiraled. A Freedmen's Bureau official in Mobile reported that "the fee charged is twelve dollars whereas the law explicitly states that four should be paid on *making application* under the Homestead act, and five more *when the patent issues.*" He noted that homesteaders also had to pay surveyors' fees of fifteen to twenty-five dollars "and often the surveyors never go to show them their tracts, but issue the certificates from the maps of unoccupied land in the Land Office." The cost to the freedman of homesteading a forty-acre plot was thus twenty-seven to thirty-seven dollars, "while they can buy a [*sic*] similar farms in the simple for the same money and secure titles at once."[28] In Montgomery, the situation was equally discouraging. The Bureau assistant commissioner reported "many applications are made by Freedmen for public lands, but the Land Offices not being fully opened for business nothing can be done."[29]

The failure of the Southern Homestead Act to provide easy access to landownership for freedmen meant that only relatively well-to-do blacks who had managed to save some money were able to acquire land. Sharecroppers who had a series of good years and artisans who managed to accumulate small savings hastened to purchase their own farms. In 1867, Swayne noted that "many freedmen" had already secured land of their own, and a year later the Republican *Daily State Sentinel*, in an apparently exaggerated claim, stated that there were "several thousand" black landowners in the state.[30] The proportion of Negro landowners varied greatly from area to area, but the percentage of those able to secure land throughout the state as a whole was tiny. In general, the proportion of blacks owning land varied inversely with the quality of the land and the number of blacks in the population. In the blackbelt, there was only a scattering of black landowners;[31] but where land was relatively cheap, Negroes few, and black labor not heavily in demand — especially in the mountain counties — it was much easier for the few freedmen to acquire land of their own.[32] A small number of urban blacks, frequently artisans, also acquired real estate.[33]

Like the Negro artisans, black landowners were rarely wealthy. Their holdings were usually worth very little — fifty, a hundred, or perhaps two hundred dollars. Frequently, landowners also had small savings of an equivalent value. The Manuscript Census Returns of 1870 reveal the majority of them to have been illiterate, although more of them could read and write than among the black population as a whole.

If the servants were the most subservient element of the black middle class, the landowners were commonly recognized as the most independent. They could afford to be; they were among the very few Negroes who did not depend directly on whites for their livelihoods. It was for this reason above all others that freedmen desired to acquire land and white planters viewed the prospect with such trepidation. "In order to become independent," the *Nationalist* insisted of Negroes, "they must become their own employers. . . . What we want is to see them get farms of their own."[34] A Talladega planter, however, felt that "it is a false step to allow them land to cultivate."[35] His views were supported by Probate Judge J. F. Waddell, who had already aroused the opposition of freedmen by readily apprenticing their children. "Everywhere throughout the country where they can obtain permission, you see little rude huts erected in isolated and barren localities," complained Waddell, "and all of them promising anything but comfort and happiness to their mistaken inmates."[36]

V

A very small number of Negroes — less than 1 percent of the black population — formed what amounted to the black upper class. This upper class was made up of two generally distinct groups. The first and by far the smaller of the two was a status elite of blacks who enjoyed unusual prominence and prestige among Negroes because of their occupations. Teachers, ministers, and government officials — all of whom were in natural positions of leadership within the black community — were the components of this group. The second was an economic elite of blacks who had managed to acquire enough property to set themselves off radically from the rest of the black population.[37]

The status elite was confined almost entirely to the blackbelt, the Tennessee Valley, and especially the cities, where the demand for teachers and preachers was greatest and where freed-

Table 14   *Members of the Black Status Elite in Twelve Selected Counties, 1870*

	NUMBER OF BLACKS IN STATUS ELITE	PERCENTAGE OF BLACK POPULATION
Four cities	29	0.24%
Four blackbelt counties (rural)	26	0.03%
Madison County (rural)	3	0.02%
Two piedmont counties (rural)	12[a]	0.11%[a]
Two wiregrass counties	0	0.00%
Three mountain counties	0	0.00%

[a]This unusually high figure reflects the influence of Talladega Normal School.

SOURCES: Manuscript Census Returns of 1870; U.S. Census Office, *Ninth Census: Population*, pp. 11-12.

men were numerous enough to elect blacks to public office. In other sections of the state — with the exception of certain special areas such as Talladega County, where the influence of Talladega Normal School was felt — black teachers and ministers were very few and black public officials virtually nonexistent.[38] Both in the cities and the countryside, the status elite was fairly evenly divided between teachers and preachers, with a much smaller number of government officials.[39]

The black economic elite is somewhat harder to define, since any standard of wealth used as a criterion is of necessity somewhat arbitrary. I have classified Negroes as members of this elite if they possessed at least $500 of real and personal property combined, unless they lived in the blackbelt or Tennessee Valley, in which case they had to possess $750, or in a city, in which case they had to own $1,000. These levels represented substantial wealth to a population that had, with very few exceptions, been entirely propertyless five years earlier. It should be kept in mind, however, that this economic elite was an elite in relative terms only. Few of its members would have been considered wealthy had they been white.[40]

Like the teachers, preachers, and politicians, the wealthy blacks were most evident in the towns and cities. Unlike the status elite, however, the economic elite represented at least as great a proportion of the black population in the predominantly white counties as in the blackbelt. Although most wealthy Negroes lived in the blackbelt or Tennessee Valley — simply because most Negroes lived there — the smaller number of blacks in the piney woods-wiregrass region, the piedmont, and the mountains evidently found it just as easy to become financially independent (Table 15).

The makeup of this economic elite differed in urban and rural areas. In the cities, the economic elite was composed primarily of artisans and wealthy unmarried or widowed women who kept house.[41] They were a well-educated group compared with most blacks: about half of them could read and write.[42] In the countryside, the economic elite was primarily a landowning, farming group, with larger holdings and savings than the landowners in the middle class. The most successful of them were

Table 15 *Members of the Black Economic Elite in Twelve Selected Counties, 1870*

	NUMBER OF BLACKS IN ECONOMIC ELITE	PERCENTAGE OF BLACK POPULATION
Four cities	56	0.46%
Four blackbelt counties (rural)	84	0.10%
Madison County (rural)	49	0.36%
Two piedmont counties (rural)	19	0.18%
Two wiregrass counties	15	0.53%
Three mountain counties	1	0.13%

SOURCES: Manuscript Census Returns of 1870; U.S. Census Office, *Ninth Census: Population*, pp. 11-12.

able to hire farm help or contract with sharecroppers much as white planters did.[43] Among the rural economic elite, the literacy rate was much lower than it was for the urban group, although it was still higher than that of the black population as a whole.[44]

Both in the country and in the cities, the status and economic elites were two separate groups with very little overlap. None of the thirty-three teachers in the twelve counties was wealthy enough to qualify for membership in the economic elite, and only four of the thirty ministers were. While teachers and preachers were the acknowledged leaders of the black community, to whom freedmen turned for guidance in social and moral as well as religious and educational matters, they had not by 1870 taken any great material advantage of their position. Conversely, blacks did not usually turn for leadership to the wealthiest and most economically independent men within the black community.

By the late 1860s, then, two strikingly diverse groups had emerged within the Negro upper class. The status elite consisted primarily of idealistic black teachers, preachers, and politicians dedicated to serving the black community, and embodying many

of the characteristics that W. E. B. Du Bois would later attribute
to the "talented tenth." The economic elite, on the other hand,
was made up of men who displayed the virtues later celebrated
by Booker T. Washington. They were a pragmatic group; they
worked hard, improved the land, learned a trade, and generally
avoided controversial situations in which they would be likely
to antagonize powerful whites.

VI

Unlike most other areas of Alabama, Mobile had long had a large
number of free and relatively educated blacks. In 1860, almost
one-half of the state's free black population lived in Mobile County.[45] Many of these free Negroes were Creole descendants of the
French and Spaniards who had once occupied the area. Under
the terms of the treaty by which the United States acquired Mobile from Spain in 1819, the descendants of these early Negro
settlers were guaranteed the rights of American citizens.[46] Some
of them became wealthy and even owned slaves. The Chastang
family, for example, was descended from the eighteenth-century
French settler Jean Chastang, who married a slave.[47] By 1860,
there were twenty-two mulatto Chastang males over eighteen
years old living in Mobile County. They included farmers, artisans, and traders, and some of them were wealthy.[48] Unlike other
Negroes before the war, many of the Mobile Creoles were able
to send their children to special schools set aside for them.

It is not surprising, then, that after the war the Negro upper
class was slightly larger in Mobile than in most other areas of
the state, nor that the black upper class there differed in several
respects from that which existed elsewhere.[49] The literacy rate
of the economic elite in Mobile was substantially higher: sixty-six
of them could read and write and eight could read, while only
forty-four were illiterate. There was an unusually large number of
businessmen — eleven cotton merchants, retail merchants, and
grocers — among them. Several members of the Negro upper class
in Mobile held important governmental positions; these included
a customs inspector, inspector of weights and measures, assistant chief of police, circuit court judge, deputy sheriff, and

state senator. The Mobile economic elite was also considerably wealthier than that of the rest of the state: twenty-four of its members were worth over $3,000. Unlike the rest of Alabama, there was a significant overlap between the two elites in Mobile. Of twenty-four members of the status elite, nine were also members of the economic elite.

Many of the special characteristics of the black upper class in Mobile stemmed from the presence of a large number of Negroes who had been free before the war. Some of the most distinguished members of the Mobile upper class came from these free Negroes. In addition to politician Ovid Gregory, these included James Summerville, who before the war had been a cotton sampler and after the war became a customs inspector owning property valued at $7,000 in 1870. Constantine Perez worked as a master tinner before the war; in 1870 he was inspector of weights and measures, and had accumulated $7,500. Cleveland Moulton was also born free — in New York. In 1870, he was a circuit court judge in Mobile with property valued at $9,000; his Massachusetts-born wife also owned property valued at $9,000.[50]

It would be a mistake to conclude, however, that Mobile's upper class was dominated by Negroes who had been free before the war. Indeed, while a few exceptional free Negroes assumed positions of leadership after the war, the vast majority did not. Of 133 upper-class Mobile blacks in 1870, only 19 had been free in 1860.[51] With a few important exceptions, the new black upper class was not drawn from those who had been at the top of the Negro hierarchy before the war. In fact, the process of Civil War, emancipation, and Reconstruction may have seriously undercut the established position of many Creoles. A study of one of the largest and most prominent of the Creole families of Mobile, the Chastangs, reveals how the fortunes of this group suffered. None of the Chastangs belonged to the new status elite in 1870, and only six of them were in the economic elite. Five of these six were farmers of only modest means — in all cases under $1,000 — and one kept house in Mobile.[52] Several other Chastangs continued to follow their old occupations, but frequently fared less well financially than they had before the war. In 1860, Edward Chastang for example, had been a brickmason with property valued at $250; in 1870 he was still working as a brickmason, but according to the census returns he owned no property at all. Francis Chastang, who before the war had been a farmer with $3,000, in 1870 claimed only $500. Other Chastangs died or left the county; in 1870 there were only sixteen adult male Chastangs in Mobile, compared with twenty-two in 1860. Certainly the Chastangs were still better off than most blacks in 1870, but the difference appeared much less striking than it had ten years earlier.

Negroes who had been free before the war, and especially Mobile's Creoles, who had prided themselves on their lineage and superiority to the bulk of the blacks, were placed in an ambiguous position after the war. On the one hand, they seemed ideally suited by training and experience to be the natural leaders of the freedmen. On the other, their position of privilege within the black community now seemed threatened by an emancipation that made all blacks their equals. A few Creoles, such as Ovid Gregory, wholeheartedly embraced the new order and became leading Radicals.[53] More often, however, Creoles continued to stress their distinction from the mass of the freedmen.

Mobile's elitist Creole Fire Company Number 1 was the most glaring example of Creole efforts to recapture a dying age. Formed in 1821, the Creole Fire Company continued to hold meetings and parades which received conspicuous notice in the white press.[54] T. U. Bernard, a leading officer of the company and also first vice president of Mobile's Colored Democratic Club Number 1, explained that "he had always been, and all his people had been, true to the South. In time of war, as well as of peace, he was and had always been a Southern man."[55] The Radical *Nationalist* made the Creole Fire Company a subject of frequent and blistering attack. "It does seem almost incredible that any persons having even the form of men could thus get upon their bellies and crawl on their faces," the paper declared of the Creole firemen, "for the poor privilege of occasionally securing a smile from one of the men who are doing all in their power to keep them down to the level of brutes."[56] But it was less for their actions than for symbolizing Creole snobbery that the firemen were denounced. The *Nationalist* expressed the resentment of many freedmen when it attacked those Creoles who, "inflated with pride at their supposed superiority to 'common niggers,' have assumed such airs that sensible people are heartily disgusted at them. These easily become the tools of the enemies of their whole race."[57]

VII

The Negro upper class as a whole was subject to similar if less extreme pressures. True, its members were products of the new order rather than remnants of a bygone age. They were the leaders of Alabama's blacks: the politicians represented them; the teachers and preachers gave them moral and social, as well as religious and intellectual, guidance; the prosperous artisans and farmers were looked upon as the pillars of the black community. All of them were black success stories, and their achievements seemed to reflect favorably upon the whole race. Consequently, their interests were in many ways closely tied to those of other blacks. But members of the black upper class were also acutely conscious of their elevation above the masses, and they were proud of their achievements. Their racial views were often closely intertwined with class feelings. To add to their confusion, many of them were mulattoes who simultaneously considered themselves leaders of the blacks and prided themselves on the lightness of their skin.[58]

Light, educated, and wealthy Negroes resented being automatically lumped with the mass of the freedmen. In opposing racial discrimination on railroads, for example, Negro delegates to the Constitutional Convention stressed their objection to being forced to ride in second-class carriages with lower-class blacks and whites as much as their opposition to the principle of racial segregation. James K. Green pointed out that "[i]t was a common thing for colored people to be put into a smoking car, with drunkeness and low white men. He thought they ought to be allowed to go among decent white people." John Carraway similarly complained that a "colored man could not send his wife from one point of the State to the other, because she would be placed in a smoking car and exposed to the insults of low and obscene white men." Other Negro delegates emphasized that they were civilized men who deserved the right to travel first class. Gregory noted that "Napoleon on his throne was not a better man than he," and James T. Rapier reminded the other delegates that he "had dined with Lords in England in his lifetime."[59]

In general, most black leaders tended to support the goal of integration during the early part of the Reconstruction period. During the summer of 1868, for example, Gregory and Carraway tried repeatedly to get the state legislature to pass a common carrier bill that would prohibit any racial discrimination on railroads and steamboats. Gregory insisted that "the colored man certainly had as much right in a first class car as the dirty Irishman who were allowed this privilege." Their efforts were supported by the simultaneous but unsuccessful attempt of Mobile Negroes to enter the all-white streetcars of that city. Although the house finally passed the antidiscrimination measure, the legislature adjourned before the senate voted.[60]

Among some black leaders, integrationist sentiment reached the point of complete assimilationism and rejection of the concept of race. Prominent Mobile Negro L. S. Berry opposed the idea of holding conventions representing only blacks, explaining that "[t]he sooner we as a people forget our sable complexion, and the sooner we cease to meet as a class in conventions, the better it will be for us as a race."[61]

At the same time, however, separatist tendencies were present. Many members of the black upper class, such as teachers and preachers, had a strong vested interest in the existence of the separate black institutions that supported them. Black politicians became increasingly disillusioned with their subordinate role within the Republican party. Occasional overt acts of black nationalism were evident as well. A white resident of the blackbelt town of Greensboro noted that black politician James K. Green was "trying to induce all the negroes to go with him to Liberia," and added that "the negroes all over the state have been put up to the same trick."[62] Whites also encouraged racial separation. When the Montgomery City Council elected twenty-four new policemen, half of whom were black, it was agreed "that the colored police be instructed by the Mayor to arrest only colored parties, in the discharge of their duties, except when called upon by the marshal or police." As an afterthought, the council determined that "white police be instructed the same way."[63]

Despite the interest of some Negroes in integration and the fear of many whites of "social equality," most blacks had relatively little contact with whites. Although of great interest to upper-class Negroes, whether or not theaters, restaurants, steamboats, and first-class railroad cars were integrated had little impact on the bulk of Alabama's freedmen. There were two institutions — the churches and the schools — in which integration would have had widespread repercussions, but in both of these segregation prevailed, in one case because most blacks wanted it that way, and in the other because most whites did.

VIII

The emergence of the black upper class reflected many of the changes taking place within the black community. Unlike the middle and lower classes, the Negro upper class consisted of new groups that owed their prominence to the new opportunities for Negroes made possible by the overthrow of slavery. Before the war, there had been no black teachers or politicians and only a handful of black preachers and landowners. By 1870 there were hundreds. Unlike many middle-class and almost all lower-class blacks, members of the Negro upper class were not dependent upon whites for their immediate livelihoods. The politicians were elected by, and represented, black voters; the teachers had black students; the ministers had black congregations; the wealthy black landowners were not under the constant supervision of white employers. Upper-class blacks could consequently afford to be more independent and less subservient than other Negroes.

It is hardly surprising, then, that on every level the efforts of exceptional Negroes — members of the black upper class — to achieve independence were met by a white counteroffensive.

Black politicians were murdered; black schools and churches were burned; black landownership was opposed. Realizing that the success of any Negro proved that ultimately all blacks could manage without white supervision and protection, whites complained often and loudly of Negroes who no longer knew their place, and who would no longer take the advice of decent Southern whites. As black politician George W. Cox observed, whites persisted in "branding the colored man as being lazy and improvident," but "as soon as a colored man finds out how to seek redress and SUE for his rights and obtain them, just so soon do[es] the respect that those swindlers pretend to have for him disappear."[64] The successful, independent black man threatened the very basis of white racial ideology.

Notes

1. In 3 sample urban wards (Mobile's 2d, Huntsville's 2d, and Tuscaloosa's 1st), more than half the working blacks listed in the Manuscript Census Returns of 1870 were servants. The majority of these servants were women.

2. For slaves working in mining and manufacturing before the war, see Robert S. Starobin, *Industrial Slavery in the Old South* (New York: Oxford University Press, 1970).

3. One small-town newspaper, for example, complained on such an occasion that "there are at present in this town about two hundred specimens of the genus African engaged in the interesting occupation of doing nothing." Union Springs *Times*, 18 January 1867.

4. W. L. Coleman, Mayor of Montgomery, to Governor Parsons, Montgomery, 15 August 1865, Parsons Papers, Alabama State Department of Archives and History; A. L. Brown, Assistant Superintendent, to Colonel Cadle, Assistant Adjutant-General, Greenville, 14 September 1865, FBP, Alabama Operations Reports; *Daily Selma Times*, 18 October 1865.

5. Montgomery *Weekly Advertiser*, 12 March 1867, quoting the Selma *Times*.

6. Mobile *Advertiser and Register*, 31 March 1867, 2 April 1867; Montgomery *Weekly Advertiser*, 9 April 1867.

7. Tuscaloosa, 17 December 1865, FBP, Alabama Letters Received.

8. Josiah Gorgas, Journal, 19 May 1867, University of Alabama Library.

9. *Daily Selma Times*, 5 August 1865; Montgomery *Daily Advertiser*, 6 September, 19 July 1866.

10. These servants, who were usually trained as domestics from childhood, are to be distinguished from the larger number of blacks who held jobs as porters, washers, maids. etc., in the cities after the war, who were part of the lower class.

11. James B. Sellers, *Slavery in Alabama* (University, Alabama: University of Alabama Press, 1950), pp. 74-75.

12. Mary F. Clay to Virginia Caroline Clay, Huntsville, 21 January 1866, Clement Claiborne Clay Papers, Duke University Library.

13. Ibid., Huntsville, 12 February 1866, Clay Papers.

14. Montgomery *Daily Advertiser*, 12, 13 December 1867.

15. *Ku Klux Conspiracy*, IX, 1072-1078.

16. Mrs. W. D. Chadick, diary, 27 March 1864, Alabama State Department of Archives and History.

17. *Southern Advertiser*, 14 September 1866; *Alabama Beacon*, 10 August 1867.

18. U.S., Congress, Senate, *Report of the Committee of the Senate Upon the Relations Between Labor and Capital* (Washington, D.C.: Government Printing Office, 1885), IV, 26.

19. Charles Buckley to Carl Schurz, Montgomery, 15 August 1865, Schurz Papers, Library of Congress.

20. The word "artisan" is used here and elsewhere in this chapter in the broadest possible sense to include skilled workers and members of certain service occupations, such as barbers. In Lowndes County, Beat No. 1, 1.1 percent of the working Negroes over eighteen years old listed in the Manuscript Census Returns of 1870 were artisans; in Madison County, Township 3, Range 2 West, the figure was also 1.1 percent. In urban areas, the number of artisans was much greater. In Demopolis, 5.5 percent of the black adult working population were artisans; in Mobile's Ward No. 2, 7.8 percent were.

21. Very few of the artisans listed in the Manuscript Census Returns of 1870 were literate. Even fewer of them owned any land. Of 15 artisans in Lowndes County, Beat No. 1, only 1 owned any real property. Only 1 out of 26 did in Demopolis, and 2 out of 18 in Mobile's Ward No. 2.

22. May W. Lankford et al. to Swayne, Mobile, 14 June 1867, FBP, Alabama Letters Received.

23. *Nationalist*, 29 November 1866.

24. See Martin Abbott, "Free Land, Free Labor, and the Freedmen's Bureau," *Agricultural History* 30 (1956): 150-156, and LaWanda Cox, "The Promise of Land for the Freedmen," *Mississippi Valley Historical Review* 45 (1958): 413-440.

25. Paul Wallace Gates, "Federal Land Policy in the South, 1866-1888," *Journal of Southern History* 6 (1940): 307.

26. Register of Homestead Entries, Huntsville, United States Land Office Records, Alabama Department of Archives and History. The Huntsville office covered Blount, Jackson, Jefferson, Lawrence, Limestone. Madison, Marshall, Morgan, Walker, and Winston counties.

27. *Nationalist*, 30 September 1866.

28. James Gillette, Sub-Assistant Commissioner, Mobile, 21 May 1868, FBP, Alabama Operations Reports. See also the *Nationalist*, 23 April 1868, on the Mobile Land Office.

29. O. L. Shepherd to Howard, Montgomery, 10 June 1868, FBP, Assistant Adjutant General's Office, Annual Report.

30. Swayne to Howard, 30 September 1867, FBP, Assistant Adjutant General's Office, Annual Report; *Daily State Sentinel*, 12 March 1868.

31. In Lowndes County, Beat 1, 9 Negroes, or 1.1 percent, of the black adult male population, were listed in the Manuscript Census Returns of 1870 as owning land. In Marengo County, Hills Beat, there were no black landowners.

32. In Walker County, in the mountains, the Manuscript Census Returns of 1870 listed 57 black males eighteen years old and over. Of these, 13, or 22.8 percent, owned land.

33. The Manuscript Census of 1870 listed 7 Negroes in Demopolis, or 1.9 percent of the adult black males, as owning real estate. In Huntsville's Ward 2, only 1 Negro, or 0.87 percent of the adult black males, owned real estate. In Mobile's Ward 2, the figure was 3 blacks, or 2.7 percent of the adult black males.

34. *Nationalist*, 1 May 1868.

35. James Mallory, diary, 1 January 1866, Southern Historical Collection, University of North Carolina.

36. Waddell to Bvt. Major S. Greene, Crawford, 14 January 1868, FBP, Alabama Letters Received.

37. The following generalizations concerning the Negro elites are based entirely on the Manuscript Census Returns, even when additional or conflicting information is available elsewhere, in order that the data should be as consistent as possible. For the analysis of the elites, it should be noted that in addition to possible errors discussed previously, the Census Returns were especially liable to omit government officials. Some, such as members of the state legislature, were frequently away from home; others, who occupied part-time local offices, may often have been listed under their permanent occupations.

The sampling technique used here differs from that employed in previous chapters. For the study of the black elites, I have used entire counties and cities, rather than selected wards, beats, and townships. In addition to Mobile, which will be treated separately, I have studied four cities: Montgomery, Selma, Huntsville, and Talladega; four blackbelt counties: Montgomery, Dallas, Macon, and Sumter; one Tennessee Valley county: Madison; two piedmont counties: St. Clair and Talladega; three mountain counties: Dekalb, Winston, and Walker; and two wiregrass counties: Dale and Coffee.

38. In the three sample mountain counties and two sample wiregrass counties, there was not one member of the black status elite. See Table 14. As a percentage of the black population, the status elite was so infinitesimal as to make statistics almost meaningless, but I have listed the percentages for comparative purposes, to show where the black elite was strong and where it was not.

39. In Montgomery, Selma, Huntsville, and Talladega, of 29 members of the status elite 14 were teachers, 12 ministers, and 3 government officials. In the sample rural areas, of 41 members, 19 were teachers, 18 ministers, and 4 government officials.

40. In the 12 selected counties, there were only 26 Negroes who owned more than $3,000, and all of them were concentrated in 3 counties.

41. Of 56 members of the economic elite in Montgomery, Huntsville, Selma, and Talladega, 30 were artisans and 13 were women who kept house. There were also 3 laborers, 2 merchants, 2 farm laborers, 1 railroad superintendent, 1 street overseer, 1 cotton classer, 1 servant, 1 policeman, and 1 man with no occupation.

42. Of the 56, 27 could read and write, 6 could read, and 23 were totally illiterate.

43. Of 169 rural blacks in the economic elite in the 12 counties, 120 were farmers, 17 farm laborers, 14 artisans, 6 servants, 4 ministers, 4 women who kept house, 3 merchants, and 1 a laborer.

44. Of the 169, 47 could read and write, 18 could read but not write, and 104 were totally illiterate.

45. Of the state's 2,690 free blacks, 1,193 lived in Mobile. See Lewy Dorman, "The Free Negro in Alabama from 1819 to 1861" (Master's thesis, University of Alabama, 1916).

46. Sellers, *Slavery in Alabama*, p. 384.

47. Mary Taresa Austin Carroll, *A Catholic History of Alabama and the Floridas* (New York: P. J. Kennedy & Sons, 1908), pp. 339-340.

48. See the Manuscript Census Returns of 1860. Gene Chastang, for example, a seventy-eight year old farmer, owned $3,900 of real and $30,000 of personal property.

49. Twenty-four Mobile blacks — constituting 0.11 percent of the county's Negro population — were in the status elite. Of these, 12 were ministers, 5 teachers, and 7 government workers. One hundred and eighteen blacks — or 0.56

percent of the black population — were members of the economic elite. Of these, the largest groups were artisans (37), women keeping house (17), laborers and farm laborers (17), farmers (16), and businessmen (11). Because many free Negroes — including virtually all of the Chastangs — lived in rural Mobile County, the city and county are here treated together.

50. Manuscript Census Returns, 1860, 1870. See Chapter 7 for a brief biographical sketch of Gregory.

51. The situation was similar in other counties containing substantial numbers of free Negroes. In Dallas County, of 74 free Negroes in 1860, only 1 was included in the new black upper class in 1870. In Montgomery County, only 4 of 62 free blacks belonged to the upper class, and in Madison County, only 8 of 163 did. In Talladega County, of 21 free Negroes in 1860, not one was a member of the upper class in 1870.

52. By contrast, in 1860 5 Chastangs had owned property valued at more than $3,000, and 2 more had owned property valued at between $2,000 and $3,000.

53. The conservative Mobile *Advertiser and Register*, 30 November 1867, denounced him as a "deserter and renegade from his own (creole) class." In a typical attempt to divide Negroes, the paper insisted that "he is no black man, nor the prototype or friend of the blacks. He never was a slave himself."

54. For example, the Mobile *Advertiser and Register*, 30 April 1867, and the Mobile *Daily Register*, 29 April 1868.

55. Mobile *Advertiser and Register*, 20 April 1867.

56. *Nationalist*, 3 May 1866.

57. Ibid., 26 April 1866.

58. Although mulattoes constituted only about 12 percent of the state's Negro population and 16 percent of the rural upper class in the twelve sample counties, in the four largest cities, between one-quarter and two-thirds of the upper class members were mulattoes. The figures were as follows: Selma, 23.5 percent; Huntsville, 38.1 percent; Mobile, 54.9 percent; Montgomery, 62.9 percent.

59. Montgomery *Daily Advertiser*, 26 November 1867.

60. Ibid., 31 July, 1, 4, 5, 13 August 1868.

61. *Nationalist*, 30 November 1868.

62. John Parrish to Henry Watson, 30 September 1867, Watson Papers, Duke University Library. Parrish considered Green's efforts "an excuse for him to stump the country in the interest of the Radical party."

63. Montgomery *Daily Advertiser*, 15 August 1868.

64. Letter to the *Daily State Sentinel*, 17 August 1867.

7

The Awakening of
Black Political Consciousness

I

Alabama's Negroes were slower to become actively involved in politics than in some other fields of endeavor. In great measure, this was because they were specifically excluded from participating in the political life of the state until the passage of the congressional Reconstruction Acts of 1867. For the first two years after the Civil War, the ballot box, the state legislature, and countless lesser offices were the exclusive preserve of white men.

Even before blacks legally entered politics, however, they had begun to express themselves politically through rallies, barbecues, and conventions. When the barriers were finally removed, they emerged as the backbone of the Republican party. At first, black political leaders were unsure of themselves and frequently turned for instruction and guidance to their white benefactors. Soon, however, Negro politicians began to pursue their own

aims, aims that were sometimes at odds with those of their carpetbagger mentors and in outright conflict with those of their
scalawag allies. Black leaders voiced, along with their appeals
for greater black power, increasingly Radical demands.

II

Alabama freedmen held quasipolitical meetings as early as the
autumn of 1865. Their ability to hold conventions was as much
a test and symbol of their freedom as was changing employers
or leaving the old plantations, for mass meetings of blacks had
been strictly prohibited in the days of slavery. With this prohibition lifted, blacks naturally got together to discuss common
problems which previously they could only have whispered about
in slave quarters.

All-black local meetings were held in several regions of the
state in 1865. These early conventions, which were well attended
by freedmen, were cautious in tone. Still unsure of their position in society, Negroes were careful to avoid giving the appearance of challenging their former masters. In October, a public meeting of blacks in Selma, for example, adopted resolutions that advised freedmen to behave themselves and seek good
relations with whites. In a gesture perhaps designed to win the
goodwill of the anti-Northern white community, the convention protested the beating and robbing of freedmen by Union
Soldiers.[1] When the Selma gathering chose one of its members
to serve as a delegate to a statewide convention of Negroes, he
declined, explaining that he had "no desire to enter politics,
feeling that the time has not arrived for extending the elective
franchise to the whole colored race."[2]

This moderate spirit was fully maintained at the first statewide
Colored Convention, which met in Mobile in November 1865.[3]
Most of the fifty-six delegates, who had been chosen at local
meetings, were ministers, and the president of the convention,
E. S. Winn, was a Methodist elder who would later be one of
the participants at the first convention of the AME Zion Church.[4]
The resolutions adopted at the convention did not contain the
slightest hint of anything white Alabama might consider objec-

tionable. The delegates urged a policy of "peace, friendship, and good will toward all men — especially toward our white fellow-citizens among whom our lot is cast," reassured whites that "it will continue to be our purpose to work industriously and honestly," and recognized that freedom "imposes new obligations upon us to cultivate all the virtues of good citizenship."[5]

The moderate tone continued through 1866, as blacks made themselves heard throughout the state in parades, meetings, and celebrations. Public holidays provided Negroes with one of their few opportunities to get together without being accused of plotting some mischief. These celebrations were primarily urban affairs. Although plantation blacks occasionally came to the nearest town to celebrate the holidays, most field hands remained, for the time being, in the dark politically.

A typical celebration occurred in Montgomery on New Year's day 1866 when large crowds of freedmen turned out for a parade to celebrate their "independence day." After the parade there were several speeches by Negro leaders, the most prominent of whom was ex-slave Baptist preacher Holland Thompson. Thompson, who was later to serve three terms in the state legislature, urged blacks to prove they were worthy of their freedom. The Montgomery *Daily Advertiser* was pleased that the black leaders had given the freedmen "good advice."[6]

A similar gathering occurred in Huntsville, where Negroes celebrated the anniversary of the abolition of slavery in the West Indies with a procession "with regalia, banners, marshals, music, &c.," followed by a barbecue dinner. During the dinner there were addresses by several speakers, including a white Northern Methodist minister who "gave the negroes much good advice as to their duties, responsibilities, conduct, &c." A black visitor from Nashville advocated universal suffrage.[7] Such Radical views were unusual in 1866, however, and it is significant that in this case they were expressed by an out-of-state black.

In general, while political power rested in the hands of local whites, Negroes found it safest to tell them what they wanted to hear. In August 1866, several Negroes "representing the better class in Mobile" called upon the mayor and "tendered their services to aid in preserving law and order in the event of any distur-

bance being raised by any portion of the negro population."[8]
Even some early black organizations seemed designed as much
to reassure anxious whites as to benefit the freedmen. When
blacks in Athens formed a benevolent aid association, the local
newspaper noted with pleasure that the president of the new
organization was someone they knew and trusted, "John Tyre,
our barber."[9] Occasionally there were hints of an incipient black
Radicalism, but they were only hints, and could easily be explained away. When Holland Thompson published a letter calling for a national Negro convention because "[w]e need to
know each other as friends and allies," the *Southern Advertiser* concluded that it was probably written by a "mean white."[10]

III

The 1867 Reconstruction Acts, which provided for the division
of the Southern states into five military districts to be ruled by
military commanders until those states had approved constitutions granting full black suffrage and had ratified the Fourteenth
Amendment, introduced the period of black participation in Alabama politics. Not only could Negroes now take part in elect-
ing officials and governing the state, but their participation was
essential for the success of the new Republican party the victorious
North expected would come to power. From 1 April 1867, when
General John Pope arrived in Montgomery to assume command
of the Third Military District of Alabama and Georgia, political
activity was intense.

One of the chief instruments through which the Republican
party was established in Alabama was the Union League, an
organization that had originated in the North during the war as
a patriotic association, but which after the war rapidly became
a bulwark of the Republican party in most Southern states. It
was the Union League that first enlisted most blacks behind the
Republican party. Its period of effective political influence in
Alabama lasted only about a year. By late 1868, because of at-
tacks by the Ku Klux Klan and because its purposes were served
just as well by the Republican party, it had practically ceased
to exist. But during the early organizational period its role was

vital. It aroused intense controversy, and opponents charged that it manipulated and intimidated Negroes through secret rituals.[11]

The earliest successes of the Union League in Alabama, however, were among whites in the northern part of the state. There had long been a regional split in Alabama politics. The isolated, predominantly white regions of the north had resented the political control of the state by the large cotton planters of the south. In 1861, the northern delegates to the secession convention voted unanimously against immediate secession, but the southern majority carried the day. During the war, many northerners defected to the Union side, and the north sent Radical, pro-Union delegates to the restoration Constitutional Convention of 1865, while the southern majority was Conservative.[12] Under such conditions, the Union League found widespread support in the northern part of the state, and even before the end of the war federal authorities began to organize League chapters in occupied areas. After the war, the League grew rapidly. By late 1865, approximately 40 percent of the white population in the north were members.[13] At the time, the League's organization in the north attracted relatively little attention.[14]

With the passage of the Reconstruction Acts, blacks became fair game politically. As they began forming Union League clubs in the south and joining the already existing ones in the north, many white northerners began to desert the organization.[15] The process was remarkably disorganized, and there was a surprising lack of information in certain areas about what was going on in others. Late in May 1867, for example, the secretary of the Union League in one piedmont county wrote to Governor Patton expressing his surprise that in some locations Negroes were being admitted to the League. "[T]he negro question has come up before this League," he explained; "it has been laid over untill the next meeting of our U.L. to be considered and ... we have no means of ascertaining whether it has sprung up among in some of the Leagus to initiate the negro or whether they have authority for it. Some of our neighboring Leggs have been initiating them but they have failed to explain to us by what authority they do it."[16]

White reaction to the enlistment of blacks varied. In some areas, where there were relatively few Negroes, many whites remained in the League and continued to support the Republican party during the early stages of Reconstruction. Race simply was not a major issue where there were very few blacks, and there the Republican party continued to represent the aspirations of the small white farmer. Winston County, for example, which contained only twenty-one blacks in 1870, remained staunchly Republican after most of the northern counties had turned Democratic. Elsewhere, however, there was a general white exodus from the Leagues, and it was mainly in the blackbelt region where Negro majorities were large that the Republicans could expect success.

The original impetus for the formation of the Union Leagues in the blackbelt came from whites. The Grand Secretary of the League in Alabama was John C. Keffer, a carpetbagger from Pennsylvania and a Freedmen's Bureau official.[17] Other Bureau agents also played key roles in the League. One wrote to Swayne from a small town, "[w]e keep the ball in motion here. Last Saturday night we organized a U.L. for the colored people at this place. Thirty six were initiated, and they had a very short notice of the meeting."[18] Another white League organizer reported from Talladega, "I am doing very well about making voters of the Blacks. I have taken about five hundred in the *League* and am taking them in about one hundred a week."[19]

Negroes also played a secondary role at the early Republican rallies and meetings. Although they supplied the bulk of the actual Republican manpower, the politically inexperienced freedmen seemed content at first to listen to the exhortations of their Northern white mentors. Occasionally one or two black leaders would speak, but for the most part, during the first few weeks they just listened. At a Republican rally in Montgomery on 26 March, for example, although most of the audience was black, all of the speakers, including Swayne and Keffer, were white.[20]

When Negroes first spoke at Republican gatherings, they tended to be extremely cautious and moderate. Hamp Shuford, for example, a black speaker at a rally in Hayneville, drew the praise of the conservative Montgomery *Weekly Advertiser* for his

"practical wisdom. He exhorted his people to be honest, indus-
trious, and frugal, and save their money to buy land," rejoiced
the paper. "They should also be magnanimous. They had rights
which some of the smartest men in the country were denied;
and . . . they must now endeavor to have the disabilities of those
very men removed, in order that they might have wise men to
make laws for them." A Selma newspaper noted that at a Republican meeting in that city "[a]lmost all the colored men who
spoke made conservative speeches."[21]

Gradually, however, especially in the larger cities, some
Negroes grew bolder. At a huge Republican rally held in Mobile,
thousands of blacks, many of them armed, listened to Radical
speeches from both whites and blacks.[22] One Negro speaker
who would later serve as an alderman in Mobile declared, "[w]e
are here tonight to tell the world that after being enfranchised
we are wise enough to know our rights and we are going to claim
those rights." He listed among them sitting on juries and riding
with whites in public conveyances.[23] When William V. Turner,
a black teacher and future state legislator, spoke at a rally in
his home town of Wetumpka, he noticed "the more Radical the
speeches, the better the colored people like them."[24] A letter to
the *Nationalist* advising Negroes on the use of firearms captured
the increasingly militant mood of many blacks; the author concluded that in case of trouble they should not risk firing into the
air but should aim to hit.[25]

IV

In May 1867, the second statewide Colored Convention met in
Mobile. The differences between it and the 1865 convention
were indicative of the growing Radicalism of black political
leaders. The convention was not entirely representative of the
state's Negro population: one-half of the delegates were from
Mobile and the remainder came from only twelve other counties. Most of the blackbelt counties, however, were represented,
and many of the delegates were typical of a new breed of semi-
professional black politicians. At least twelve of them would
later hold some political office, and others were influential in

their own communities. Holland Thompson was elected president of the convention.[26]

After two days of debate and deliberation, the convention adopted a series of resolutions affiliating itself with the Republican party, praising Generals Pope and Swayne, calling for the establishment of a public-school system and a program of relief for the aged and homeless, and requesting military protection from election day abuses. The delegates also expressed their desire for the maintenance of good relations between freedmen and employers, and proclaimed that "it is our undeniable right to hold office, sit on juries, to ride on all public conveyances, to sit at public tables, and in public places of amusement." The convention later issued an address to the people of Alabama supporting the Republican party and claiming for blacks the same legal rights as whites.[27]

The Colored Convention was followed less than a month later by the first Republican State Convention. In late May, Union men held county meetings throughout the state to elect delegates to the state convention; in most cases, several blacks were among those chosen. The Radical nature of the convention was evident when Ovid Gregory, a Mobile Negro, objected to the seating of federal Judge Richard Busteed because he was not sufficiently Radical to be a true Republican. By a vote of 146 to 25, Busteed was denied the right to speak.[28] From the convention emerged the new Republican State Executive Committee, of which four out of twenty-three members were blacks. In addition to Holland Thompson, they included Moses B. Avery, a Methodist minister from Mobile, Samuel Blandon of Lee County, who would later serve in the Constitutional Convention and state legislature, and Lafayette Robinson of Huntsville, a future Constitutional Convention delegate and cashier of the Freedmen's Savings Bank.

During the summer of 1867 Negroes were appointed to several police forces for the first time. Selma became the first Alabama city to have a black policeman when five Negroes were appointed to serve with six whites.[29] Mobile followed soon after. Swayne had suggested the appointment of black policemen to Mayor Horton, and on 1 June the mayor indicated his agreement, declaring "it is but *right* — as well as *politic* that they should have a fair showing, and the sooner it can be prudently done, the better."[30] A month later five freedmen were appointed to the Mobile police force, and in August fourteen more were added.[31] Montgomery and other cities also appointed black policemen.

Unlike other blacks in positions of authority, few of the policemen had been prominent community leaders before their appointments. Few if any of them went on to successful careers in politics. Of the twelve black Montgomery policemen listed in the Manuscript Census Returns of 1870, only one had any other political experience (he had served as a registrar during the 1867 and 1868 elections), and five were illiterate. A similar situation existed in Selma, where none of the four policemen listed was especially distinguished, and two were illiterate.

Although many blacks were becoming increasingly bold in their political demands, some remained cautious and reluctant to push their luck. In June, when Swayne asked eleven prominent Mobile Negroes, including Moses B. Avery and Ovid Gregory, for advice on the appointment of a black alderman, they declined to recommend a candidate and explained that they desired that the most capable person — presumably a white man — be chosen.[32] Their letter proved extremely embarrassing to Radicals. A leading Huntsville scalawag wrote Swayne, "it is pointed to by the rebels as an evidence of the negroes['] want of confidence in us & their subservience to rebel influence. If another occur[r]ence of this same kind takes place for the sake of our party and Cause, do not let it get into the papers," he continued. "This Mobile letter of the negroes to you is doing our cause great injury up here."[33]

All blacks, however, did not subscribe to such a cautious approach to power. Less than two weeks after the appearance of the letter declining the appointment of a black alderman, nine prominent Mobile Negroes, including two who had signed the letter, demanded that one-half the policemen in Mobile be blacks and complained to Swayne that blacks were being denied their legitimate rights in court. "The policy which some of our leaders think best," they wrote, "viz: to pander to a conservative element, at the expense of our rights and privileges, we think neither wise nor just."³⁴

V

Most Alabama freedmen came in contact with politics for the first time in the summer of 1867, during registration for the election to the Constitutional Convention. The registration process also marked a new stage of involvement for black political leaders. General Supervisor of Registration William H. Smith, a prominent scalawag and future governor, determined that in each of the state's forty-two election districts the board of registration should consist of one black and two white registrars. These forty-two black registrars were the first Negroes to serve in an official political capacity.

In some cases, the appointment of Negro registrars gave rise to serious disputes between Republican factions. Especially interesting was the struggle in Madison County, because it presaged future factional fights between carpetbaggers and scalawags. Joseph C. Bradley, a leading Unionist during the war and the Tennessee Valley's most important scalawag, first advised Keffer that because of anti-Negro sentiment among whites it would be harmful to appoint black registrars in northern Alabama. On the same day, John B. Callis, the Freedmen's Bureau sub-assistant commissioner in Huntsville and a future congressman, recommended the appointment of one Henderson Hill as the Negro registrar for Madison County. When Bradley found that Callis had recommended a Negro, he came up with one of his own, Reverend Alfred Barnett, whom he praised to Swayne as "the most influential man of his color in our State." In fact, Barnett was an elderly Methodist minister of Huntsville, "poor as a matter of course, with an education equal if not superior" to that of most Huntsville blacks. Evidently he was not, however, the choice of the black population. "The colored people ask me to write you and represent that they in convention have chosen Henderson Hill col[ore]d to represent the new voting element in the registration of voters for Madison Co.," exulted Callis. "They say that Bradley and Davis [another scalawag] have clandestinely recommended a man by the name

of Barnett who is supremely distasteful to them and in the confidence of the worst negro hating element in the county, with
whom Bradley and Davis are coalecing for political power."[35]
Hill received the appointment, but the factional split among the
Madison County Republicans was later to grow still more violent.

In some other areas, the problem was not one of selecting
from two competing candidates but rather of finding any blacks
qualified for the job. While most cities had a small number of
at least semiliterate Negroes, in many of the more remote counties — especially the predominantly white ones — there were few
if any literate blacks. Consequently, it was necessary to choose
some of the registrars from counties other than those in which
they served. At least five of them came from Montgomery.[36]

The plight of a sophisticated Negro relegated to the Siberia
of provincial Alabama was well illustrated by a letter from
George W. Cox, the black registrar in Tuscaloosa County. A
one-time resident of Tuscaloosa, Cox had been a slave blacksmith until freed by the war, at which time he still "did not know
a letter in the book." By the time of his appointment as registrar,
he had moved to Montgomery where "by close application"
he had "learned to read and write."[37] Upon his return to Tuscaloosa, he was very unhappy with the primitive level of black
consciousness. "The colored men are few & far apart & ought
to have the light sent to them in this dark part of the country,"
he wrote. "I want to get through & get back to Montgomery so
bad I don[']t know what to do — this place is too far in the woods
for me now — it can never be my home any more."[38]

Freedmen's Bureau officials played a major part in expediting
the registration of blacks. By 1 August, Superintendent of Registration Smith reported that Bureau sub-assistant commissioners
had visited nearly all of the state's election districts.[39] Their
reports on the process of registration among freedmen varied.[40]
In general, however, while blacks in the major population centers
were well informed about registration and voting procedures,
in some of the more remote areas they were in total ignorance
of their political rights. In many districts, whites tried to intimi-
date them from registering by warning them that if they did
"they would be put in the army, pay more taxes, etc."[41]

Most Alabama whites viewed the black registrars with great antagonism. In some cases, the white registrars concurred in this sentiment. One of Tuscaloosa's white registrars resigned because he found George W. Cox "unacceptable."[42] On 13 June, Alex Webb, the Negro registrar for the two western blackbelt counties of Hale and Greene, was murdered. Conservatives denied that politics had anything to do with the murder and explained that the atrocity had been the result of a private dispute in which Webb insulted a white man in a Greensboro store.[43]

Many whites were increasingly alarmed by the growing number of political meetings that blacks began attending during the registration period. They were also disturbed by the evident Radicalization of the freedmen. Not only did blacks refuse to stay quietly in the cotton fields, but they were no longer satisfied with issuing vague resolutions urging education, self-help, and the maintenance of harmonious relations between laborers and employers. Now, they were increasingly likely to issue strident demands for their own rights. After registrar Webb's murder, James K. Green, another black leader of the area, frightened whites by making "one of the most incendiary speeches ever delivered to an infuriated crowd." He warned that he would probably be the next Negro to be murdered, and he called on freedmen to be ready to avenge his death. *"He has...,"* the Greensboro *Alabama Beacon* declared, *"rendered himself exceedingly obnoxious to the community."*[44] Even the *Nationalist* denounced James B. Gibbs, a Negro who declared that the Republican party should become a black man's party and that blacks should refuse to vote for whites.[45]

In July and August, the Republicans held a series of mass meetings throughout the state. These gatherings were attended primarily by blacks, many of whom came armed, although most of the speakers were white.[46] At a Greensboro meeting, for example, four whites and James K. Green spoke, and Green was chosen as one of two candidates for delegates to the coming Constitutional Convention.[47] A white resident of Greensboro who observed the proceedings thought that the "most disgusting, low down, *incendiary* speeches were made calculated to make the most bitter feelings of hostility on the part of the negroes toward the white race." He blamed the situation primarily on "Yankee traveling agents, the meanest looking men you ever saw, who eat[,] drink and sleep with the negroes and teach them their peculiar doctrin[e]s[,] establish 'Loyal Leagues' &c."[48]

The result of the election was never in doubt. Although the initial registration figures listed 88,243 blacks and 72,748 whites, after the boards of registration met to revise the voting lists, "striking off the names of those not entitled to vote, and adding the names of those who are," the black advantage was much greater. With the convention certain to be called, most whites and all but a few Conservatives boycotted the polls. Voting for the convention were 71,730 blacks and 18,553 whites; against it were 5,583 whites.[49] The overwhelming majority of the ninety-eight convention delegates were Republicans; only four, according to the Republican *Daily State Sentinel,* were "Rebel[s]."[50] Seventeen of the delegates were Negroes.[51]

VI

By the autumn of 1867, a new group of black political leaders had emerged. It was a small group; while almost every community had some leader whom blacks trusted and to whom they turned for guidance, in most counties there were only one or two blacks of more than local prominence, and in some there was none. It was also a new group. Few of them had attended the state's first Colored Convention in 1865, which had consisted largely of Negroes trained as preachers before the war. The fifty-seven blacks who served as voting registrars or delegates to the Constitutional Convention in general were the most important early black politicians in the state.[52] The seventeen Convention delegates were especially prominent. Ten of them continued to play active roles in politics, most in the state legislature.[53]

Almost all of the black politicians came from the blackbelt, the Tennessee Valley, and Mobile — areas with heavy concentrations of Negroes.[54] In the predominantly white counties there was little opportunity for blacks to take an active part in politics, even if there had been a group of politically conscious freedmen. Mobile, where there had been many free and relatively well-educated Negroes before the war, offered the largest reserve from which the new black political leadership could be drawn.

The origins of the new Negro politicians, and their roads to prominence, varied, but in general they came from relatively privileged backgrounds, especially those from the cities and most of all those from Mobile.[55] Two Negroes in Mobile achieved special prominence. One was Ovid Gregory, a free-born Creole and light mulatto who spoke French and Spanish and owned a cigar store in Mobile.[56] Initially appearing "mild and rational and most conservative in his views," he was among the eleven Mobile Negroes who wrote to Swayne declining to recommend a black alderman. By the autumn of 1867, however, after his appointment by Mayor Horton as assistant chief of police, he had acquired a reputation — which he would maintain in the Constitutional Convention and later in the state legislature — as a fiery Radical. Mobile's leading newspaper bitterly denounced him as "a deserter and renegade from his own (creole) class. They neither agree with his politics," continued the paper, "nor admire his affiliation with mean white men and seditious negroes."[57]

John Carraway, Gregory's closest political ally, came from a similar privileged background. Born in North Carolina the son of a wealthy white planter, he was freed upon his father's death, along with his mother and two sisters. Moving north, he settled in Brooklyn, where he became a tailor. During the war, he enlisted in the Massachusetts Fifty-fourth Regiment and composed a song called "Colored Volunteers," which became a favorite among the black troops. After the war he settled in Mobile, where he became active in state politics, serving as secretary of the Colored Convention of 1867 and attending the Republican State Convention in June of that year. He also worked as assistant editor of the *Nationalist*. Like Gregory, Carraway was known as an ardent Radical. During the Constitutional Convention he would be a leading integrationist, and later he would distinguish himself as Speaker of the Alabama House of Representatives.[58]

The Tennessee Valley was the one other region of the state where there had been a sizable number of free Negroes before the war, and some of the Negro politicians from the Valley consequently resembled their Mobile colleagues in background. All four of the Convention delegates who had been free before the war came from Mobile or the Tennessee Valley. Ovid Gregory and John Carraway were from Mobile; James T. Rapier and Lafayette Robinson were from the Tennessee Valley. The most prominent north Alabama politician was James T. Rapier, who would later be one of three Alabama blacks to serve in the United States Congress. Born in Florence in the northwestern corner of the state, Rapier was the son of free mulatto farmers. He was taught by a private tutor and then sent to Canada to complete his education. When he reentered Alabama, it was as a newspaper correspondent with Federal troops. He returned to the family home in Florence, where he was soon "classed among the extensive and successful planters in the Tennessee Valley."[59] When it came time to send a delegate to the Constitutional Convention, he was the choice of Lauderdale County.[60]

Most of the black politicians from the blackbelt or piedmont regions of the state came from different backgrounds. In many of the small towns and villages, teachers were central figures within the black community, and it was natural for freedmen to turn to them for leadership.[61] Such was the case with William V. Turner, who taught school in Wetumpka, not far from Montgomery, in 1866 and 1867. The freedmen of Elmore County chose him as their representative to the Colored Convention of 1867, and shortly thereafter he was appointed registrar for Elmore and Autauga counties. Later he would serve two years in the state legislature. Like many other black leaders, Turner became increasingly militant in 1867. Before the passage of the congressional Reconstruction Acts, he made "a pretty little conservative speech" opposing black participation in politics. In January 1868, however, in an "incendiary" address, "he said that the time was passed when the white people of the South could be looked upon as the friend of the negro." The Elmore *Standard* pointed out the inconsistency of his thought. "[N]ow, all at once," jibed the paper, "he has discovered that he was wrong then, and that he is a suitable representative of intelligent white people."[62]

Preachers occupied a position similar to that of teachers in the small towns of the blackbelt, and at least six black ministers served as registrars and Convention delegates. Although some of these preacher-politicians were totally uneducated,[63] most of those who were registrars or delegates were literate, and some were quite learned. John Dozier, a Baptist minister who was appointed a registrar and would later serve in the state legislature, had learned to read Greek while still a slave.[64] Moses B. Avery, a Methodist minister who served as registrar from Mobile and then as assistant secretary of the Constitutional Convention, had been raised as a free man in Mobile, where he went to school. During the war he served on the federal gunboat *Clifton* and was injured in the battle of Galveston. After the war he went to New Orleans, where he became assistant editor of the New Orleans *Tribune,* the nation's leading black newspaper. In 1866, he entered the ministry and moved to Mobile.[65]

The largest single group of black politicians had been trained as artisans.[66] Although not so well educated as the preachers, teachers, or free-born Negroes, they still had privileged backgrounds in comparison with those of the mass of Alabama's blacks. They had not been anonymous laborers toiling endlessly and monotonously in the cotton fields.[67] Frequently they had received preferential treatment from their masters.

Typical of these blackbelt politicians was James H. Alston, registrar and later state legislator from heavily black Macon County. Before emancipation, Alston belonged to Confederate General Cullen A. Battle, who considered him "quite an orderly negro, a good boot-maker and a valuable servant." He also learned to read and became something of a musician. After the war, because of his unusual training and abilities, Alston became the most influential black in Macon County. Later he would be shot at by political enemies and forced to flee to Montgomery.[68] A similar artisan-politician was George W. Houston, a registrar and state legislator from Sumter County, in the blackbelt. As a slave, he had been trained to be a tailor because he was crippled and unfit for strenuous physical labor. Under slavery "[h]is general character . . . was very fair. He was a negro who commanded the respect of the white people to probably as great an extent as any other negro in the country." After the war, however, when he became leader of the Union League in Sumter

County, whites began to find him "aggressive in his social ideals," or "domineering and turbulent."[69] He too would later be shot by political enemies, but would recover.

The black politicians who became active in 1867 were, then, in general a highly privileged group of Negroes. Few of them had shared the lot of the mass of slaves by toiling in the cotton fields. Most could read and write, and a few were highly educated. A disproportionately large number were mulattoes. Some were artisans, others teachers or ministers, and several had been either born free or freed before the war. Almost all of them had received some form of preferential treatment or training. They had been well prepared for political leadership, but many of them had interests and desires different from, if not at odds with, those of the constituents they were supposedly representing.

VII

The Constitutional Convention met in Montgomery on 5 November 1867. Both at the time and later, there were numerous charges that the Convention was an extremist body, that "the carpet-bag element had control of the negro vote" and "with a few extreme scalawags were disposed to resort to extreme measures."[70] Nevertheless, the majority of the delegates were Southern-born, and at no time was the Convention totally controlled by Radicals.[71] There was a precarious balance among Radicals, Moderates, and Conservatives; Radicals always had to hope for the support of a number of Moderates to get their way. In some instances that support was forth coming and in others it was not. The constitution that finally emerged was the result of a series of compromises between Radicals and Moderates.[72]

There was a distinctive geographic basis to the voting, which reflected the longstanding political hostility between the northern and southern parts of the state. White delegates from the Tennessee Valley and mountain regions of the state tended to be much more Radical on political issues than those from the south.[73] There was much less sectional division of white delegates on civil-rights measures.[74] Such a voting pattern suggests

Table 16 *White Voting on Twenty Roll Calls Relating to Political Issues in the 1867 Constitutional Convention*

REGION	WHITE DELE-GATES	EXTREME RADI-CALS	RADI-CALS	MODER-ATES	CONSER-VATIVES	NOT CLAS-SIFIED
Tennessee Valley	6	1	4	0	1	
Mountains	16	4	4	7	1	
Piedmont	11	0	2	6	3	
Blackbelt	34	0	6	15	11	2
Piney woods-wiregrass	10	1	3	3	1	2
Mobile County	3	0	2	1	0	
Total	81[a]	6	21	32	18[a]	4

[a]I was unable to determine the region of one white delegate.

SOURCE: *Convention Journal.*

that, at least in the early stages of Reconstruction, political Radicalism was as much a class and sectional force as a racial one, and that the Radicalism of many of the delegates from white, mountain counties represented a desire to break the power of the blackbelt planter rather than a strong commitment to the rights of the Negro.

Black delegates tended to vote together much more than other delegates did, especially on issues involving politics or civil rights.[75] Although this voting cohesion among blacks was no doubt in part the result of their common interest in a Radical Reconstruction program containing basic guarantees for the freedmen, black delegates tended to stick together on many nonpolitical issues as well. On two motions to reduce the per diem and mileage allowances of the delegates, for example, every Negro voted in opposition, although the white delegates were evenly split.[76]

Despite the general cohesiveness of the black delegates, there were certain differences among them. The best-known Negroes

Table 17 *White Voting on Four Roll Calls Relating to Civil Rights Issues in the 1867 Constitutional Convention*

REGION	WHITE DELEGATES	RADICALS	MODER-ATES	CONSERVA-TIVES	NOT CLAS-SIFIED
Tennessee Valley	6	4	2	0	
Mountains	16	4	5	6	1
Piedmont	11	3	2	5	1
Blackbelt	34	10	11	9	4
Piney woods-wiregrass	10	3	2	2	3
Mobile	3	2	1	0	
Total	81[a]	26	23	22	10[a]

[a]I was unable to determine the region of one white delegate.

SOURCE: *Convention Journal.*

— the educated mulatto delegates from Mobile and the Tennessee Valley, who were generally considered by whites to be the most extreme and offensive of the Negro delegates — spoke most often and most eloquently. Carraway, for example, delivered a ringing address in which he denounced the opponents of Reconstruction as "just as bitter, just as arrogant, and just as vindictive as they were in 1861."[77] Many whites, unused to having their views challenged by blacks, branded such speeches by "Rapier, Gregory, Carraway, and other blacks" as "violent and highly inflammatory harangues."[78]

Though articulate and prominent, the Mobile and Tennessee Valley mulattoes were not the most Radical of the Negro delegates. Not one of them was among the Convention's eleven extreme Radicals on political questions. All five of the Negroes in that group were relatively obscure blacks from the blackbelt. They did not make so many speeches as the better-known mulattoes, but their votes were more consistently Radical. Their Radicalism cannot be explained by arguing, as one historian has, that the "uneducated Negroes followed the Radical Carpetbag leaders" while "the three Negroes [Gregory, Carraway, and

Rapier] with educational and cultural advantages expressed opinions of their own," because of the numerous prominent carpetbaggers in the Convention, several of whom had served in the Freedmen's Bureau, only one was an extreme Radical.[79] The five most Radical black delegates were not pawns of the leading Convention carpetbaggers.

There were relatively few votes on questions of civil rights or integration, but on four key votes Negroes were strongly united. All but three blacks supported the prohibition of peonage and contract labor for a period of more than one year, which passed on one vote and failed on another by narrow margins, and was thus defeated.[80] All Negro delegates voted to table a motion that would have required the establishment of segregated schools. As a result of this successful vote, the Convention left to the new state board of education the decision concerning the establishment of separate schools. It was generally understood, however, that the schools would be segregated, and the board of education wasted little time in confirming these expectations. Black delegates also voted unanimously in a successful effort to table a bill providing for the segregation of "hotels, steamboats, railroads, and places of public amusement."[81]

Despite the unanimity of the black delegates, the lead in the struggle for integration was clearly taken by the light-skinned Negroes from Mobile and the Tennessee Valley. While on strictly political matters the rural blackbelt Negroes tended to be more Radical, integration seemed to offer the greatest appeal to the cultivated mulattoes who would be most likely to take advantage of the opportunities afforded by integrated theaters, restaurants, railroads, and places of public amusement. On the third day of the Convention, Gregory offered a resolution, which was never acted upon, urging "a special ordinance abolishing and removing all laws, regulations and customs heretofore or at present in existence, wherein distinctions are made on account of caste, color, or former condition of servitude." Rapier and Carraway were also active in pushing what whites referred to as "social equality."[82]

A paradoxical reversal of this pattern occurred over the question of mixed marriages. Twice, Conservatives attempted to include in the constitution a provision barring marriages between blacks and whites, and both times the Convention defeated these measures. Most blacks voted against banning mixed marriages, but in addition to the thirty white delegates who voted at least once for the proposal, there were seven Negroes, among them the five from Mobile and the Tennessee Valley. Gregory even introduced an amendment to the proposed measure, that "any white man intermarrying or cohabitating with colored women, shall be imprisoned for life."[83] Evidently the mulatto delegates were especially sensitive, because of their backgrounds, to the question of miscegenation.

VIII

Although the constitution drafted by the Convention was not an entirely Radical document, it contained several features that most white Alabamians found obnoxious. Chief of these was the suffrage article enfranchising blacks and disenfranchising whites unable to hold office under the Fourteenth Amendment.[84] Nine Conservative delegates finally voted against the adoption of the constitution and twenty-two more failed to vote. Thirteen of the delegates issued an address to the people of Alabama protesting against the constitution, universal suffrage, and white dis-franchisement.[85] The adoption of the constitution was the signal for the revival of the Democratic-Conservative opposition. Their strategy was to organize a massive boycott of the polls, since the constitution could be defeated if it was not approved by the majority of registered voters.[86]

In the campaign, Conservatives attempted to play up every possible difference between blacks and white Republicans. Democrats repeatedly informed Negroes that they were merely serving as the pawns of self-seeking politicians. They sarcastically suggested that Negroes be given greater influence within the Republican party and rejoiced openly over every evidence of black disaffection with their white allies.[87] "We understand," exulted the Montgomery *Daily Advertiser*, "there has been considerable discussion among the colored people in relation to the nominations for office made by the Radical Republicans of the

Convention in this city last week; and that many of them have expressed dissatisfaction at the result."[88] Occasionally, in their enthusiasm, Conservatives simply fabricated reports of Negro defections, as when several newspapers printed a letter supposedly written by Holland Thompson in which he announced his resignation from the Union League and his support for the Conservatives. Thompson denied having written the letter, which he claimed was a forgery, and remained a Republican.[89]

Some blacks, in fact, did have doubts about the sincerity of their white allies. As early as 2 December, all three of the Negro delegates from the Tennessee Valley refused to participate in a Radical caucus.[90] The blacks' suspicion that they were being used grew when the Republican party chose its candidates for the February 1868 elections. Nine of the seventeen black delegates were among the Negroes receiving nominations, but of these eight were to the state house of representatives and only one to the state senate.[91] Although blacks would obviously provide the bulk of the Republican votes, the higher offices were reserved exclusively for white Republicans. Not one Negro was nominated for Congress. In Tuscaloosa, where the Republicans nominated C. W. Pierce, a Freedmen's Bureau agent, for Congress, the county's Freedmen's Executive Committee met and denounced him as "a stranger in Alabama, whose interests are not identified with ours." They nominated instead S. W. Jones, a black barber and AME preacher, but he was soon forced to withdraw from the race for lack of funds.[92]

These early hints of black political disenchantment with the white Republicans mirrored a growing spirit of restlessness among the freedmen. In November, a group of Tuskegee blacks tried to interfere with a constable who was arresting several Negroes for theft.[93] In Blandon Springs, not far from Mobile, according to the Mobile *Times* "unemployed negroes" began congregating "in large bodies, armed with guns, swords, and by bludgeons, camping in front of private residences, discharging their muskets singly and in volleys without any *cause*, and threatening to help themselves to whatever they want."[94] Blacks formed an insurrectionary government in the blackbelt community of Perote, where rebel leaders "went to plantations and forced laborers to join them for vengeance, showing pretended orders from Gen. Swayne that they had a right to kill all resisting their authority." Swayne finally sent troops to put down the rebellion, and fifteen blacks were arrested.[95]

Although there was some black discontent over the paucity of high-level Negro nominations, blackbelt Negroes did receive many nominations for lower offices. Freedmen predominated at most local Republican nominating conventions held across the state in December and January. In Selma, where according to a local newspaper "a few hundred of town niggers and a dozen or two white office seekers constituted the 'nominating convention,'" blacks were nominated for state legislator, county commissioner, and tax collector. In Montgomery, the process was similar.[96]

Republican nominations did not, however, always go so smoothly. In the Tennessee Valley, where there were many blacks but where the native white Republicans were numerous enough to make a bid for power on their own, there was considerable tension among blacks, carpetbaggers, and scalawags. On 30 December, the scalawags met and nominated ex-Confederate General J. W. Burke for Congressman from the Sixth Congressional District, which included most of the eastern Tennessee Valley and mountain counties. Several days later, a rival faction of carpetbaggers and blacks met and nominated John B. Callis, a Freedmen's Bureau agent, for the same position, and denounced Burke as a rebel. The Republican Huntsville *Advocate,* which strongly supported Burke, complained that "the Bolters have prepared and are circulating as secretly as possible among the colored voters a nameless Address or Circular, charging Gen. J. W. Burke with having whipped on the public square in Huntsville, in 1862, a negro man or woman, &c. This is done," the paper continued, "to prejudice the colored voters against him as the Republican nominee for Congress! And is done by those who seek to array the colored voters against native white Unionists!"[97]

The elections were held over a four-day period starting on 4 February. At issue were both the ratification of the constitution and the election of government officials to serve in the new government. The Conservatives concentrated all of their efforts on defeating the constitution through a massive election boycott. They made no nominations for office, and in effect conceded the elections to the Republicans.[98]

In addition to boycotting the polls, Democrats made strenuous although generally unsuccessful efforts to keep blacks from voting.[99] Planters could most effectively apply pressure. One labor contract between a planter and three freedmen included the provision that they would not join the Union League "or *attend elections* or political meetings without the consent of the employer."[100] More frequently, planters threatened to discharge, and in some cases did fire, laborers who insisted upon voting. Many such freedmen complained to the Freedmen's Bureau, and these complaints became so numerous that a Bureau official in Washington wired Assistant Commissioner Hayden: "See that nobody starves in consequence of having done his duty." Hayden confirmed that many blacks had been fired for voting, but claimed that most of them had already "been employed by others, and in general upon much better terms."[101]

Because of the Democratic boycott of the polls, the Republican candidates were successful throughout the state. In the Tennessee Valley, Callis easily overwhelmed his scalawag opponent.[102] In the blackbelt Negroes were elected to numerous local offices. "All the magistrates elected in Shelby county are negroes," exaggerated the Selma *Times and Messenger,* "and not one of them can read and write."[103] Although no blacks were elected to Congress and only one to the state Senate, they would have a sizable vote in the new House of Representatives, where the Speaker would be John Carraway.

The Negroes placed in positions of power in 1868 were a politically experienced group. With few exceptions, they had been among the black political leaders during the previous year. Of twenty-four blacks elected to the state legislature, fifteen had been registrars of election or delegates to the Constitutional Convention.[104] Others, such as Holland Thompson, had been active politically even though they had not served in either of those two capacities. When the Republican State Convention in July chose four blacks among twelve vice presidents, three of them had served in the Constitutional Convention and the other one had been a registrar. All four were currently in the legislature.[105]

As a consequence of the white voting boycott and the intimidation of black voters in many areas, the vote cast in favor of the constitution was substantially smaller than the vote for calling the Constitutional Convention had been.[106] As fewer than one-half the registered voters approved the constitution, General George G. Meade, who had replaced General Pope as commander of the Third Military District, officially reported that the people of Alabama had rejected the constitution.[107] It was only after considerable debate that Congress, in the so-called Omnibus Bill, voted to consider the constitution adopted by a majority of the voters, and readmitted Alabama to congressional representation along with Georgia, Louisiana, North Carolina and South Carolina. On 13 July, William H. Smith was sworn in as governor, and the new state legislature assembled.[108]

With the inauguration of the Republican government, a new political era seemed to be dawning for Alabama's blacks. A transitional period of three years, which had seen the growth of black interest in politics and the emergence of the Negro politician, was over. A Republican coalition of carpetbaggers, scalawags, and blacks, based largely on the united vote of the freedmen, was firmly in control of the state. It was not yet apparent just how shaky this coalition would prove, although hints of future trouble were already evident in the disappointment of blacks over the paucity of offices allotted to them and in the discord between carpetbaggers and scalawags in the Tennessee Valley.

For the purposes of this analysis, however, the greatest significance of the Republican coalition lay not in its future success or failure, but in the basis of its initial triumph. When given the opportunity, blacks had quickly shown their concern with the political life of the state. They had, to the surprise and consternation of many whites, refused to follow passively the political lead of their ex-owners. Instead, they had rushed to join the Republican party, which to them was the party of freedom. The realization that it was black manpower that provided the basis of Republican success led black politicians to take an increasingly independent and increasingly militant position within the party. Once aroused, black political consciousness proved to have a momentum all its own.

Notes

1. *Daily Selma Times*, 21 October 1865.

2. *Alabama Beacon*, 24 November 1865, quoting his statement published in the Selma *Times*. "Sensible negro, that!" commented the *Alabama Beacon*.

3. See August Meier, *Negro Thought in America, 1880-1915* (Ann Arbor: University of Michigan Press, 1963), pp. 4-10, for an analysis of the Reconstruction convention movement among Negroes.

4. *Nationalist*, 14 December 1865.

5. New York *Daily Tribune*, 12 December 1865. The conservative *Daily Selma Times*, 28 November 1865, rejoiced that the resolutions "inculcate morality, the duty of labor, and the obligation to render conscientious obedience to the civil law."

6. Montgomery *Daily Advertiser*, 2 January 1866; *Nationalist*, 25 January 1866.

7. Huntsville *Advocate*, 4 August 1866.

8. Mobile *Advertiser and Register*, 18 August 1866.

9. Athens *Post*, 16 June 1866.

10. *Southern Advertiser*, 14 September 1866.

11. See Walter L. Fleming, *Civil War and Reconstruction in Alabama* (New York: Columbia University Press, 1905), pp. 553-568, and Clement Mario Silvestro, "None But Patriots: The Union Leagues in Civil War and Reconstruction" (Ph.D. diss., University of Wisconsin, 1959), passim.

12. See Fleming, *Civil War and Reconstruction*, pp. 3-143, passim.; Hugh C. Bailey, "Disloyalty in Early Confederate Alabama," *Journal of Southern History* 23 (1957): 522-528; Bessie Martin, *Desertion of Alabama Troops from the Confederate Army: A Study in Sectionalism* (New York: Columbia University Press, 1932).

13. Fleming, *Civil War and Reconstruction*, p. 556.

14. Occasional complaints were made, however, of "tories" who refused to recognize state authority. One citizen wrote Governor Patton of "secret political organizations . . . called Union Leagues or Union Circles. . . . [T]his party is mostly composed of the most ignorant portion of our people." Anonymous to Patton, St. Clair County, 31 July 1866, Patton Papers, Alabama State Department of Archives and History.

15. Fleming, *Civil War and Reconstruction,* p. 558.

16. J. M. Hare to Patton, Shelby County, 29 May 1867. Patton Papers.

17. Silvestro, "None But Patriots," pp. 311-312.

18. W. E. Connelly to Swayne, Roanoke, 15 April 1867, Swayne Papers, Alabama State Department of Archives and History.

19. A. Bingham to William H. Smith, 14 April 1867, Swayne Papers.

20. Mobile *Advertiser and Register,* 29 March 1867; Montgomery *Weekly Advertiser,* 2 April 1867.

21. Montgomery *Weekly Advertiser,* 23 April 1867; *Daily Selma Messenger,* 16 April 1867.

22. New York *Daily Tribune,* 19 April 1867.

23. L. S. Berry, in the *Nationalist,* 25 April 1867.

24. *Daily State Sentinel,* 24 May 1867.

25. *Nationalist,* 30 May 1867; see also the New York *Daily Tribune,* 5 June 1867.

26. For a list of delegates, see the Montgomery *Weekly Advertiser,* 7 May 1867.

27. Mobile *Advertiser and Register,* 3 May 1867; *Daily State Sentinel,* 21 May 1867.

28. Mobile *Advertiser and Register,* 6 June 1867.

29. *Daily State Sentinel,* 1 June 1867; Montgomery *Daily Advertiser,* 1 June 1867.

30. Horton to Swayne, Mobile, 1 June 1867, Swayne Papers.

31. New York *Daily Tribune,* 2 July, 10 August 1867.

32. Montgomery *Weekly Advertiser,* 18 June 1867.

33. Joseph C. Bradley to Swayne, Huntsville, 19 June 1867, Swayne Papers.

34. Mobile *Advertiser and Register,* 4 July 1867, quoting the *Daily State Sentinel.*

35. Bradley to Keffer, Huntsville, 17 April 1867; Callis to C. C. Cadle, Huntsville, 17 April 1867; Bradley to Swayne, Huntsville, 18 April 1867; Bradley, M. C. H. Davis, and J. W. Burke to Swayne, Huntsville, 16 April 1867; Callis to Swayne, Huntsville, 22 April 1867: Swayne Papers. The Colored Executive Committee of the Republican party in Madison County did, in fact, unanimously recommend the appointment of Hill. Joint Executive Committee of the Union Republican Party of Madison County to Swayne, 22 April 1867, Swayne papers.

36. Montgomery *Weekly Advertiser,* 28 May 1867; Robert S. Rhodes, "The Registration of Voters and the Election of Delegates to the Reconstruction Convention in Alabama," *Alabama Review* 8 (1955): 125.

37. *Daily State Sentinel,* 24 June 1867.

38. Cox to Keffer, Tuscaloosa, 29 June 1867, Swayne Papers.

39. Smith to General Samuel C. Green, Acting Assistant Adjutant General, Montgomery, 1 August 1867, FBP, Alabama Book Records, Letters Sent.

40. See, for example, G. H. Tracy to O. D. Kinsman, Mobile, 1 July 1867, Swayne Papers; George Reese to Kinsman, Opelika, 23 July 1867, FBP, Alabama Letters Received; J. F. McGogy to Kinsman, Centre, Cherokee County, 17 July 1867, Swayne Papers.

41. C. W. Pierce, Sub-Assistant Commissioner, to Kinsman, Demopolis, 18 July 1867, Swayne Papers.

42. William Miller to Kinsman, Tuscaloosa, 27 June 1867, Patton Papers.

43. *Alabama Beacon,* 22 June 1867; Montgomery *Weekly Advertiser,* 18 June 1867. The *Alabama Beacon,* 1 June 1867, had previously praised the ex-slave as "a man of good character" and predicted that he would "discharge the duties of his office acceptably."

44. Greensboro *Alabama Beacon,* 22 June 1867.

45. *Nationalist,* 26 September 1867.

46. Whites were especially incensed when Negroes went armed to political meetings. See, for example, the complaint of F. C. Hall, Sheriff of Bullock County, to Patton, Union Springs, 3 July 1867, Patton Papers; Selma *Daily Messenger,* 3 August 1867.

47. *Alabama Beacon,* 17 August 1867.

48. John H. Parrish to Henry Watson, Greensboro, 13 August 1867, Watson Papers, Duke University Library.

49. New York *Daily Tribune,* 2, 4 September 1867. The final registration figures listed 104,518 blacks and 61,295 whites. Fleming, *Civil War and Reconstruction,* p. 491.

50. *Daily State Sentinel,* 17 October 1867.

51. There has been some disagreement over the precise number of black delegates. Malcolm Cook McMillan, *Constitutional Development in Alabama, 1798-1901: A Study in Politics, the Negro, and Sectionalism,* The James Sprunt Studies in History and Political Science, Vol. XXXVII (Chapel Hill: University of North Carolina Press, 1955), p. 17, states that there were eighteen Negroes in the convention. Fleming first declares that there were eighteen, then lists twenty-two, and finally explains that "[t]here is doubt about four or five men, whether they were black or white" *(Civil War and Reconstruction.* pp. 517-518). Newspapers at the time were equally vague. One black who was elected to the convention never appeared or served as a delegate. My most accurate estimate is that seventeen Negroes actually participated in the Convention.

52. A few important black leaders, however, occupied neither of these two offices. Holland Thompson, for example, Montgomery's leading Negro politician, was neither a registrar nor a Convention delegate. Supposedly registrars were ineligible to serve in the Convention, but in fact two Negroes served as both registrars and delegates.

53. Others continued to play important semipolitical roles. Lafayette Robinson, for example, served for several years as cashier of the Freedmen's Savings Bank in Huntsville.

54. Of the seventeen Convention delegates, twelve were from the blackbelt, three from the Tennessee Valley, and two from Mobile.

55. Despite their relative prominence, the origins of many of the black politicians remain obscure. Little or no information is available concerning eighteen of the fifty-seven, and for some of the remaining thirty-nine information is very sketchy. More accurate information can be gained for most of the Convention delegates, but the backgrounds of even some of them are hazy. The following generalizations may slightly exaggerate the privileged background of the group, since those for whom information is available may have been the most prominent and best educated.

56. *Daily State Sentinel,* 22 November 1867. Mulattoes were more prominent among the fifty-seven leaders than among the state's Negro population as a whole. At least ten of the leaders were mulattoes, and at least four of the convention delegates were. Of these four, two were from Mobile and two from the Tennessee Valley. They had all either been born free or freed before the war. Twelve percent of the state's Negro population were mulattoes.

57. Mobile *Advertiser and Register,* 30 November 1867.

58. *Daily State Sentinel,* 27 November 1867; *Nationalist,* 26 September 1867; McMillan, *Constitutional Development,* pp. 117-118; Benjamin H. Screws, *The "Loil" Legislature of Alabama: Its Ridiculous Doings and Nonsensical Sayings* (Montgomery: R. W. Offut and Co., 1868), p. 25.

59. *Daily State Sentinel,* 25 November 1867.

60. Ibid.; McMillan, *Constitutional Development,* p. 117; Joseph Matt Brittain, "Negro Suffrage and Politics in Alabama since 1870" (Ph.D. diss., Indiana University, 1958), pp. 34-35.

61. At least four of the black registrars, for whom literacy was an essential requirement, were teachers. On the other hand, none of the Constitutional Convention delegates was a teacher.

62. Elmore *Standard,* 17 January 1868.

63. See, for example, the testimony of George Roper *(Ku Klux Conspiracy,* IX, 691), an illiterate black Republican from Huntsville who claimed his political ability from "going and seeking to God. . . . Many has come this way," he ex-

plained, "and some of them said the Lord sent them to preach the Gospel but they can't read or write."

64. Charles Octavius Boothe, *The Cyclopedia of the Colored Baptists of Alabama: Their Leaders and Their Work* (Birmingham: Alabama Publishing Company, 1895), pp. 138-139.

65. *Daily State Sentinel*, 3 December 1867.

66. Three Convention delegates and six registrars were artisans. Of these, only two had been free before the war, and only two came from outside the blackbelt. There were two blacksmiths, two tailors, one shoemaker, one carpenter, one barber, one carriage driver, and one bridge builder.

67. Five of the Convention delegates, according to Fleming *(Civil War and Reconstruction,* p. 518), were common field hands. There is some reason to question his assertion; one of the delegates he lists as a field hand was in fact a grocer, and Fleming is generally imprecise in his treatment of black delegates.

68. *Ku Klux Conspiracy,* IX, 1061. On Alston, see ibid., 1016-1072.

69. Ibid., testimony of Benjamin F. Herr, X, 1664-1665; testimony of Edward W. Smith, X, 1664.

70. Fleming, *Civil War and Reconstruction,* p. 530.

71. Of the ninety-seven delegates whose places of birth could be determined by the *Daily State Sentinel*, sixty-four were Southern-born. Although the conservative New York *Herald*, 29 November 1867, sneered that "[t]hree-fourths of the delegates are men possessed of scarcely any property, and in many cases of no property at all," almost one-half of the delegates were planters, and three-quarters were either planters, lawyers, physicians, or manufacturers. *Daily State Sentinel*, 16 November 1867.

72. In the following study, I have called a bill or vote Radical if it tended to support a far-reaching Reconstruction program, or civil and political rights for blacks, and Conservative if it tended to impede these goals. I classified each delegate according to an index of Radicalism $I=R-C$ where R is the number of Radical votes he cast and C the number of Conservative votes. On twenty votes pertaining to political questions (for example, votes on restricting the franchise), I rated a delegate an extreme Radical if his index of Radicalism was at least 15 out of a possible 20; Radical if it was between 7 and 14; Moderate if it was between -6 and 6; and Conservative if it was -7 or less. Eleven delegates were extreme Radicals under this classification and thirty-three were Radicals, for a total of fourty-four. Thirty-two delegates were Moderates and eighteen Conservatives, for a total of fifty. Four delegates missed too many votes — at least ten of the twenty — to be classified.

There was a similar division of delegates on four civil-rights votes. I classified a delegate a Radical if his index of Radicalism was 2, 3, or 4; a Moderate if it was -1, 0, or 1; and a Conservative if it was -2, -3, or -4. Forty-two delegates were Radicals twenty-six were Moderates, and twenty were Conservatives. Ten delegates missed too many votes — at least three of the four — to be classified.

I did not include roll calls in the study if they were unanimous or nearly unanimous (with four or fewer delegates dissenting); if they were entirely procedural, with no Radical or Conservative implications; or if the significance of the measure was obscure. All roll-call information was taken from the *Official Journal of the Constitutional Convention of the State of Alabama* (Montgomery: Barrett and Brown, 1868), hereafter cited as *Convention Journal.*

73. Of the six whites who were extreme Radicals on political issues, five came from the Tennessee Valley or mountain regions, while of the eighteen whites who were Conservatives, only two were from those regions. See Table 16. (Four delegates did not vote often enough to be classified, and I have been unable to determine the region of one other.)

74. For the breakdown of white delegates according to their votes on four civil-rights issues, see Table 17. (Ten delegates did not vote often enough to be classified.)

75. I have rated the black delegates according to the Rice index of voting cohesion, which measures the extent to which a group votes together. The index is derived by dividing the difference between the number of yeas and nays the group casts by the total number of votes it casts, and multiplying by 100:

$$I = 100 \ \times \ \frac{\sum_{i=1}^{n} |a_i - b_i|}{\sum_{i=1}^{n} c_i}$$

where n is the number of roll calls, a_i the number of yea votes in the ith roll call, b_i the number of nay votes in the ith roll call, and c_i the number of votes cast in the ith roll call.

If all members of a group vote together, the index of cohesion is 100; if they split evenly, the index is 0. For a discussion of indexes of cohesion, see Lee F. Anderson et al., *Legislative Roll-Call Analysis* (Evanston: Northwestern University Press, 1966), pp. 32-44.

On twenty votes pertaining to political issues, the index of cohesion among Negroes was 72.0, compared with an index of 26.3 for the Convention delegates as a whole. On four civil-rights votes, the index among blacks was even higher: 85.7.

76. *Convention Journal,* pp. 79-80. On seven votes concerning economic issues, the index of cohesion among black delegates was 44.7, compared with an index of 29.8 for the convention as a whole. Some economic votes seem to have been primarily sectional and others ideological. On a series of votes relating to divorce

ordinances, Negroes divided among themselves very much as the Convention did: the index of cohesion among black delegates was 39.2. compared to 31.6 for the whole Convention.

77. *Daily State Sentinel,* 16 November 1867.

78. Mobile *Advertiser and Register,* 27 November 1867.

79. McMillan, *Constitutional Development,* p. 118. One Negro delegate, James K. Green, fell into the Moderate category as a result of five abstentions.

80. One of the three blacks split his vote. *Convention Journal,* pp. 145, 226-227.

81. Ibid., pp. 152-153, 223-224.

82. Ibid., p. 15; Mobile *Advertiser and Register,* 27 November 1867.

83. *Convention Journal,* pp. 188-189, 218.

84. *Reprint of the Official Constitution of the State of Alabama . . . , p. 10, Art. VII, Section 3.*

85. *Convention Journal,* p. 240; Montgomery *Weekly Advertiser,* 17 December 1867. Most of the protesting delegates came from the blackbelt, and only one was from the Tennessee Valley or mountains.

86. Fleming, *Civil War and Reconstruction,* p. 537.

87. See, for example, the Mobile *Advertiser and Register,* 25 December 1867, which noted that Rapier was "about as elevated as a black, helped by a strong infusion of white blood, can become in the scale of being," and suggested that he run for lieutenant-governor to test the sincerity of the white Radicals.

88. Montgomery *Daily Advertiser,* 10 December 1867.

89. Mobile *Advertiser and Register,* 24 December, 1867; *Daily State Sentinel,* 21 December 1867.

90. Mobile *Advertiser and Register,* 5 December 1867.

91. See the Montgomery *Weekly Advertiser,* 3 March 1868, for a list of Convention delegates who were nominated for political office.

92. *Alabama Beacon,* 18 January, 1 February 1868. Among the signers of this statement were such prominent Negroes as Allen A. Williams, the founder of the first freedmen's school in Tuscaloosa; William Shortridge, a Methodist minister and registrar of elections; and Prince Murrell, a teacher and Baptist minister.

93. Montgomery *Daily Advertiser,* 17 November 1867.

94. Ibid., 10 January 1868, quoting the Mobile *Times.*

95. Montgomery *Daily Advertiser,* 4, 15 December 1867; New York *Daily Tribune,* 5 December 1867.

96. Selma *Daily Messenger,* 29 December 1867; Montgomery *Weekly Advertiser,* 31 December 1867.

97. Huntsville *Advocate,* 10, 14 January 1868.

98. Fleming, *Civil War and Reconstruction,* pp. 535-537.

99. New York *Daily Tribune,* 15 February, 17 February 1868.

100. Jacob Black, Chairman, Board of Registrars, Barbour County, to Thaddeus Stevens, Eufaula, 22 February 1868, Stevens Papers, Library of Congress.

101. E. Whittlesey, Acting Assistant Adjutant General, 19 February 1868, FBP, Alabama Telegrams Received; Hayden to Howard, Montgomery, 7 March 1868, FBP, Assistant Adjutant General's Office, Letters Received. On freedmen's complaints to the Freedmen's Bureau, see, for example, the report of James Gillette, Sub-Assistant Commissioner, Mobile, 26 February 1868, FBP, Alabama Letters Received.

102. In the district's largest county, Madison, Callis received 2,100 votes to 23 for Burke. Burke fared better in the predominantly white counties, receiving 360 votes to 617 for Callis in Jackson County, and 237 to 250 for Callis in Marshall County. Huntsville *Advocate,* 14 February 1868.

103. Selma *Times and Messenger,* 8 July 1868.

104. Fleming maintains (*Civil War and Reconstruction,* p. 738) that of 100 House members, 26 were black, but as usual this figure is open to debate. I have verified 23 Negro representatives. In the 33-man Senate, there was only one black.

105. Montgomery *Daily Advertiser,* 16 July 1868. The four were Ovid Gregory, Thomas Diggs, William V. Turner, and Columbus Jones.

106. Voting for the constitution were 62,089 blacks, 5,802 whites, and 2,911 voters of unspecified color. Voting against the constitution were 900 whites and 105 blacks. The previous year, 71,730 blacks and 18,553 whites had voted to call the Convention. New York *Daily Tribune,* 30 March 1868.

107. Ibid. The total number of registered voters in the state was 170,631. In four counties, the vote was invalidated, so a total of 156,945 registered voters remained. The number of votes needed for ratification was therefore 78,473. The vote for the constitution was 70,802.

108. Ibid., 20 July 1868.

8

Black Reconstruction
in Perspective

I

In 1883, a committee of the United States Senate held extensive hearings on labor relations throughout the United States,
which were published two years later in four bulky volumes.[1]
In the course of its investigation, the committee spent several
weeks in Alabama hearing testimony from various witnesses,
mostly white but some black, who provided an enlightening
picture of Alabama's black population eighteen years after emancipation.

One white witness after another testified that the new gener-
ation of blacks was a restless, troublesome one. "The young
negroes here are growing up very worthless," declared a white
carriage manufacturer in the blackbelt town of Opelika. "You
can't get them to work."[2] Former Governor Robert Patton agreed
that "[t]he negroes raised and educated before the war are much
more capable, learn better, and work better than those that are
now growing up." He complained that the young blacks "are run-

ning about night and day, and if you go out...on a Saturday evening, you can hardly get along the pavement on account of the crowd of these young people." He further noted that "they are not willing to be controlled or guided by their employers, because they have an idea that that is submitting to slavery again."[3]

Patton was not alone in observing that blacks resisted control by their employers. A white cotton commissioner stated that young Negroes were not content to work long on one plantation. Instead, "they want to go and see something of the world, so they start off to another plantation, or go to work on a railroad or in a coal mine."[4] A planter who employed blacks on shares explained that the shortage of labor was one reason Negroes found it so easy to take advantage of their employers.[5] Willard Warner, an ex-Senator, also testified that blacks were unhappy under planter domination. He recalled that upon emancipation blacks "seemed to have an intuition" that led them to try to acquire land, or barring that to rent or work for shares. Negroes "wanted to do anything of this kind rather than to work for wages." When Warner was asked if that was still the case, he replied: "Yes, sir, that is still so. They want to get just as far as possible from the old condition of slavery; they have a great desire to become landowners."[6]

James K. Green, the black former politician, who was now a successful carpenter and contractor in Montgomery, also testified. He recalled that at the end of the Civil War he had been "entirely ignorant; I knew nothing more than to obey my master; and there were thousands of us in the same attitude, that didn't know the Lord's Prayer, but the tocsin of freedom sounded and knocked at the door and we walked out like free men and we met the exigencies as they grew up, and shouldered the responsibilities." Green stressed that the one great need of the blacks was education. "I am not educated at all myself, but I know the value of the schools," he declared.[7] Other blacks also testified to their continued enthusiasm for education.[8] When the Senate committee visited a Negro school in Opelika, its members were surprised to see three adults in the class along with the black children. The Negro teacher explained that "[a]ll of those three are married ladies . . . [a]bout forty-seven or forty-eight." When he was asked why they came to school at that age, he replied, "[w]ell, their object is just to learn to read and write, so they can act for themselves."[9]

The striking thing about much of this testimony is that it revealed black attitudes — hopes, aspirations, fears, and frustrations — remarkably similar to those of the late 1860s. Whites also, in their comments about blacks, displayed very much the same views they had fifteen years earlier. With a few exceptions, almost all of the testimony before the Senate committee could have been given unchanged in 1868 or 1870.

That such was the case should not be surprising, for the period immediately following the Civil War was a decisive one during which the main patterns of a new social order emerged. Radically changed social conditions, virtually all of which were connected with the emancipation of the slaves and the transition from a slave to a free labor society, made necessary sudden readjustments in the relationship of both blacks to whites and blacks to each other. This revolution profoundly affected almost all areas of life among the ex-slaves.

Not all of these developments were permanent. There were false starts, as in politics, where the bright prospects of the late 1860s were not fulfilled. Perhaps it was too much to expect a party based on the tenuous alliance of such diverse groups as blacks, carpetbaggers, and scalawags (who themselves consisted of the unlikely combination of blackbelt planters seeking to maintain control over their ex-slaves and northern Alabama farmers resentful of the large planters) to remain in power for long. Blacks, who formed the vast majority of Republican voters, were by the early 1870s demanding the increased share of offices to which they thought their numbers entitled them. These demands, however, met the formidable opposition of most scalawags, few of whom sympathized with the bid for greater black power. Scalawags, in turn, chafed at the prominent position of carpetbaggers within the party.[10]

Such dissension within the Republican party was largely responsible for the renewed strength of the Democrats, who in 1868 had not even bothered to contest the state elections. From

1870 to 1874 Republicans and Democrats struggled for control of the state, and in 1874, through a combination of Republican disunity, Democratic intimidation of black voters, and the appeal for all whites to band together behind the "white man's party," the Republicans were permanently driven from power. In Alabama, as in other Southern states, black participation in politics had been greatly reduced by the late 1870s and would later be almost entirely eliminated.

Most of the new developments of the late 1860s, however, were not primarily the result of Republican ascendancy, and unless one regards Reconstruction in a narrow, political sense, to speak of its overthrow in 1874 in Alabama — or in 1877 in the South as a whole — is misleading. The more significant Reconstruction — the restructuring of patterns of life following the war — resulted not from the temporary triumph of the Radical Republicans, but from the overthrow of slavery. It is for this reason that the late 1860s constituted such an important transition period for Alabama blacks, during which the outlines of the new social order took shape. The transition period cannot be given a precise time span; if the basic pattern of sharecropping was set by 1867, the public-school system was not fully operating until 1871, and both continued to undergo modifications in subsequent years. But in general, by 1869 the nature of the new system which the overthrow of slavery made possible was fairly clear. Developments after that date more often consisted of variations on themes already suggested than radical new departures.

II

A review of this process of social Reconstruction casts light upon the previous history of Southern blacks and the nature of American slavery. Historians have long debated, for example, whether slavery was a brutal system of repression creating among its victims only fear and hatred of the oppressors, or a paternalistic, often kindly, system in which slave and master shared many common experiences and felt real affection for each other. No doubt it was both; we need not assume that all masters treated their slaves alike, that all slaves reacted identically, or that life on a large plantation was the equivalent of the more informal relationships likely to prevail on a small farm.

Still, the responses of freedmen after the war should lead us to question how common and how real the bonds of affection between slave owner and slave had ever been. They were not strong enough to prevent masses of blacks — including trusted servants — from leaving their former homes when given a choice. Few planters hesitated to expel old and sick freedmen who were now useless to them. The attempts of planters to underpay their hands, or to drive them away from their plantations before the division of the crop, and the complaints of blacks to the Freedmen's Bureau about the activities of their employers, were too common to be regarded as mere aberrations or exceptions. It is conceivable, of course, that the ties that had previously held master and slave together were snapped by the new animosities and conflicts created by emancipation. Ties that could be broken so quickly and easily, however, could never have been more than tenuous to begin with. The master's concern for his slave seemed essentially the owner's concern for his property; once that property was free, the concern vanished remarkably quickly in most cases. Similarly, the slave's love for his master probably existed most often in the planter's own imagination.

The Reconstruction experience can also serve as a test of the validity of the Sambo thesis propounded by Stanley Elkins in his controversial book, *Slavery: A Problem in American Institutional and Intellectual Life*.[11] According to Elkins, American slavery was such a brutalizing experience that it changed the very personality of the slaves, rendering them childlike and submissive. Cut off from all contacts, deprived of any independent activity or existence, and totally dominated by the slaveowner, blacks internalized his values and came to see him as a father figure whom they should try to please. They were not merely role-playing; their character had actually been transformed by slavery. "Sambo, the typical plantation slave," wrote Elkins, "was docile but irresponsible, loyal but lazy, humble but chronically given to lying and stealing; his behavior was full of infantile silliness, and his talk inflated with childish exaggeration. His relationship with his master was one of utter dependence and childlike attachment: it was indeed this childlike quality that was the very key to his being."[12]

Once again, common sense warns us not to adopt an all-or-nothing position. The experiences of slaves varied so greatly depending on the region, size of plantation, attitude of the planter, and character of the slave that it would be foolish to assign all slaves one personality — as foolish as to assign all slave owners one personality. No doubt Samboes did exist. Their existence was not limited to slavery; they are recognizable even today as smiling, shuffling, good-natured Uncle Toms.

But the behavior of blacks in Reconstruction should lead us to question how pervasive Sambo could have been before the war. As soon as they were free, most blacks behaved not in a childlike, dependent manner, but in one that showed their passionate attachment to freedom and their desire to live as independently as possible. If they had indeed been Samboes under slavery, it is remarkable how quickly they were able to discard their old personalities. In all walks of life — whether in forming their own churches, seeking to improve their position vis-á-vis their planter employers, becoming active politically, acting to strengthen the family as a social unit, supporting the education of their children — freedmen struggled for an independence based upon human dignity and self-respect.

It might be suggested that Sambo had indeed existed before the war, but that the experience of liberation actually changed the character of Southern blacks and enabled them to stand on their own. Doubtless this process did occur; men and women who formerly had no choice but to labor on their plantations now saw a new world of potential opportunities appear before them. The sudden overturning of an established system, the new hopes engendered, and the fact that for the first time they had a choice and did not have to do as they were told must have aroused new feelings of pride and solidarity among many blacks, and led them to act in a way they would not have thought possible a few years earlier.[13]

That all of this could occur, however, casts serious doubt upon the basis of the Elkins thesis — that slaves not only acted like Samboes but actually were Samboes, who had internalized all the values of the slave system. It is difficult to believe that blacks whose character had been as stunted and warped as Elkins suggested they were ever could have acted the way they did after the war. As soon as they were free, these supposedly dependent, childlike Negroes began acting like independent men and women. Such a rapid transformation strongly suggests that most antebellum Samboes were merely playing the roles expected of them, telling whites what they wanted to hear.

During Reconstruction, Southern whites repeatedly and bitterly complained about the changed character of Negroes they had known before the war. "When I knew him before the war," stated ex-Confederate General Cullen A. Battle of black legislator James Alston, "when he belonged to me, he was quite an orderly negro, a good boot-maker and a valuable servant. Since then I have heard of his being exceedingly turbulent and sometimes . . . overbearing in his manner to his own people and insolent in his manner toward white people, though that is not his manner toward me."[14] Numerous other whites voiced similar complaints.

It was this refusal to play the accustomed role, this transference of the "good darkey" into the "uppity nigger," that more than anything else enraged the white South. It was no accident that black politicians, black ministers, educated blacks, black landowners, black males who asserted themselves — in short, those blacks who were most successful by accepted white standards — became the prime targets of white attack and intimidation. By their actions they, and all other freedmen who refused to play Sambo, dispelled the myth that had been the white South's most compelling defense of slavery. That many whites continued to cling to that myth only testifies to man's almost unlimited ability to believe what he wants, whatever the evidence may suggest.

III

An understanding of developments among the freedmen during Reconstruction can also help us better evaluate interpretations of the subsequent history of blacks in America. Many writers have assumed that the roots of most current black problems lie in the experience of slavery. In order to explain the position of blacks in the United States today, scholars frequently point to the slave past. Surely, they reason, an experience as different from that of other Americans as slavery must be at the heart of the major differences between black and white Americans in the twentieth century. Historians, too, find such a mode of explanation congenial, since by emphasizing the importance of understanding the past in order to explain the present it seems to justify — indeed, add "relevance" to — the historian's occupation.

A good example is the analysis of the modern black family. Social scientists have paid much attention in recent years to the instability of the contemporary black family. Daniel Patrick Moynihan, in his controversial report, *The Negro Family: The Case for National Action,* is perhaps best known, but he has been far from alone.[15] Thomas Pettigrew, Kenneth Clark, Abram Kardiner and Lionel Ovesey, and many others have stressed that the contemporary black family is matrifocal; is marked by high rates of divorce, desertion, and illigitimacy; and does not provide a satisfactory role for the male.[16]

These authors have been curiously ambivalent in explaining the reasons for family disorganization among contemporary blacks. On the one hand, they have all pointed to the peculiar problems blacks face in the twentieth-century ghetto, including poor housing, urban congestion, job discrimination, unemployment, and the emasculating psychological impact of these factors upon black men. On the other hand, they have stressed the continuing legacy of slavery and family patterns common among slaves. Thus, in the same chapter that Clark ascribes black family disorganization to the ghetto environment, he suggests that modern blacks have inherited family relations originally developed under slavery.[17] Similarly, Pettigrew, after describing how slavery fostered a matriarchal family structure, notes that "[b]oth poverty and migration also act to maintain the old slave pattern of a mother-centered family."[18] These social scientists have made little serious effort to weigh the relative importance of the historical legacy of slavery versus the impact of contemporary urban conditions in explaining modern family relations. It is almost as if the disruptive effects of slavery blend so smooth-

ly into the disruptive effects of the twentieth-century ghetto
that there is no real need to distinguish between them.

The problems with which the twentieth-century ghetto con-
fronts the urban black, however, are quite different from those
of slavery that faced the rural Southern Negro in the middle of
the nineteenth century. It is difficult to avoid wondering whether
there is any functional relationship between two very different
phenomena separated in time by almost a century, even if they
are said to have contributed to similar developments. It is not
enough merely to say that slavery disrupted the family lives of
slaves; in order to establish that slavery was one of the principal
factors leading to contemporary family instability among blacks,
presumably one must show some sort of direct continuity between
the two.

The history of the black family in Alabama during Reconstruction suggests it is unlikely that the legacy of slavery was a major
cause of twentieth-century family weakness among urban blacks.
Even if one grants that slavery was as destructive to Negro family relations as the social scientists have assumed — and some
historians are no longer sure that this was the case — there is
still little direct connection between the disrupted slave family
and the disrupted ghetto family.[19] After emancipation blacks
strove, for the most part successfully, to create a more unified
family pattern along conventional white lines. Relations between
husbands and wives and those between parents and children
were affected. By 1870, family structure among Alabama blacks
did not appear to differ appreciably from that among Alabama
whites.

If during Reconstruction a relatively stable black family had begun to develop, whatever family instability there is among
twentieth-century urban blacks must be the result of the disruptive conditions faced by those families in the ghetto, not the per-
petuation of slave patterns.[20] It is likely that only with the massive twentieth-century migration to the cities did the disorganized family that has so intrigued recent scholars appear. The logic
that assigns to slavery responsibility for the ills of the modern
ghetto ignores the developments of nearly a century.

IV

In ignoring historical developments of Reconstruction, scholars investigating the contemporary black family have been in good company. The assumptions of historical continuity and of slow, gradual change have been so strong among historians that they have almost intuitively sought to explain the current situation among blacks by pointing to the experience of slavery. The tendency to regard Reconstruction as a political movement that ultimately failed has also contributed to the illusion of continuity. I would suggest, therefore, that the greatest significance of the story of black Reconstruction — in the broad sense of the word — lies in its revealing the revolutionary nature of the period.

Few historians today believe — as most did in the 1920s, 1930s, and 1940s — that the Civil War and Reconstruction constituted a "second American Revolution" in which the capitalists of the Northeast, represented in Congress by the Radical Republicans, seized control of the federal government from the agrarian slaveholders of the South.[21] While once historians regarded the war as a spur to American economic development, more recent scholars have argued that the war did not further American industrialization and may in fact have retarded it.[22] While once historians saw the Radical Republicans as conspirators whose Reconstruction policies, although couched in the language of civil rights and black equality, were really designed to promote the interests of Northern businessmen, recent scholars have pointed out that both the Radicals and businessmen were hopelessly divided on virtually all important economic issues of the day, and that businessmen were not on the whole especially pleased with the political policies of the Radical Republicans.[23] In short, most historians now agree that Radical Reconstruction simply cannot be explained as a capitalist revolution designed to protect the interests of Northern industrialists.

There is a certain danger in pushing the argument too far, however, and assuming that the Civil War and Reconstruction were mere ripples on an otherwise calm sea of American historical continuity. There is a difference between refuting a narrowly conceived economic interpretation of the second American

Revolution and proving that there was no revolution at all. A good case can still be made that the Civil War did represent a fundamental clash of interest between a conservative, traditionally oriented slave South and an aggressive, dynamic, democratic, capitalistic North.[24]

Certainly, as far as the South was concerned, the period was a revolutionary one. The slaveholding system that had dominated the section for some two hundred years was forcibly overthrown and replaced by a free labor, or capitalist, system. The overturning of slavery, which had been the very basis of Southern society, was a momentous event which could not fail to require substantial changes in social organization, as men groped toward redefining their patterns of life to be more in tune with the new social reality. At the same time, however, old ideas sometimes lingered on long after new conditions had made them obsolete. Many whites found it especially difficult to accept or even comprehend the new relationships required by emancipation, and continued to expect the freedmen to behave as slaves. This tension between new circumstances and old attitudes made the period a particularly frustrating one for those unable to adjust to change.

The revolution was especially sweeping, as I hope I have shown, for black Southerners. In almost all areas of life their social relationships — both with whites and with each other — underwent dramatic and rapid change. The changes were not so much narrowly economic — it is not obvious that most blacks were better off materially after the war than before — as social, political, legal, and psychological. Negroes could now work at their own pace, rather than under the lash of the overseer. They could leave home at will without being stopped by patrols of whites and asked for identification. They could marry without running the risk of being forcibly separated, perhaps forever, from their mates. They could attend their own churches, where they could listen to black preachers. They could send their sons and daughters to school. They could (at least for the time being) elect their own representatives to the state government, and have a voice in its political decisions. A few of the more fortunate ones could, either through luck, skill, or perseverance, become prosperous or prominent citizens in their communities. In short, they were free, and freedom, even when it is accompanied by oppression and discrimination, is very different from slavery.

By 1870, then, as a result of innumerable changes affecting the lives of the freedmen, a new black society had emerged. The great majority of these changes were the result not of Radical rule or of any particular action taken by the Republican government — indeed, most of them had already occurred before the Republicans came to power in 1868 and continued after they were overthrown — but of emancipation itself. Because emancipation was so sudden, the changes that ensued from it were also sudden. But once the new patterns were established they proved remarkably enduring, and were modified only slowly, over the course of decades. So it is with revolutions; they take a long time to arrive, but when their time has come the changes they bring are sudden, dramatic, and irresistible.

Notes

1. U.S., Congress, Senate, *Report of the Committee of the Senate Upon the Relations between Labor and Capital* (Washington, D.C.: Government Printing Office, 1885).

2. Ibid., IV, 656.

3. Ibid., pp. 48-50.

4. Ibid., p. 70.

5. Ibid., p. 146.

6. Ibid., p. 274.

7. Ibid., pp. 451-452.

8. For example, see the testimony of J. G. Going, a barber in Birmingham, Ibid., p. 401.

9. Ibid., pp. 651-652.

10. On Alabama scalawags, see Sarah Van Voorhis Woolfolk, "The Role of the Scalawag in Alabama Reconstruction" (Ph.D. diss., Louisiana State University, 1965).

11. For a collection of largely negative responses to Elkins' theories, see Ann J. Lane, ed., *The Debate over Slavery: Stanley Elkins and His Critics* (Urbana: University of Illinois Press, 1971).

12. Stanley Elkins, *Slavery: A Problem in American Institutional and Intellectual Life* (Chicago: The University of Chicago Press, 1959), p. 82.

13. For a suggestive account of how a revolution can change the character of a people, see Frantz Fanon, *A Dying Colonialism* (New York: Grove Press, 1967). Fanon describes how Algerians, who under French colonial rule had exhibited many of the characteristics attributed to Sambo, were totally transformed by their common struggle for independence during the 1950s.

14. *Ku Klux Conspiracy*, IX, 1061.

15. U.S., Department of Labor, Office of Policy Planning and Research, *The Negro Family: The Case for National Action* (Washington, D.C.: Government Printing Office, 1965).

16. Thomas F. Pettigrew, *A Profile of the Negro American* (Princeton: D. Van Nostrand Company, Inc., 1964); Kenneth B. Clark, *Dark Ghetto: Dilemmas of Social Power* (New York: Harper and Row, 1965); Abram Kardiner and Lionel Ovesey, *The Mark of Oppression: A Psychological Study of the American Negro* (New York: W. W. Norton and Company, Inc., 1951). I hope it is clear that I am not here passing judgment on whether these authors have been correct in their descriptions of contemporary family weakness. For conflicting, mostly hostile, reactions to the Moynihan Report, see Lee Rainwater and William L. Yancey, eds., *The Moynihan Report and the Politics of Controversy* (Cambridge, Mass.: The M.I.T. Press, 1967).

17. Clark, *Dark Ghetto*, p. 70.

18. Pettigrew, *A Profile of the Negro American*, p. 15.

19. See Bobby Frank Jones, "A Cultural Middle Passage: Slave Marriage and Family in the Ante-Bellum South" (Ph.D. diss., University of North Carolina, 1965).

20. On the greater stability of the rural Southern black family, see Lee Rainwater, "Crucible of Identity: The Negro Lower-Class Family," in Talcott Parsons and Kenneth B. Clark, eds., *The Negro American* (Boston: Houghton Mifflin Co., 1966), pp. 160-204.

21. For a general statement of the Civil War as a second American Revolution, see Charles A. Beard and Mary R. Beard, *The Rise of American Civilization*, rev. ed. (New York: The Macmillan Company, 1935). II, chap. XVIII. The best, most restrained, application of the economic interpretation to the Reconstruction period is Howard K. Beale, *The Critical Year: A Study of Andrew Johnson and Reconstruction* (New York: Harcourt, Brace and Co., 1930).

22. See the selections in Ralph Andreano, ed., *The Economic Impact of the American Civil War* (Cambridge: Schenkman Publishing Co., 1962), especially that of Thomas C. Cochran, "Did the Civil War Retard Industrialization?" pp. 148-160.

23. See Stanley Coben, "Northeastern Business and Radical Reconstruction: A Re-examination," *Mississippi Valley Historical Review* 46 (June 1959): 67-90; Robert P. Sharkey, *Money, Class, and Party: An Economic Study of Civil War and Reconstruction* (Baltimore: The Johns Hopkins Press, 1959); Irwin Unger, *The Greenback Era: A Social and Political History of American Finance, 1865-1879* (Princeton: Princeton University Press, 1964); Glenn M. Linden, "Congressmen, 'Radicalism' and Economic Issues, 1861-1873" (Ph.D. diss. University of Washington, 1963); and Peter Kolchin, "The Business Press and Reconstruction, 1865-1868," *Journal of Southern History* 33 (May 1967): 183-196.

24. Two provocative studies, one dealing with the South and one with the North, present precisely such an interpretation. See Eugene D. Genovese, *The Political Economy of Slavery: Studies in the Economy and Society of the Slave South* (New York: Random House, 1965), and Eric Foner, *Free Soil, Free Labor, Free Men: The Ideology of the Republican Party before the Civil War* (New York: Oxford University Press, 1970).

Bibliographical Essay

This essay includes only the most important sources I have used. For a full list of sources consulted, see the bibliography of my Ph.D. dissertation, "First Freedom: The Responses of Alabama's Blacks to Emancipation and Reconstruction" (Johns Hopkins University, 1970).

The most important materials for this study were the voluminous Papers of the United States Bureau of Refugees, Freedmen, and Abandoned Lands (Freedmen's Bureau), classified as Record Group 105 in the National Archives. Fortunately, most of this vast collection is arranged and subdivided by state. The most useful categories of the Alabama records were the Letters Received, containing letters and reports sent to the assistant commissioner from his agents in the field, as well as miscellaneous contracts, questions, complaints, and other correspondence from planters and occasionally from freedmen; the Operations Reports, weekly and monthly reports to the assistant commissioner from his sub-assistant commissioners, superintendents, and assistant superintendents; the Letters Received by the state superintendent of education; and the weekly and monthly Teachers' School Reports sent to the superintendent of education. Important information was also found in the Letters Received by the Assistant Adjutant General's Office, containing letters sent to Commissioner Howard and his staff in Washington, D.C.; and the Letters Received by the Education Division, consisting of letters sent to General Superintendent of Education John W. Alvord, also in Washington. The Freedmen's Bureau Papers are described in detail in a *Preliminary Checklist of the Records of the Bureau of Refugees, Freedmen, and Abandoned Lands, 1865-1872,* compiled in 1946 by Elizabeth Bethel, Sara Dunlap, and Lucille Pendall.

The American Missionary Association Papers at Fisk University in Nashville provided an important supplement to the Freedmen's Bureau Papers on educational matters. Especially useful were the letters from AMA missionaries in Alabama describing their efforts and the condition of blacks to their Northern superiors. The Freedmen's Aid Society Papers for Western Georgia and Alabama of the Methodist Episcopal Church, located at the Interdenominational Theological Seminary in Atlanta, chronicle the efforts of Northern Methodists to establish their church among the freedmen and contain some interesting observations on their religious practices.

In general, private manuscript collections for Alabama proved disappointing, and not among the most helpful sources for this study. Among those used, the papers of blackbelt planter Henry Watson, at Duke University Library, were most useful. The letters to Watson from his brother-in-law John Parrish were especially revealing of conditions among the freedmen. Also informative were the diary of Talladega County planter James Mallory, located in the Southern Historical Collection at the University of North Carolina, and the diary of Tuscumbia planter J. B. Moore, a typed copy of which is at the Alabama Department of Archives and History. Information on political, social, and economic conditions in Alabama following the war can be found in the papers of Provisional Governor Lewis E. Parsons, Governor Robert M. Patton, and Assistant Commissioner Wager Swayne, all located at the Alabama State Department of Archives and History.

Of great value in the study of family relations, social structure, and migration patterns were the Population Schedules of the Manuscript Census Returns of the Eighth Census (1860) and the Ninth Census (1870), taken by the United States Census Office. These returns, located in the National Archives and available on microfilm, list each individual's age, sex, color (white, mulatto, or black), occupation, real property owned, personal property owned, literacy, and state of birth. Although the returns depended for their accuracy on the skill and interest of numerous different census takers, and therefore undoubtedly contain some errors, they still provide the best overall picture of the population. The Manuscript Returns for the Alabama State Census of 1866, located in the Alabama State Department of Archives and History, proved much less useful. The returns were taken by race, with blacks and whites listed in separate volumes. Unfortunately, the state census of blacks was merely an enumeration of individuals, listing heads of households by county, without giving their townships, beats, or wards.

The published census returns were also useful, especially for determining patterns of migration. These returns included U.S. Census Office, *Eighth Census: Population* (Washington, D.C.: Government Printing Office, 1864) and its *Ninth Census: Population* (Washington, D.C.: Government Printing Office, 1872); and two slightly different versions of the Alabama State Census of 1866, listing the black and white population by counties, in the Montgomery *Daily Advertiser* of 21 March 1868 and in U. S., Congress, Senate, Ex. Doc. No. 6, 39th Cong., 2d sess., pp. 21-22.

Of the many Alabama newspapers used, the most helpful were two Democratic ones, the Montgomery *Daily Advertiser* and the Mobile *Advertiser and Register,* and two Republican ones, the *Nationalist* (Mobile) and the *Daily State Sentinel* (Montgomery). Also informative were the *Alabama Beacon*

(Greensboro), the Selma *Daily Messenger,* and the *Clark County Journal* (all Democratic), and the Huntsville *Advocate* (Republican). The *Official Journal of the Constitutional Convention of the State of Alabama . . . 1867* (Montgomery: Barrett & Brown, 1868) contains the votes of delegates on the convention roll calls.

Three United States government publications were valuable. *The War of the Rebellion: A Compilation of the Official Records of the Union and Confederate Army,* Ser. I, Vol. XLIX, Pt. II (Washington, D.C.: Government Printing Office, 1897) contains interesting observations of army officers on the state of affairs in Alabama when federal troops first arrived in the spring of 1865. The *Testimony Taken by the Joint Select Committee to Inquire into the Condition of Affairs in the Late Insurrectionary States* (Washington, D.C.: Government Printing Office, 1872), Vols. VIII, IX, and X, contain much interesting information on violence and other matters during the late 1860s. The U.S., Congress, Senate, *Report of the Committee of the Senate upon the Relations between Labor and Capital* (Washington, D.C.: Government Printing Office, 1885), Vol. IV, provides a good description of conditions in Alabama eighteen years after emancipation.

Secondary accounts were not especially useful, with the important exception of those dealing with religion. Numerous obscure volumes chronicle the development of various churches and church organizations in Alabama. Many of these books, although quite unsophisticated as history, contain valuable information about persons or events, and can be used as primary sources. A few examples of the many such works used are Charles Octavius Boothe, *The Cyclopedia of the Colored Baptists of Alabama: Their Leaders and Their Work* (Birmingham: Alabama Publishing Co., 1895); W. P. Harrison, *The Gospel among the Slaves: A Short Account of Missionary Operations among the African Slaves of the Southern States* (Nashville: Publishing House of the M. E. Church, South, 1893); W. H. Mixon, *History of the African Methodist Episcopal Church in Alabama with Biographical Sketches* (Nashville: A.M.E. Church Sunday School Union, 1902); and Josephus Shackelford, *History of the Muscle Shoals Baptist Association* (Trinity, Alabama: published by the author, 1891).

Three secondary accounts should receive special mention. Walter L. Fleming, *Civil War and Reconstruction in Alabama* (New York: Columbia University Press, 1905), although written from a conservative, antiblack perspective, remains the most thorough and informative account of the period. Horace Mann Bond, *Negro Education in Alabama: A Study in Cotton and Steel* (Washington, D.C.: The Associated Publishers, Inc., 1939), is an excellent study of Reconstruction and post-Reconstruction Alabama, dealing with topics far broader than those suggested by the title. Robert Gilmour, "The Other Emancipation: Studies in the Society and Economy of Alabama Whites during Reconstruction" (Ph.D. dissertation, Johns Hopkins University, 1972) is a perceptive social history of Alabama's whites, covering the same years as this volume, and therefore in many ways complementary to it.

Index

African Methodist Episcopal
Church, 108, 115, 116
organized in Alabama, 111
African Methodist Episcopal
Zion Church, 108, 116
organized in Alabama, 110-
111
Alston, James H., 166, 190
Alvord, John W., 85, 89, 98
American Missionary Associa-
tion, 80, 82, 86, 92, 99
establishes Talladega Nor-
mal School, 90-91
promotes Congregational-
ism, 113-114
Apprenticing of black children,
63-67
Arkansas, 21, 111, 114
Army of the United States. *See*
Union Army
Artisans, black
in economic elite, 138
middle class, 133-134
in politics, 167-168
Ashby, Nathan, 110, 116
Athens, 43, 81, 154
Atrocities, 121-122, 146
Autauga County, 165
Avery, Moses B., 158, 159, 166

Baptist State Convention
(black), 110